# INFORMATION ARCHITECTURE

## An Emerging 21st Century Profession

# INFORMATION ARCHITECTURE

## An Emerging 21$^{st}$ Century Profession

**Earl Morrogh**

*Florida State University*

Prentice Hall

Upper Saddle River, New Jersey 07458

Library of Congress Cataloging-in-Publication Data
Morrogh, Earl.
    Information architecture: an emerging 21st century profession/Earl Morrogh.
        p. cm.
    Includes bibliographical references and index.
    ISBN 0-13-096746-7 (paper adhesive)
    1. Information technology—History. I. Title.
    T58.5 .M68 2002
    004'.09—dc21

                                                        2002028529

**Editor-in-Chief:** Stephen Helba
**Director of Production and Manufacturing:** Bruce Johnson
**Executive Editor:** Elizabeth Sugg
**Managing Editor—Editorial:** Judy Casillo
**Editorial Assistant:** Anita Rhodes
**Marketing Manager:** Leigh Ann Sims
**Managing Editor—Production:** Mary Carnis
**Manufacturing Buyer:** Cathleen Petersen
**Production Liaison:** Denise Brown
**Production Editor:** Bridget Lulay
**Production Management and Composition:** Carlisle Communications, Ltd.
**Design Director:** Cheryl Asherman
**Design Coordinator/Cover Design:** Christopher Weigand
**Cover Printer:** Phoenix Color
**Printer/Binder:** Phoenix Book Tech

Pearson Education Ltd.
Pearson Education Australia PTY, Limited
Pearson Education Singapore, Pte. Ltd.
Pearson Education North Asia, Ltd.
Pearson Education Canada, Ltd.
Pearson Education de Mexico, S.A. de C.V.
Pearson Education—Japan
Pearson Education Malaysia, Pte. Ltd.

10 9 8 7 6 5 4 3 2 1
ISBN 0-13-096746-7

# Contents

## PART 4

### COMPUTER NETWORKS:
Communication and Computing
Systems Converge   71

## CHAPTER 13

### Internauts: Architects of the Intergalactic Network   73

## CHAPTER 14

### ARPAnet: The Birth of the Internet   77

## CHAPTER 15

### Email: The First Killer "App"   83

## CHAPTER 16

### WWW: The World Wide Web   88

## PART 5

### INFO AILMENTS: Unintended
Consequences of the Information
Age   95

## CHAPTER 17

### Info Glut, Info Trash, Info Hype, and Info Stress   97

# Foreword

I am obsessed with the three tools of understanding:

* Questions,
* Conversations, and
* Stories.

## QUESTIONS: THERE IS ALWAYS A QUESTION

Questions can enlighten our world, expand our understanding of the universe, and help us assess what we know and what we do not. I have always found that asking the right question will take you a lot further than getting the right answer, yet the emphasis of most educational institutions is on finding answers. In my consideration of what to say to you, the reader, when introducing the author of this book and all that follows in this foreword, I asked myself the question, "What *is* the purpose of an introduction to any book, or in this case, my introduction to a book about information architecture?" From this question came the following answers:

> **Answer 1**   The author, Earl, did write his own excellent introduction—Chapter 1.

> **Answer 2**   A second way to approaching an introduction of a book is an endorsement. My name, Richard Saul Wurman, attached to this endorsement, acts to substantiate the chapters that follow—either by celebrity, reputation, or position. I think that the table of contents of this book encapsulates a rich journey through the ordered mind of the author and defines a new field of human endeavor. It is also my opinion that this book serves the new universe of information architecture in the most thorough manner yet published.

> **Answer 3**   The third purpose an introduction can serve is to add a slightly obtuse point of view to that of the author—advice on how to read the book, an epiphany about the subject itself, or a story, as in a comic saying, "on my way to the theater I met so and so. . . ." This is a book to cherry-pick through and create your individual journey by going in and out of the interesting and stand-alone chapters, which then allows you to discover your personal definition of information architecture.

## CONVERSATIONS: TALK IS DEEP

My particular view and my passion focuses on Chapter 2—"Let's Talk About It: The Spoken Word." Ninety percent of future discoveries to be made in information architecture and communication are metaphorically to be found embedded in two individuals having a conversation. Nothing we do or invent is more clearly a seed of solutions than the 35,000-plus-year exercise of telling stories to each other.

## STORIES: DEFINING INFORMATION ARCHITECTURE

The stories being told about the emerging profession of IA are filled with comment and response in a search for the stickiness that connects interesting words and ideas to each other. This communication enables the creation of clear patterns of understanding and the potential for new ideas. Ideas need a rigor of Velcro-like attachments that celebrate new patterns of understanding. And, fundamental to understanding are the diagramming of these patterns as well as the visualization of their natural hierarchical order of importance.

## FORMULATING YOUR OWN QUESTIONS

I believe there will soon be a computer that can simulate the human nod of understanding and organize concepts to position them in an understandable orientation to each other. This important step in the crossover of man/machine conversation is in your future. When this time comes, the ideas defining information architecture will then become paramount. Now is the time for you to formulate your own questions, engage in the IA conversations—the social construction of IA, and listen to the IA stories being told (as well as tell your own).

The *Information Architecture: An Emerging 21ˢᵗ Profession* story begins with a question about the roots of IA and invites the reader to consider the origins of speech as where it all began. The story ends with questions about the future of a new profession and information society.

Richard Saul Wurman, FAIA

### Author's Note:

In 1975 Richard Saul Wurman coined the term and the concept of information architecture. It is not surprising that his career spans the fields of both information design and architecture.

He has practiced and taught architecture and received both M.Arch. and B.Arch. degrees from the University of Pennsylvania. He is also a fellow of the American Institute of Architects. It was while practicing architecture in Philadelphia that he began producing a series of highly regarded architecturally oriented books on building comparisons, city analyses, and Louis Kahn (with whom he had a deep personal and professional relationship).

Leaving his architecture practice, in 1981 he founded Access Press in Los Angeles and began producing his revolutionary Access Guides for which in 1991 he was honored with the Kevin Lynch Award from MIT. He has also been awarded several grants from the National Endowment for the Arts and a Guggenheim Fellowship.

Wurman is the author of the 1990 best-selling book dedicated to managing the influences of the information age, *Information Anxiety,* and the more recent sequel, *Information Anxiety 2.* He is the founder, chairman, and creative director of the TED Conferences on Technology, Entertainment, and Design—a conference that has been characterized as representing the new coalition of energies that "information" now requires.

# Preface

## ABOUT MY INTEREST IN IA

My interest in information architecture as an emerging profession began with reading the popular book by Peter Morville and Louis Rosenfeld, *Information Architecture: Designing Large-Scale Web Sites.* After reviewing a number of guides to Web site design, I decided that this book would serve me best. Having worked on many computer-mediated education projects practically since the invention of the PC, I had learned that one of the major problems in starting new team-based multimedia design projects is communication. Representing a different discipline, each team member brings to the table a different, specialized, technical language and unique design methodology. My experience also taught me that before a group (often consisting of graphic designers, computer programmers, video and sound specialists, and instructional designers) can work effectively as a team, they must come to share a common design terminology and methodology. I also knew that, with the exception of a few new technical issues, most of what I had learned about design and management issues that are related to multimedia projects would transfer well to large-scale Web site projects. Faced with managing the design of a large-scale Web site intended to support a variety of activities and audiences associated with the distance learning initiative of a major university, I thought adopting Morville's and Rosenfeld's information architecture philosophy, terminology, and methodology would help the project team pull together quickly. Enjoying a satisfactory degree of success, I held onto the book for future reference.

As I reread the book, I became more and more intrigued with the idea of information architecture as an emerging profession. The following definition of "information architect" by Richard Saul Wurman, included in the Morville book, generated a number of questions and fueled more inquiry into the subject of IA and eventually led to my authoring this book.

Information Architect:

1. "The individual who organizes the patterns inherent in data, making the complex clear";
2. "A person who creates the structure or map of information which allows others to find their personal paths to knowledge"; and

3. "The emerging 21$^{st}$ century professional occupation addressing the needs of the age focused upon clarity, human understanding, and the science of the organization of information."

The questions this definition generated that I am attempting to answer are:

1. What constitutes a professional occupation?
2. From what context is the professional occupation of information architect emerging?
3. In what stage of emergence is it?
4. What are the "needs of the age" it is emerging to address?
5. How will it address these needs?

Having studied architecture, I began to compare my professional experiences as an information designer and what I was discovering about information architecture to what I had learned about architectural theory, history, design, and practice as a student. As a result of that comparison, I came to view information architecture as a field with strong similarities to architecture. I have also come to believe that the professionalization of information architecture will prove to be as important and as integral to American society as was the professionalization of architecture.

## ABOUT THIS BOOK

This book is written for an audience of American college students studying in the fields of information and library science, computer science, communications, and visual design. It is designed to introduce the reader to key innovations in the history of communications systems and technologies leading to the information age; the fields of information design; human–computer interaction design and user experience design; and the emerging profession of information architecture by:

- Presenting an abbreviated history of revolutionary communication systems and technologies;
- Identifying social and technology-related factors in information creation, communication, storage, and retrieval throughout history;
- Identifying information age-related problems;
- Defining information environment, information space, and information architecture;
- Presenting existing information architecture courses and curriculum; and
- Envisioning the future of information architecture.

It is divided into six parts:

### Part 1—"Information Architecture"

Part 1 introduces and sets information architecture in an historical context by drawing an analogy between its evolution and the evolution of architecture.

**Parts 2–4—"Human Interactions," "Human and Computer Interactions," and "Computer Networks"**

Parts 2 through 4 focus on the history of communication systems and technologies and cover the evolution of communication systems, the evolution of computing systems, and the convergence of communication and computing systems. To understand this history is to understand the roots of today's information marketplace. Each chapter concludes with a brief evaluation of the information-processing capacity of the system or technology featured. The evaluation is based on the premise that communication systems and technologies have varying capacities for communicating, storing, and retrieving information.

**Part 5—"Info Ailments"**

Part 5 presents a range of issues that have arisen from the relentless hype associated with new communication technologies as well as the unorganized and uncontrolled flood of data unleashed by them.

**Part 6—"Toward a New Discipline"**

Part 6 focuses on the emergence of the professional occupation of information architecture and proposes that the "solutions" to many of the issues presented in Part 5, "Info Ailments," will be designed by information architects. Trained to be conceptual thinkers, information architects will foremost be design professionals who are well-versed in the history, theory, skills, and science of their field. They will have the education, experience, and vision necessary to manage entire design and implementation processes. They will clarify and define clients' and users' needs, develop design specifications, draft construction documents, and ultimately help maximize the cost effectiveness of information environments. They will be creative problem solvers.

## UNDERLYING ASSUMPTIONS

My research and writing were based on the following assumptions:

- Human existence is a continuously evolving interplay between environmental and technological influences, formal and informal institutions and practices, and personal values and beliefs.
- The struggle to create, communicate, manage, and preserve information is integral to the process of building civilizations.
- There have been four major communication epochs: oral, writing, printing, and electronic.
- The medium of communication has a significant influence on the nature and content of human communication.
- Social forces, in conjunction with available material resources and technical knowledge, influence the invention and constructions of new technologies.

- New technologies may, in turn, influence society.
- The properties of a communications environment—the unique ways in which information can be stored, transmitted, and distributed in that environment—may "favor" the interests of some social forces and ideas over others and, consequently, affect social organization.
- Change in communication environments may also affect humans' "internal" worlds of ideas and ways of thinking.

Changes in information and communications technology are one among many other important innovations that influence the way we live. Yet because communication is so vital to human existence, these changes will likely have far-reaching implications. Information architecture is the emerging profession focusing on realizing the full value—the human worth—of these changes.

## ACKNOWLEDGMENTS

Many acknowledgments end by thanking one's spouse. In this case I want to reverse the traditional order for Judye (McCalman), who has always challenged me to question the traditional order of most everything. Not only has Judye been a fantastic editor, but, without her encouragement and remarkable patience, I would never have started nor could I have finished this project. For her invaluable contributions and accepting her life as a "book widow" for the better part of a year, she has my deepest love and gratitude.

I also owe thanks to a number of my friends and colleagues who took a special interest in this book, offering their insights, suggestions, or encouragement: I would like to thank Bob and Wings Benton, Joyce Kincannon, David Lebow, Sally McCrorie, Mary Anne Havriluk, Phil Pollock, Dawn Pollock, Judith Harriss, and Sara Golinveaux.

I also wish to thank my LIS 4910-03 students (Tyler Appleby, Jean-Paul Lepez, Arnetia Thomas, Richard Araujo, and Vickie Trice) who reviewed and commented on the first draft of this manuscript. Their interest was encouraging, but, perhaps more importantly, their senses of humor reminded me to lighten up and remember that, "It's just a textbook."

To Professor Keith Belton of the Florida State University School of Information Studies, who reviewed the manuscript over the 2001 Christmas and New Year's holidays, your advice was extremely helpful and your contributions to the book deeply appreciated. Also, many thanks to Arnie Lund of Sapient, Inc., Karyn Young of IBM, and Lillian Svec of Walmart.com for their valuable contributions to this text and for helping me maintain a balanced point of view, and to Paula Thornton and Jason Withrow whose comments helped shape the manuscript in its early stages.

Special thanks to Richard Saul Wurman whom I admire and respect and from whom I drew a great deal of inspiration. Also special thanks to Dean Jane Robbins and Associate Dean Cathy Burnett of the Florida State University School of Information Studies for supporting my research activities over the summer of 2001.

Many thanks, finally, to my parents, Earl and Lillian Morrogh, to whom this book is dedicated. Their gift of love has made all the difference.

# About the Author

Earl Morrogh is a writer, designer, and educator who has studied and worked for 30 years in several fields including architectural and visual design, multimedia design, communications, and education. He considers these areas of professional interest to be interrelated and his knowledge of them essential for informing his research of the emerging profession of information architecture.

He has worked in both the public and private sectors in a variety of capacities including: art director of an internationally distributed sports magazine (*Surf* magazine); communications director of the Florida component of the American Institute of Architects; project manager of a National Science Foundation-funded project (the Interactive Media Science Project) in partnership with Apple Computer, Inc., Pioneer, Inc., and Houghton-Mifflin Publishing, Inc.; associate director of the Florida Department of Education's distance learning initiative (Florida Remote Learning Services); and assistant director of Florida State University's distance learning office (Office of Distributed and Distance Learning).

He holds an undergraduate degree in sociology with a minor in architecture and a master's degree in mass communication with a specialization in interactive communications. At present he is a consultant and visiting scholar in Florida State University's School of Information Studies where he has taught undergraduate courses in information architecture and design theory.

Born in southwest Louisiana, "Acadiana," Mr. Morrogh has lived in the Florida panhandle since 1972 where he enjoys living in a rural setting in a house he and his wife of 23 years designed and built. He also enjoys sea kayaking, sailing, scuba diving, and other water-related recreational activities.

## PART 1

# INFORMATION ARCHITECTURE

## An Introduction

"It is hard to say where the concept of information architecture originated, since people have been [practicing] information architecture in one form or another for centuries. The structure and organization of books, maps, libraries, museums, and cities are all artifacts, in one sense, of an information architecture process."

Peter Morville

## CHAPTER 1

# Information Architecture
## From Craft to Profession

For thousands of years humans have struggled to create, communicate, manage, and preserve information. This struggle is as old as civilization itself and throughout it extend the roots of information architecture. Being aware of this history benefits our understanding of information architecture and broadens our perspective on humanity's cultural evolution. From these events of the past we can also come to better understand today's information environments and to ultimately improve them.

## THE ARCHITECTURE METAPHOR

The metaphors we use constantly in our everyday language profoundly influence what we do because they shape our understanding. They help us describe and explore new ideas in terms and concepts found in more familiar domains. Because architecture, architects, and the profession of architecture are already well-defined concepts in the minds of many people, the architecture metaphor enables the quick construction of a conceptual model of information architecture. The metaphor capitalizes on common knowledge that architects are highly respected professionals in a very complex field of work, require rigorous specialized education and training, and are designers concerned with the occupants, aesthetics, structure, and proper mechanical functioning of buildings as well as the efficient and effective use of space. Perhaps this is why the architecture metaphor as used to help define information architecture has been adopted by so many so easily: it provides an established framework upon which a new concept—information architecture—can be quickly constructed and understood. In fact, when used as metaphors, other real-world or place-based concepts, such as environment and space, are helpful to both information architects and users in visually summarizing complex information systems.

When using electronic information systems we often hear of information-seeking behavior referred to as "wayfinding" or "navigating."

"The metaphors we use constantly in our everyday language profoundly influence what we do, because they shape our understanding. [It is said] that metaphors are pervasive because they reflect how we think, perhaps embodying deeply unconscious archetypes of personality and vision. When we change metaphors, therefore, we change how we think about things. Because metaphors can guide our imagination about a new invention [or profession], they influence what it can be even before it exists."

*Mark Stefik*

## KEYWORDS

cyberspace
information age
information space
information
  superhighway

Both references are based on the commonly used spatial metaphor "information space." By further extending this metaphor, it is easy to imagine occupants of an information space needing to have a sense of place in order to remain oriented; a sense of space so as to know where it is possible to go; and navigation devices commonly seen in physical environments such as maps, signs, paths, and landmarks for navigation. Information systems have even been referred to metaphorically as information cities, and, of course, we've all heard the infrastructure of the Internet referred to as the "Information Super Highway." These are all spatial metaphors used to assist in the visualization of technologies and professions that are too new or complex for us to understand easily.

Some information architects believe that the practice of information architecture is very much like what architects do in that "[they] design spaces for human beings to live, work, and play in" with the primary differences being in the materials they work with (Christina Wodke, 2000). Or, that information architects in reality, not just metaphorically, are very much like architects in that they too are concerned with spatial relationships and "setting structure to an element to be built that combines components that are grouped together based on users' understandings and expectations" (Van Der Wal, 2001). Architecture and information architecture are, in fact, similar in many ways; consequently, numerous analogies can be drawn between them, including their histories.

## ARCHITECTURE

Architects are responsible for a major portion of our built environment. They design and create not only buildings but entire blocks and even cities. They plan the places where we live our lives—where we raise our families, work, socialize, worship, play, learn, and dream. Architecture is a holistic field, and aspiring architects are trained in a wide range of skills, knowledge, and sensitivities that are essential to planning, organizing, and managing the design-build process. They have long been highly respected in most cultures of the world. Indeed, rarely is a work of architecture with any historical, cultural, technical, or aesthetic significance mentioned without giving credit to the architect.

Given this present-day context, it is difficult to imagine that a great Gothic cathedral like, for example, Notre Dame de Paris with its dramatic archways, ribbed vaults, flying buttresses, large stained-glass windows, and ornate spires would not be the work of a brilliant, highly trained architect. In fact, no one in 1163 A.D. had yet been trained as an architect; there were no architecture schools and no architecture profession. The individual responsible for the design and construction of Notre Dame was known as a cementer, a stone worker, or simply a master mason.

These are all labels descriptive of a craft. Through a crafts tradition, a master mason would generally have learned his trade by advancing through three levels of expertise:

"People have been developing information architecture ever since a stylus was first applied to a clay tablet. All information systems have an architecture, planned or otherwise. Books for example, have sequential numbered pagination, move top-to-bottom and left-to-right, use title pages, table of contents, and back-of-the-book indices. These are all architectural conventions that we take for granted. But, their acceptance took decades after Gutenberg's revolution."

*Louis Rosenfeld*

1. Mastering various stone-crafting techniques,
2. Mastering the processes of stone construction, and
3. Mastering the art of design.

Stonecutters, woodcarvers, and metalsmiths might all work under a master mason to build, as well as furnish, a cathedral. Consequently, the work of master masons was highly valued, and many enjoyed an elevated status typically not given to craftsmen. In fact, their names were often inscribed along with community dignitaries in prominent places in cathedrals and public works.

Gothic architecture evolved during a time of dramatic social and economic change in western Europe. In the late 11th and 12th centuries, trade and industry were booming, resulting in improved communications between neighboring towns and cities as well as more distant communities. Taller and larger than most community structures, Gothic cathedrals were visible from the surrounding countryside and were dramatic symbols of the Church's powerful influence. At the same time, a new intellectual movement was rising. The outcome of these influences was the end of the isolationism of the feudal era and the emergence of a more cosmopolitan world. This era in history is known as the *Medieval Ages*. From this rich mix also emerged a profession concerned with designing buildings and spaces that are both beautiful and functional—architecture.

## INFORMATION ARCHITECTURE

For perhaps as long as two million years, our ancestors have struggled to communicate information across time and space and to preserve valuable legacies of experience for the benefit of future generations. Throughout this history, great innovations have occurred that dramatically improved humankind's abilities to create, communicate, manage, and preserve information. Each innovation coincided with major social and economic change. They are often referred to as communication epochs: oral, writing, printing, and electronic. With the exception of the oral epoch, each has built upon its predecessor, leading to the technologically sophisticated, complex, and dense information "environments" we experience today.

Now, we are all living in a time of dramatic social and economic change. A global economy and sophisticated new communication and network technologies have resulted in practically instantaneous communication among governments, businesses, and individuals anywhere on the planet. The great towers and spires that dominate the skylines of today's cities are symbolic of the powerful influence of corporations in contemporary culture. The generation, distribution, and management of information are significant factors in today's "knowledge" economy, and consumers are being presented with, and have instantaneous access to, more information than at any other time in history. This era in human

"The notion of design arose during the fourteenth and fifteenth centuries in Europe and connoted the separation of thinking and doing. That is not to suggest that designing was a new activity. Rather it was separated out from a wider productive activity [craftswork] and recognized as an activity in its own right. Design can be said to constitute a separation of hand and brain, of manual and intellectual work, of the conceptual part of work from the labor process." Up until this point in history great structures were designed and built by master builders. Subsequently, the design-build process became more specialized and more and more buildings were designed by architects and constructed by builders.

*Robert Jacobson*

"More and more of work depends on the effective use of information. New possibilities to access information are affecting our daily lives, not only at work but also at home and during leisure time. Social functions have become more and more specialized, creating greater complexity and, consequently, new needs for information. The urban and architectural environment has also grown more perplexing; just finding our way around our built environment, a trivial task in the past, is now a distinct challenge. Thus the design of information and its efficient communication are more essential than ever before."

*Robert Jacobson*

The complexity of today's information design problems is pushing information designers to integrate concepts and methodologies from other disciplines into their design practices. These other fields include communications, cognitive psychology, computer science, visual design, journalism, information studies and library science, and even anthropology.

history is often referred to as the *Information Age*. Another new profession is emerging to meet the needs of the times—information architecture.

Information architecture is primarily about the design of information environments and the management of an information environment design process. Information architecture's roots are in multiple fields, including visual design, information design, library science, computer science, social informatics, and engineering psychology (more commonly known as "human factors"). All are occupations focused on the creation, communication (presentation and organization), management (storage, retrieval, and distribution), and preservation of information or maximizing the relationship between humans and technology. Each has its own history, traditions, best practices, and technical languages. Until the advent of personal computers, the digitization of all media, and the maturation of the Internet, these disciplines were worlds unto themselves.

Now, many information and communication professionals, no matter what their field, are being forced by the demands of the marketplace to solve information environment design problems requiring knowledge that spans all these disciplines. Mastery of any one requires a great deal of time, practice, and knowledge. To expect mastery of *all* is more than can be required of an individual.

Such is the plight of many designers today. Most are too specialized in one discipline to understand fully how to organize and present information in an effective and compelling way when using a variety of media in one integrated, networked, and often interactive, environment. Yet, a rapidly growing and evolving information marketplace is putting these demands on individuals who have not been trained to handle such complex design issues nor have the knowledge to manage effectively teams of individual experts. Master masons must have faced a similar set of circumstances that pressured them to move beyond their craft (requiring highly specific knowledge) and invent a profession that required a more comprehensive knowledge of an entire design-build process using a variety of materials other than stone—architecture. Now, professionals from multiple disciplines, like master masons in the early stages of architecture's evolution, are moving toward inventing a profession that requires a more comprehensive knowledge of an entire design-build process, using a variety of media and technologies, for the purpose of creating information environments that are beautiful, valuable to users and sponsors, and easy to use—information architecture.

## PART 2

# HUMAN INTERACTIONS
## The Evolution of Communication Systems

"Speaking and writing seem to us such natural acts that at first it seems inconceivable that they are the most complex inventions achieved by the human brain. And, in the last analysis, the most fundamental tools that have made all the rest possible."

Henri-Jean Martin

## CHAPTER 2

# Let's Talk About It
## The Spoken Word

> "Human society first formed itself with the aid of oral speech, becoming literate (a writing culture) very late in its history. . . . *Homo sapiens* were capable of articulate language 35,000 years ago. The earliest writing dates from only 6,000 years ago."
>
> Walter J. Ong

## HISTORY: 2,500,000 B.C.–Present

Speaking seems to have originated with the emergence of the genus *Homo* some 2.5 million years ago and involved four species in this evolutionary order: *habilis, erectus, neanderthalensis* (Neanderthal), and *sapiens.* Many experts claim that the genus *Homo* evolved from a species of the genus *Australopithecus. Australopithecines* were great walking apes; they were not great talking apes.

### *Homo habilis* (2.4 million years ago)

*Homo habilis* had a larger brain and longer limbs than *Australopithecus.* These two attributes alone apparently helped *habilis* adapt to climatic changes that *Australopithecus* could not. Although *habilis* did not develop weapons, he could make simple stone tools and was the first to control fire. *Habilis'* bigger brain advantage improved his survivability, and his numbers increased. Larger and more complex groups led to more complex societies. *Habilis* societies, within which superior mental abilities were favored, ultimately propagated members with larger brains and perhaps the neural pathways for rudimentary language. *Habilis* would have been capable of basic gestures and vocalizations, but not of articulate speech (the systematic arrangement of significant vocal sounds).

Through specialized adaptations of mind and body, speech became possible for early humans. The subsequent development of language enabled them to define things, communicate their experiences to one another, and use symbolic reasoning. Articulate speech and sophisticated reasoning led to increasingly sophisticated societies. Ultimately, brain power would play a more significant role than brawn in the survival of the human species.

### KEYWORDS
evolution and speech
human evolution
*homo erectus*
*homo habilis*
*homo neanderthalensis*
*homo sapiens*
orality
origins of speech

### *Homo erectus* (2 million years ago)

With the exception of protruding brow ridges and a backward sloping forehead, *erectus* resembled modern humans and was smarter (larger brain), taller, and faster than *habilis*. *Erectus* was an inventor and developed many versatile tools including the world's first hand axe. Consequently, *erectus* was very adaptable and migrated to different regions of the world. In fact, it appears that *erectus,* in one well-researched instance, was both intelligent and socially organized enough to construct rafts and cross many miles of water to a distant shore. Planning of this complexity requires complex thought processes, and the social implementation of a complex plan requires a high level of cooperation among individuals. This implies the use of speech. It would not be speech as we know it because *erectus* was anatomically unable to control exhalation. However, it is conceivable that *erectus* was capable of short, meaningful utterances.

Speech formed the basis upon which all cultures have been built. However, subsequent communication technologies and systems have not replaced speech. They have all simply expanded the variety of means by which humans communicate—each having different communicative qualities and capacities for creating, communicating, and recording the human experience.

### *Homo neanderthalensis* (300,000 years ago)

Early Neanderthals (pre-Neanderthals) were tall and thin, much like *Homo erectus* but, as a result of a heat-retaining anatomical adaptation to the climate of Ice Age Europe, later Neanderthals were stocky and barrel-chested with short and powerful limbs. Neanderthals were hunters and gatherers and used cooperative hunting strategies to kill. They were capable of fashioning warm clothing from animal hides, they buried their dead, and they cared for their sick and lame. They were also highly skilled toolmakers. Experts agree that the only explanation for their sophisticated tool-manufacturing skills and complex societies is that they used a basic form of language. Recent discoveries support the possibility that they were anatomically capable of frequent and fluent speech.

### *Homo sapiens* (300,000 years ago)

The practice of creating, communicating, storing, and retrieving information is as old as civilization itself. What has changed over time are the means by which we create, communicate, store, and retrieve information.

*Homo sapiens* were almost identical to us anatomically and, like the Neanderthals, were also capable of fluent speech. Interestingly, the cultures of *Homo sapiens* and Neanderthals were virtually indistinguishable from each other until approximately 50,000 years ago. It is even possible that there was some interaction between the two cultures. However, some sort of evolutionary leap allowed *sapiens* to evolve into modern humans. Neanderthals eventually became extinct, possibly as a result of the dominance of *Homo sapiens*. There is evidence that early *sapiens* practiced art and music and lived in permanent settlements. They were capable of killing large prey with spears and developed a variety of tools, some of which were manufactured specifically for trading. They had a rich and complex knowledge of the natural world and would have used language much as we use it today.

| **TABLE 2–1   About Speech** |
|---|
| Scientific research into the uniquely human ability to use and understand language has revealed the following: |
| 1. Human speech is made possible by special adaptations of the mind and body that occurred in the course of human evolution (Pinker, 1990). <br> 2. All human beings are genetically endowed with the ability to learn and use language. <br> 3. All languages are complex systems with the same basic kinds of rules. <br> 4. The grammars of contemporary societies are no more complex than the grammars of ancient societies. <br> 5. Within societies, [most] individuals use language regardless of their intelligence, social status, or level of education (Pinker, 1990). <br> 6. Speech has tremendous utility in that it gives humans the capacity to define things and to communicate ideas, observations, and experiences to others. It has given all human activity a voice. |

## CULTURAL NOTES

It is very difficult for us to imagine a world where writing does not exist; yet, for many thousands of years, this was the case. In early oral cultures, words existed only as sounds and did not have a visual presence (like a written word). This restriction shaped communication and thought processes. For example, in an oral culture, to think through something complex (without a means to record it) would be a waste of time because it could not be recovered very effectively. It would simply be a passing thought.

In oral cultures, saying things in memorable ways became very important, and memory aids, called mnemonic devices, were devised. Walter Ong, in his text, *Orality and Literacy*, writes, "In [an] oral culture, to solve effectively the problem of retaining and retrieving carefully articulated thought, you have to do your thinking in mnemonic patterns, shaped for ready oral recurrence. Your thought must come into being in heavily rhythmic, balanced patterns, in repetitions or antitheses, in alliterations and assonances, in epithets and other formulary expressions, in standard thematic settings (the assembly, the meal, the duel, and so on), in proverbs that are constantly heard by everyone so that they come to mind readily and which themselves are patterned for retention and ready recall, or in other mnemonic form. Serious thought [in oral cultures] is intertwined with memory systems. In an oral culture, experience is intellectualized mnemonically" (Ong, 1997).

There were other significant characteristics of oral cultures:

1. Intellectual experimentation was discouraged. Traditional expressions were not broken up (analyzed) because to do so (without a recording system like writing) is to risk losing generations of hard work.

Because languages are cultural systems, individual languages may classify objects and ideas in completely different ways. Even within one language culture such as American English, there are, for example, smaller professional cultures that use highly technical languages. These technical languages are used and understood only by other members of the same professional community.

| TABLE 2–2　Information Processing—Speech |
| --- |
| Communication systems and technologies have various capacities for communicating, storing, and retrieving information. Speech is distinctly different from all other communication media. In fact, it is closer to being an internal instinctual component of human behavior than to an external conveyance. However, for the purpose of comparing speech to other communication systems and technologies, we will look at speech as a communication system. With that restriction in mind, speech has the following information-processing capacities. |
| *Information Communication*<br>　　Languages are extremely complex and adaptive and have an almost unlimited capacity for processing and communicating human experience.<br><br>*Information Storage*<br>　　The ability to store information in an oral culture was limited to an individual's memorization skills.<br><br>*Information Retrieval*<br>　　The ability to retrieve information stored in an individual's memory in an oral culture was limited to that individual's skill level for recalling information from memory. |

Because languages are cultural systems, many have disappeared along with the societies that developed them. "In the long process of evolving articulate speech there has always been an ebb and flow of human populations—the victims and beneficiaries of warfare and disease, accident, and climate. Scores of thousands of languages have come and gone without a trace."

*Steven Fischer*

2. Redundancy in storytelling was important. Redundancy helped listeners remember critical events and the opportunity to hear again what they may have not heard or understood when first spoken.
3. Knowledge was conceptualized in the context of human activity. Oral cultures did not itemize things. References to people, facts, or statistics where embedded in stories. Without texts, most learning occurred by doing and observing.
4. The oral mind was not interested in precise word definitions. Oral cultures had no dictionaries, and word meanings were shaped by the gestures, vocal inflections, and facial expressions of the speaker as well as the social context in which spoken.
5. The effective use of words was very important in oral cultures and, therefore, on human interaction. Oral communication tends to unite people in groups.

## SUMMARY

Perhaps because of improved diet, migrations, and/or changing climate, around a million years ago significant change in the cerebral capacity of early hominids was occurring. Apparently, as a consequence of this increased cerebral capacity, changes in their vocalizations were also occurring. From indistinct sounds, a simple language system emerged; from then on, human vocal language developed concurrently with the human brain. As the brain enlarged, speech became more articulate and, in turn, enabled societies to become more complex. As societies became more complex, brain capacities increased to accommodate the increasing complexity of society.

Using primitive speech, early *Homo erectus* was capable of basic social planning and organization in order to achieve cooperative projects. As his speech grew more sophisticated, he settled into permanent villages and developed a rich variety of technologies and rituals. Later, *erectus* developed the capacity to use articulate speech with a more complex syntax (the way in which words are put together to form phrases, clauses, or sentences) which was inherited and further developed by *Homo neanderthalensis* and *Homo sapiens*.

About 35,000 years ago, *Homo sapiens* attained a capacity for human thought and language usage comparable to the capacity we have today. Twenty thousand years later, *Homo sapiens* was the only hominid species to survive evolution.

By this time, thousands of languages were being spoken. In another two thousand years, Earth would warm, triggering a biological revolution that resulted in permanent farming communities. This ultimately led to agriculture's becoming the primary means of subsistence for many people, and humans settled into one place for generations. As agricultural practices became more sophisticated and successful, surpluses of food became available, and human populations grew even larger and social complexity increased. As humans became more attached to the land, so did language. Eventually, languages came to be known as the "tongue" of the people and the region they inhabited. Speech formed the basis upon which all cultures have since been built (Fischer, 1999).

# INFORMATION ARCHITECTURE (IA) AND THE SPOKEN WORD

Some innovations in information and communication technologies (ICT) have a direct historical relevance to the IA profession, while the relevance of others has more to do with the facilitation of the IA process. The information organization, navigation, interaction, and flow characteristics of ICT innovations (ancient and modern) influence the shape of today's information spaces and are therefore also relevant to understanding information architecture.

Throughout the history of the human species, there have been many individuals, both famous and unknown, who have made significant contributions toward making all forms of communication, including speech, more effective. These individuals are the predecessors of today's information architects.

## The Information Space: Organization, Navigation, Interaction, and Flows

The original information space

would have been within the brain, in the air transmitting sound between people, or as part of artistic/cultural ritual manifestations like painting and dance. The information technologies used then were "soft" technologies, based on what has been called the "wetware" of our brains rather than on any hardware. Communication occurred through the use of spoken language, and processing took place without any technical assistance. (Andrew Treloar, 1994)

In oral cultures, information was organized into the linear narrative forms we know as stories to enhance storage (memorizing) and retrieval (remembering). Storytellers used a variety of techniques for recalling stories including rhythm, repetition, alliteration, and standard themes. Listeners used similar techniques for remembering stories and for navigating through and recalling the information embedded in stories. In the storytelling information space, the storyteller controls the experience, and the listener's interaction level with the information resource, the storyteller, is generally low. Interaction with the information embedded in stories is an internalized personal activity. The flow of information in storytelling is primarily one way: from the storyteller to the listener(s). Today, when we watch movies and television, listen to music and radio programs, or attend plays and operas, we are experiencing the storytelling information space.

Language systems are a generative form of communication in that they allow humans to generate sentences of any desired complexity to convey an unlimited number of ideas, observations, or imaginations. Language systems are also adaptive and expand or change to cope with the expression of new meanings.

In another information space that involves speech—the conversational information space—information organizational and navigational schemes, interaction levels, and flows of information are controlled by more than one individual. Consequently, the conversational information space is much more dynamic and adaptive than the storytelling information space. Conversationalists can organize and reorganize the information they are attempting to communicate depending on direct and indirect feedback received in the course of a conversation. Navigation decisions in conversations are negotiable. The potential for interaction in any conversation is very high. Conversation flows are nonlinear and two way; the potential for branching is unlimited.

## Facilitation of the IA Process

The practice of IA often involves teams of individuals representing various disciplines and stakeholders. In such circumstances, IA is a very social process, and communication plays a vital role. IAs are often responsible for facilitating communication among a design team's members, the members of the organization within which design activities take place, between the design team and the client, and between the design team and users. One very important form of communication in this process is talking.

Talking is effective for one-to-one and one-to-many communication for the purposes of:

- Disseminating information
- Exchanging ideas
- Sharing stories
- Motivating individuals and groups
- Ad hoc problem solving

## CHAPTER 3

# Put It in Writing
## The Written Word

> "Writing . . . was and is the most momentous of all human technological inventions. It is not a mere appendage to speech. Because it moves speech from the oral-aural to a new sensory world, that of vision, it transforms speech and thought as well."
>
> Walter J. Ong

## HISTORY: 3500 B.C.–Present

Writing, as we currently know it, is a relatively recent development in human history. There is general agreement that the earliest known script, or true writing (a representation of words spoken or imagined as spoken), developed as a consequence of the demands of a booming economy in the early cities of Mesopotamia about three thousand five hundred years ago. Experts theorize that the complexity of trading began to exceed Sumerian traders' memories, prompting the development of a system for recording transactions in a permanent form.

This writing as accountancy theory is based on the discovery of clay tablets upon which listings of raw materials and products, field areas and their owners, and laborers and their tasks were inscribed. The same tablets contained financial and administrative calculations. It seems that although this particular script did not spread around the world, the concept of writing did, and many other scripts were developed (Robinson, 1999).

### Prewriting (25,000 B.C.–3500 B.C.)

Long before true writing systems were developed, oral cultures used pictures and markings as mnemonic devices for the purpose of telling stories and for counting. Some techniques for recording images and calculations included engravings or paintings on stone surfaces, notches and markings on bone, clay tokens with distinctive shapes and signs impressed into

> "Before the invention of writing, perhaps by the Sumerians in the 4th millenium B.C., information could be spread only by word of mouth, with all the accompanying limitations of time and space."
>
> *Brittanica.com*

**KEYWORDS**

evolution of writing
history of literacy
history of writing
origins of writing
pictographs, ideographs, rebus

15

the clay, signs impressed on clay containers (that held clay tokens), and signs impressed on clay tablets (Robinson, 1999).

## Pictographs, Ideographs, and Rebus Writing (3300 B.C.–present)

The first written symbols were thought to have been direct representations of specific objects—pictographs. However, without a code to enable them to represent words in various grammatical relationships to each other, these pictures or symbols could not function as true writing systems. The concept of ideographs would move pictographs a step away from direct representation of an object.

Ideographs were pictures and symbols whose meanings were established by a code. For example, "in [a Chinese ideograph] a stylized picture of two trees does not represent the words 'two trees' but the word 'woods'." A reader would not understand this without having learned the code (the meaning associated with the symbol) (Ong, 1997).

The rebus, an ingenious idea, moved pictographs even further away from direct representation. With the rebus principle, instead of a pictograph representing an object or an idea, it now represented a sound. This way, sounds could systematically be made visible (Robinson, 1999). Many pictographic systems were comprised of several thousand symbols (characters), making these systems very difficult to learn and use.

Some systems became more stylized and codified for the sake of efficiency but remained rooted to their original symbols. Other systems continued to stylize their pictographs to the point of becoming highly abstracted shapes bearing no resemblance to their originating symbols. For example, Egyptian hieroglyphics were far less abstracted than Sumerian cuneiform (wedgelike shape) which, when first discovered, was considered to be a form of ornamentation and not at all related to language or writing.

## Alphabetic Scripts (1700 B.C.–present)

Scripts seemed to have developed simultaneously but independently of each other in various parts of the world. However, there is general acceptance that alphabetic writing was invented only once and perhaps by one person around 1700 B.C. It is also commonly accepted that the invention of an alphabet was one more step (but a highly important one) toward refining and conventionalizing writing. The production of a symbolic system that represents, by single characters (rather than pictographs, ideographs, or syllables), a limited number of distinct speech sounds is the defining principle of alphabets. From what script the alphabet originated is still the source of much debate. Regardless, all agree that the invention of alphabets had revolutionary effects, particularly the

---

"The first words ever recorded were probably something like, 'Bob. Three sheep.' Scholars who trace the invention of writing say the oldest was far from poetry, but was rather an accounting record. They say it developed because ancient man needed a way of keeping records for business and government."

*ABC News*

---

Early writing systems were very complex, involving hundreds of characters. Writing, therefore, was originally practiced by a relatively few professional technicians. With few exceptions, this has proven to be true with the introduction of new communication technologies ever since.

alphabet perfected by the Greeks. "The most efficient form of written communication ever devised (for most, but not all, languages), the Greek alphabet has been adopted and imitated throughout the world for hundreds, if not thousands, of languages . . ." (Fischer, 1999).

## Early Books (3500 B.C.–15th century A.D.)

The clay tablets upon which the Sumerians made impressions were really the forerunners of books. Later, book rolls, or scrolls, made of sheets of papyrus and rolled on a stick, were developed by ancient Egyptians, Greeks, and Romans and are more closely related to modern books. Reproductions of scrolls were done by professional scribes either by copying an original text or by recording dictation from the author. However, this was a very slow, labor-intensive, and expensive process, and these early forms of books were owned primarily by temples, rulers, or very wealthy individuals. For many centuries, the majority of people learned by listening and memorizing often-told stories; cultures remained primarily oral.

Around the first century A.D., the scroll was gradually replaced by the codex. The codex, as first used by the Greeks and Romans, was a rectangular ringed notebook. Consisting of two or more wax-covered wooden tablets, a codex could be marked and smoothed over many times. Sometimes sheets made of parchment were sandwiched between the tablets. By the fourth century, the codex had replaced the use of scrolls and had come to consist of many sheets of papyrus folded, stitched, and attached to wooden boards. It strongly resembled the book as we know it today. Codexes of this type were commonly used by worshipers in religious services. In fact, from the 5th through the 15th centuries, books were used mostly by rulers and churchmen.

## CULTURAL NOTES

The shift from speech to writing was highly interrelated with concurrent developments in agriculture, trade, political organization, technological skills, education, and family organization. However, every one of these developments was more than likely deeply affected by the shift from speech to writing. Writing is truly among the greatest inventions in history.

Over the past 5,000 years, cultures have become literate to the point where it is very difficult for us to imagine a purely oral culture—a culture without writing. But the transition from orality to literacy was very slow and was often met with skepticism and resistance. Plato has Socrates say in the *Phaedrus* that writing is inhuman, pretending to establish outside the mind what in reality can only be in the mind. It is a thing, a manufactured product. Writing, originally perceived to be magical, eventually came to be recognized as an instrument of power and was used to express

The technology of writing was seen by some as a threat to the importance of human memory. It was feared that those who became too heavily dependent on it could become forgetful. There were also educators who thought that the idea of someone being able to learn something through the medium of writing was absurd.

Similar fears have surfaced with the introduction of other new communication technologies. For instance, it was feared that the telephone would put an end to written correspondence, the television an end to reading, email an end to the postal service, and with the Web, the end of universities, libraries, teachers, and cities.

Writing influenced the ways in which people had interacted for thousands of years before its introduction. Systems of communication are clearly related to what humans can make of this work both internally, in terms of thought, and externally, in terms of social and cultural organization. When these systems change, patterns of human interaction are therefore also affected. However, not all new communication technologies have been successfully socialized and woven into the cultural fabric. Many, for a variety of reasons, have fallen by the wayside.

**TABLE 3–1   About Writing**

"Writing preserves and standardizes spoken language. It also generates other language-oriented processes with social [and psychological] implications" (Fischer, 1999, 18). Listed below are more key characteristics and effects of writing:

1. Writing is a technology that calls for the use of tools.
2. Writing transforms sound (speech) to something visual (text).
3. The process of putting spoken words into written words is governed by rules.
4. Writing is an external device that has the capacity to transform internal thought processes (consciousness).
5. Writing (and print) replaced hearing dominance in the world of thought and expression with sight dominance.
6. Without writing we would not have history, science, or philosophy.

Early writing systems served primarily as mnemonic devices meant to jog the memory and had no relationship to spoken language. In order to construct a written communication system that could convey information the way speech did, it would have to be based on spoken language. The invention of the alphabetic scripts succeeded in marrying spoken language and graphic symbolism, transforming speech into something visual.

the ideologies of power-seeking groups for the purpose of domination. In some cultures it was thought writing could be dangerous to the unwary reader, and literacy was restricted to an elite few.

The 7th to the 13th centuries were an age of religious manuscript book production. Illuminated manuscripts were produced and copied by monks in monasteries across Europe. Monasteries were also the seats of intellectual life in Europe during the Middle Ages. However, given the amounts of time and energy involved in producing manuscripts, books were much too valuable to be made available to the general public. Even if one did have access to the library of a monastery, uniform cataloging systems did not exist, and knowing what was in the collection or its location would have been very difficult.

Book production became more secularized after the 13th century and often attempted to document the observable world rather than serve primarily as objects of worship. The production of secular books was influenced by the rise of universities in Europe that created a demand for books. An author often wrote in his own hand, and then his work would be copied for a fee by professional copyists who worked in small shops. Each copy of an individual's work represented a tremendous expenditure of energy. At this time most manuscripts in circulation were simply notes or copies that either students, clergymen, or "men of letters" owned for their personal use. The circulation of these precious manuscripts was not large and usually was among friends, resulting in small, self-contained groups who protected their prized works under lock and key (Martin, 1994).

Ultimately, with the manufacturing of paper and the advent of printing technology, the duplication of books became much less costly. Books consequently became much more common, cheaper, and accessible to the general population. Printers, who were also booksellers, began to publish books on a broad range of popular subjects, both religious and secular. Eventually writing had a democratizing effect and proved to be essential for the development of not only history but also science and phi-

---

**TABLE 3–2   Information Processing—Writing**

Communication systems and technologies have various capacities for communicating, storing, and retrieving information. Writing has the following information-processing capacities:

*Information Communication*
- Languages, whether spoken or written, are extremely complex and adaptive and have an almost unlimited capacity for processing and communicating human experience. However, writing lacks the phonetic qualities of speech (tones that inform us that the speaker is excited, angry, etc.), and punctuation that signals tone in writings is minimal. A writer must compensate for a lack of gesture, tone, or facial expression in order to make written words clear all by themselves. This exercise sharpens analytical skills (Ong, 1997).
- Writing has great utility primarily for two reasons: (1) It records speech in a visual dimension (text), allowing it to be an object of reflection, and (2) It makes possible the accumulation, preservation, and communication of the ideas, observations, and experiences of successive generations (culture).

*Information Storage*
- The storage of written words is limited only by the efficiency of the recording process and the availability, durability, size, and mass of the material upon which the text is recorded.
- The written word freed the mind from large memorization tasks necessary for preserving knowledge in oral cultures.

*Information Retrieval*
- Retrieval of written words is limited by the skills of the information manager and the sophistication of the information management system used for storing, organizing, and retrieving texts.

---

losophy. Society as we know it today simply could and would not exist without writing.

## SUMMARY

In the pre-writing era, depictions of objects triggered the memory of spoken words for the objects depicted. Pictographic and ideographic writing also used depictions of objects to trigger the memory, but for a sound or concept less directly related to the object depicted. When used in conjunction with a code, this innovation enabled the representation of words in various grammatical relationships and, consequently, the ability to communicate more abstracted and complex information (true writing). With the invention of alphabetic writing, the picture was abstracted to a single letter that was no longer related to an object. Letters represented only one of two different types of sounds, either a vowel or a consonant, resulting in a near total transformation of words from sound to sight.

As the technology of writing improved, more and more scripts were written, but only the elite had access to them. Also, until the advent of printing, manuscript cultures would remain primarily oral, and scripts

Writing, for a very long time, "served largely to recycle knowledge back into the oral world." It would be the introduction of printing that would lead to the replacement of "hearing-dominance in the world of thought and expression with sight-dominance which had its beginnings with writing but could not flourish with the support of writing alone."

*Walter Ong*

were generally read aloud even when reading to one's self. Consequently, books remained closely associated with the spoken word and were seen as recorded speech and not as objects that contained information.

## IA AND THE WRITTEN WORD

Writing arose along with the formation of a new type of social organization—cities and city states. Such societies required a clear division of labor and well-defined hierarchies. In these new cultural centers, communication techniques and ways to transfer knowledge took on great importance.

Some innovations in information and communication technologies (ICT) have a direct historical relevance to the IA profession, while the relevance of others has more to do with the facilitation of the IA process. The information organization, navigation, interaction, and flow characteristics of ICT innovations (ancient and modern) influence the shape of today's information spaces and are therefore also relevant to understanding information architecture.

### The Information Space: Organization, Navigation, Interaction, and Flows

> The development of external representations for information such as graphic art and writing freed information from the confines of the human brain and allowed storage and communication independently of a specific individual. A range of information could now be readily manipulated in symbolic form in information spaces external to the brain. (Andrew Treloar, 1994)

Early writing systems recorded the spoken word and organized information in the same linear structure used in storytelling. Navigation of ancient manuscripts was facilitated by the use of notes and markers inserted by readers. Interaction with textual information is an internalized personal process controlled by the reader. Although readers have no control over the content of a document authored by another, flow in the written word information space is not totally one way, in that readers can elect to read whatever they want whenever they want.

## FACILITATION OF THE IA PROCESS

Anything that serves as a representation of a person's thinking by using symbols is considered a document. Documentation in writing and in a graphic form is critical to the IA design process and is used for the purposes of:

- Communicating information (one-to-one, one-to-many, and many-to-one)
- Capturing information
- Storing information
- Disseminating information

One "primary form of written communication among all parities involved in [an IA] project comes by way of the IA deliverable. 'Deliverables' is a term used for any document given to the client for maintaining contact with the project progression" (Chris Ewing, 2002). The following is a sampling of types of IA deliverables:

- Proposals
- Business objectives
- Schedules
- Research documents
- Design documents
- Specifications
- Storyboards
- Site maps
- Paper prototypes

(Chris Ewing, 2002)

# 4 CHAPTER

# Hot Off the Press
## The Printed Word

"The first assembly line, a technique of manufacture which in a series of steps produces identical complex objects made up of replaceable parts, was not one which produced stoves or shoes or weaponry, but one which produced the printed book."

Walter J. Ong

## HISTORY: A.D. 1436–Present

Johann Gutenberg is given credit for inventing the printing press. Actually, the printing press is not a single invention but a collection of inventions that occurred over a period of 500 years. Gutenberg's idea was for using and mass-producing movable type. Other relevant inventions included the screw-type press that had been in use for many hundreds of years throughout Europe and Asia for pressing grapes or olives. The adaptation of block-print technology, mass-production papermaking techniques, and the development of oil-based inks were also critical to the advent of the printing press (Wisconsin-Milwaukee, 1996).

Completed sometime between A.D. 1450 and 1456, the Gutenberg *Bible* was the first major book printed in movable type. Printing the *Bible* took Gutenberg almost two years, but the printing press ultimately simplified book production and made it economically feasible and relatively easy. Printing technology quickly spread around Europe, and by the year 1500 approximately two hundred cities and towns had presses. It is estimated that anywhere from eight to twenty million books were printed before 1500, a number exceeding the total number of books produced in western history until that time. By 1600, printing spread to the colonies in the Americas, India, Japan, and China.

As a consequence of the variety of connections printers necessarily maintained with the worlds of politics, art, and education, printing became a new type of occupation. Contracts often came from local and state

**KEYWORDS**

Gutenberg press
history of writing
history of books
invention of the printing
    press
literacy and the printing
    press

governments, artists were required to produce woodcuts and engravings, and print shops became the gathering place for scholars. Consequently, to be a successful printer required a combination of intellectual, aesthetic, and administrative skills.

Because printing was a commercial enterprise, printers would print anything that would sell. They soon discovered markets among the general public and specialized groups and produced a wide variety of book types including legal codes, instructional books, dictionaries, cheap editions of the classics, Latin missals for the clergy, and medical treatises for doctors. The general public particularly liked religious books, and the best-selling book for many years during the Reformation (1520s) "was John Foxe's *Book of Martyrs* which described in drippy, ghastly detail the deaths of many Protestants during the reign of Mary Tudor." Other popular genres included historical romances, how-to manuals, travel guides, home remedy books, cookbooks, pornography, and the accounts of adventurous travelers (Columbus' notebooks were reprinted many times) (Wisconsin-Milwaukee, 1996).

In the 1700s, Italian Renaissance printers established a number of book-publishing conventions that continue today: lightweight covers; standard page layouts; highly readable Roman and Italic typefaces; title pages; prefaces; introductions; and, later, the table of contents, lists of illustrations, explanatory notes, bibliographies, and indices.

Book production became highly mechanized throughout the 1800s and 1900s (after the Industrial Revolution). Increasingly precise and efficient presses resulted in great numbers of books being produced at a lower and lower cost. Lower cost meant more people could afford to buy books, and more people could afford to publish. Consequently, as literacy spread, the market for books grew. And, as an increasing number of publishers attempted to satisfy the growing diversity of interests of more and more readers, the subject matter of books became universal (Microsoft, 2001).

## CULTURAL NOTES

Printing had a broad range of influences on 16th-century culture for a variety of reasons. By removing precious documents from chests and vaults and ultimately the control of the elite, printing had a democratizing effect. Now, valuable data that may have been lost or never shared would be preserved by being placed in the public domain. This notion contradicted long-established traditions, but was central to the eventual success of modern science, greater cultural diversity, and more secular societies.

Printing also contributed to increased uniformity in Western Europe and the beginnings of mass culture. A growing sense of sameness among different cultures also accentuated their differences and heightened people's sense of diversity for the first time. More books and cheaper books

Like many other new communication technologies, printing was intended for one application before its potential to be used for another was recognized. Printing's primary utility was originally seen as a means of doing away with new and different errors that were inevitably introduced into a relatively few handwritten manuscript copies. However, its potential for mass producing manuscripts soon became obvious, and it ultimately transformed the possibilities for the written word.

"A book is a written (or printed) message of considerable length, meant for public circulation and recorded on materials that are light yet durable enough to afford easy portability. Its primary purpose is to carry a message between people, depending on the twin faculties of portability and permanence. As such, the book transcends time and space, to announce, to expound, and to preserve and transmit knowledge."

*Brittanica.com*

---

**TABLE 4–1    About Printing**

The ability to produce perfect copies of textual material by the hundreds or thousands led to a range of new developments.

1. The development of typographic standards in printing made book cataloging and indexing systems more feasible and retrieval easier.
2. The large-scale distribution of identical copies of books made possible for the first time large-scale data collection for the purpose of printing improved editions.
3. The duplication powers of print brought to an end the "textual drift" that would occur in manuscripts as one copyist after another hand-duplicated them, and, consequently, served to fix and preserve text in its original form.
4. Before printing, permanent and consistent records of complex techniques (anything that required following a number of steps) were rare. Printing introduced a level of permanence and an ease of retrieval that allowed for making steady progressive changes to complex techniques (Eisenstein, 2000).
5. Printing made it possible to publish exact, detailed depictions of objects that led to exact, worded descriptions of those objects as constructed by multiple observers. This characteristic of printing contributed greatly to modern science.
6. As cultures became more literate, print reinforced the sense that language is essentially textual. Consequently, publishers produced increasingly comprehensive dictionaries fostering a desire for more "correctness" in language usage.
7. Printing produced books that were smaller and more portable than those in manuscript culture. Reading could now be done silently in a private setting whereas reading in manuscript culture tended to be done in social settings with one person reading aloud to a group.
8. A sense of private ownership of words was rare in oral cultures, as orators often drew on common themes and folklore. Printed words allowed for a new sense of ownership (Ong, 1997).

---

"With printing, books became less like records of something spoken and more like something in and of themselves—an object filled with information. This was because the exact duplication of books, that printing made possible, increased the sense of a book as an object—a manufactured thing rather than a moment preserved in time."

*Walter Ong*

meant increased access. More books and more access meant more opportunities for comparison of different texts within the same subject areas. Such comparisons often resulted in identifying contradictions or errors, which led to a weakening of old theories and opened new inquiries.

In printers' workshops, intellectual exchanges occurred among the new occupational groups (artists, scholars, and technicians) brought together by the printing process, and much innovative work outside of the academic centers began in these meetings.

Printing made possible the simultaneous distribution of hundreds of identical copies of a text. For the first time, a single document could be read by many people at the same time. This level of standardization in writing made possible by printing was also true for maps, calendars, charts, musical scores, and even dress patterns. All over Europe people could now read the same literature, become more aware of distant regional boundaries, listen to the same music, and make the same clothing. This was no less than the beginnings of mass culture (Eisenstein, 2000).

Printing had more specific effects on scholarship, science, education, art, languages, and law. The oldest and best copies of many privately held manuscripts (that relatively few people ever read or even knew existed) were found, replicated, and published. Ancient languages such as Greek and Hebrew were consequently recovered as well as many other literary treasures that may have been lost forever.

Printing speeded the publishing process and made possible the quick and broad dissemination of ideas. Consequently, a more public exchange of ideas in print was common, and scientific research became a more collaborative effort. Standardization and greater accuracy in illustrations and diagrams also assisted scientific endeavors.

As typography and printing improved, so did the readability of books, and learning to read was made much easier. More individuals could afford books, and access to more reading material resulted in higher literacy among the general population. Books also freed everyone from the constant task of memorization necessary in oral cultures. Engravings and prints, once available only to the elite, were reproduced and reached wider audiences, making some artists become very popular throughout Europe. Reproductions of original works of art held in private collections were also published and seen by most people for the first time.

Some languages were used more than others in literature and as a consequence became national languages. Those used less extensively came to be considered local dialects. Also, national languages, once adopted, tended to remain the predominantly used language and were constantly refined and codified.

Books in print culture came to be considered more like objects than books in manuscript culture (when books retained the uniqueness of a conversation or speech). Eventually, the notion that words or ideas could be owned emerged; the concepts of copyright and plagiarism followed. Recognizing that thousands of copies of a book were different from a few copies, governments attempted to control the diffusion of ideas and words by controlling printers through laws and various regulations. However, none proved to be very effective as books were published covertly and smuggled all over Europe to circumvent such attempts (Wisconsin-Milwaukee, 1996).

## IA AND THE PRINTED WORD

Some innovations in information and communication technologies (ICT) have a direct historical relevance to the IA profession, while the relevance of others has more to do with the facilitation of the IA process. The information organization, navigation, interaction, and flow characteristics of ICT innovations (ancient and modern) influence the shape of today's information spaces and are therefore also relevant to understanding information architecture.

Printing, and the mass production of books, assisted in the cultural diffusion of ideas and led to the standardization of knowledge and linguistic forms. This restructuring of literate activity is one of the earliest and most dramatic examples of a new technology influencing the social organization and production of knowledge.

"The mechanization of printing in the 19th century and its further development in the 20th, which went hand-in-hand with increasing literacy and rising standards of education, finally brought the printed word to its powerful position as a means of influencing minds and, hence, societies."

*Brittanica.com*

"Gutenberg's invention of the printing press is widely thought of as the origin of mass communication. It marked Western culture's first viable method of disseminating ideas and information from a single source to a large and far-ranging audience."

*Jones Telecommunication Multimedia Encyclopedia*

| **TABLE 4–2   Information Processing—Printing** |
|---|
| Communication systems and technologies have various capacities for communicating, storing, and retrieving information. Printing has the following information-processing capacities: |

*Information Communication*
- Printing extends the capacity writing has for communicating human experience but shares writing's lack of the phonetic qualities of speech.
- The printed word, like the written word, allows text to be an object of reflection and makes possible the accumulation, preservation, and communication of the ideas, observations, and experiences of successive generations.
- Printing also enables large-scale duplication and distribution of original works making literature affordable and widely accessible. Typographic and illustration quality in printed books exceeded that of hand-crafted manuscripts and improves readability and understanding.

*Information Storage*
- By large-scale duplication of original works, printing (although usually on less stable media than manuscripts) assures a greater probability of preservation.
- Printed books were also smaller than manuscripts and stored more efficiently.

*Information Retrieval*
- Typographic conventions introduced by early printers made possible the implementation of cataloguing and indexing systems, greatly improving the ability to find and retrieve specific information or books from large collections.

## The Information Space: Organization, Navigation, Interaction, and Flows

Books and other conventions for organizing the printed word (such as tables of content, chapters, page numbers, headings, footnotes, and indices) improved the ability of readers to navigate texts. Interaction with textual information is an internalized personal process controlled by the reader. And, although readers have no control over the content of a document authored by another, flow in the printed-word information space is not totally one way in that the readers can elect to read whatever they want whenever they want.

## Facilitation of the IA Process

The development of printing enhanced all the communication capacities of writing by "enabling the rapid duplication and transmission of information, as well as redundant storage in multiple locations" (Andrew Treloar, 1994). Because IA projects can involve many people, the ability to produce rapidly multiple identical copies of IA documentation is important to the IA process. However, what is more relevant are the ways in which the invention of the printing press influenced how documents are collected, preserved, organized, retrieved, and disseminated.

## Direct Historical Significance

Before the printing press, books were expensive to produce and available to only an elite few. The printed book brought about a variety of changes (including making books affordable and accessible to greater numbers of people) that led to a need for a more orderly, systematic approach to document management that, over hundreds of years, evolved into the fields of library science and information science. Together, these two disciplines are concerned with users of information, the organization and representation of information, information management, information technologies, and the implementation of information systems.

Numerous IA practitioners come from these fields including two individuals who have had a significant influence in shaping the field of IA: Louis Rosenfeld and Peter Morville. They see IA as being concerned with "the design of organization, labeling, navigation, and searching systems to help people find and manage information more successfully" (O'Reilly, 2001).

# 5 CHAPTER

# Wired
# The Electrical Telegraph

"If the presence of electricity can be made visible in any desired part of the circuit, I see no reason why intelligence may not be instantaneously transmitted by electricity to any distance."

Samuel F. B. Morse

## HISTORY: A.D. 1825–Present

"By uncoupling information from transportation [human courier, pony express, sailing ships], the telegraph changed the way information was formulated, and it changed the way people conceived of and used that information."

*Irving Fang*

The dream of communicating over great distances has probably been around for thousands of years, and many long-distance signaling and communication systems predate the telegraph. These include smoke signals, drum signals, flag signals, and various courier services (pigeons, runners, pony express, clipper ship mail service, etc). But the precursor of the electrical telegraph, the optical-mechanical telegraph, gave the world its first glimmer of a global, high-speed communications network.

In 1790 a French researcher, Claude Chappe, having failed to successfully devise a long-distance signaling system using electricity, took a simpler approach by using a cooking pot, two specially modified synchronized clocks with ten numbers, and a numerical code. Signals were sent by striking the pot as the arm of the clock passed a specific number. Upon hearing the banging sound of the pot's being struck, the receiver would record the number across which the arm of his clock was moving. If the clocks were closely synchronized, simple messages could be sent and translated with the use of the code dictionary. However, Chappe realized that this system was limited by the distance sound would carry and embarked on developing a visual (optical) system.

Substituting a pivoting five-foot panel painted black on one side and white on the other and flipping it as the clock arm crossed a specific num-

## KEYWORDS

optical telegraphy
telegraph history
telegraph networks
telegraphy
Samuel Morse

ber, senders and receivers, now equipped with telescopes, could transmit and receive messages over a few miles. With this success, Chappe determined that it would be possible to send messages quickly over many miles by erecting a network of towers, each a few miles apart. Recognizing the military value of this system, the French government ordered the construction of a number of optical-telegraph lines in different regions of the country. Other governments in Europe soon constructed their own networks, and before long the optical-telegraph system was heralded as a technological wonder. The 1797 edition of the *Encyclopedia Britannica* said the following about the optical telegraph: "The capitals of distant nations might be united by chains of posts, and the settling of disputes which at present take up months or years might be accomplished in as many hours."

Quickly recognizing the limitations of the optical telegraph, many inventors set out to improve upon it. Optical telegraphs required shifts of skilled operators, expensive towers, and had limited information-carrying capacity. They also did not work in the dark or dense fog. An electrical system, however, would work over any terrain, in any kind of weather, and any time of the day or night. Beginning around the year 1800, a number of breakthroughs would make the development of an electrical telegraphy system possible.

Like the printing press, the electrical telegraph was not a single invention but a collection of inventions integrated into one unique machine. And also like many of the inventions that made the printing press possible, each was developed (in the case of the telegraph) for a purpose other than communication. However, all were outcomes of the theoretical and experimental studies of electricity during the 18th and 19th centuries. The most significant among these were:

1. Electricity could be created using zinc and copper plates separated by cardboard soaked in a salt solution.
2. Electric current flowing in wires generated a magnetic field.
3. Electromagnetic fields influenced magnetic needles.

These three discoveries led to the invention of the battery, electromagnet, and galvanometer, all of which were essential components of the first electrical telegraph prototypes.

Many people claimed they invented the electrical telegraph, but it was Samuel F. B. Morse's system that would prevail. From the beginning, Morse was confident that the continents would be linked by telegraph networks saying, "If it will go ten miles without stopping, I can make it go around the globe." The secret to the success of the Morse system was his code. Morse realized that, with the technology at hand, a simple code would be easier to learn and use than trying to construct complicated electro-mechanical devices that did not require the use of a code.

"The telegraph's ability to transmit news dispatches transformed the entire newspaper industry. Before the telegraph, news gathering from distant points was time consuming, linked as it was to slow modes of transportation. Like any message, first the news had to be put in writing. Then, the written report had to be put on a steamer [steamboat], carriage, horse, or train, carried on foot, or, more likely, a combination of these to get to the printing house."
*Irving Fang*

The following is an excerpt from an article in an 1881 edition of *Scientific American* regarding the role of the telegraph in reporting the shooting of American President James Garfield and his slow decline ending in death: "The touch of the telegraphy key welded human sympathy and made possible its manifestation in a common universal, simultaneous heart throb. We have just seen the civilized world gathered as one family around a common sick bed, hope and fear alternately fluctuating in unison with electric pulsations over the continents and under the seas."
Time and again since, global communication networks have brought the world together to witness and share in the great triumphs and tragedies of individuals and nations.

| **TABLE 5–1   About the Telegraph** |
|---|
| The electrical telegraph was a great technological achievement as well as a revolutionary communications device. Its rapid dissemination was a testimony to its utility. |

1. The expansion of telegraph networks was fastest in the United States.
2. Railroads, stockbrokers, and publishers were early adopters of the telegraph.
3. In 1846 only Morse's 40-mile-long experimental line existed.
4. In 1850 12,000 miles of telegraph line were in service.
5. Before the completion of a transcontinental telegraph line in 1861, the only coast-to-coast communication system was the Pony Express.
6. The submarine cable laid across the Atlantic was 2,500 miles long.
7. In 1874 650,000 miles of telegraph wire had been strung, 30,000 miles of submarine cable laid, and over 20,000 communities around the world were connected to the network.
8. Out of dozens of telegraph company startups in 1850, by 1880 Western Union came to dominate the industry in the United States, handling 80 percent of all telegram traffic.

## CULTURAL NOTES

As has been true with many new computing and communication technologies, the advantages of telegraph were first recognized, and capitalized on, by the business community. Transactions that normally may have taken up to four weeks using the postal service could now be conducted within the course of a day. This enabled businesses to make purchases and sales that would have been of no benefit to them before simply because many opportunities would fade over a few weeks' time.

In 1846 an advocate of laying a telegraph cable across the Atlantic Ocean linking Europe and North America stated, "All the inhabitants of the earth would be brought into one intellectual neighborhood" (Standage, 1998). Actually, only telegraph operators could communicate directly with each other, and the greatest beneficiaries of the telegraph were governments, militaries, businesses, and the press. In each case, information that may have once taken days, weeks, or even months to disseminate could now be communicated almost instantly across a global network.

This fact forever erased the insulating and isolating effects of distance, and the world would never be the same. The pace of life before the telegraph was slow. News spread no faster than the winds that pushed sailing ships along or the speed at which a horse could gallop. Now, via their local newspaper, common people everywhere could read about current events from around the world. Businesspeople, who experienced the effects of the telegraph more directly each day, were flooded with the latest news about national and international markets that could potentially give them an advantage over their competitors. To stay competitive, they had to embrace telegraphy or get left behind. The same held true for military leaders engaged in warfare. More intelligence, and the latest intelligence, regarding an enemy's actions communicated via a telegraph network could now mean the difference between victory or defeat. Some governments developed their own networks for the purpose of centralizing control over their empires. "The world [had] shrunk further and faster than ever before" (Standage, 1998).

| **TABLE 5–2** Information Processing—Telegraph |
| --- |
| Communication systems and technologies have various capacities for communicating, storing, and retrieving information. The telegraph has the following information-processing capacities: |

*Information Communication*
- The telegraph had almost unlimited capacity for communicating human experience but lacked the phonetic qualities of speech.
- The telegraph offered tremendous utility primarily because of the speed at which information could be transmitted over long distances and because telegraph lines could be interconnected to form worldwide communication networks.
- Only telegraph operators trained in the use of specialized codes and with access to telegraph technology could send and receive messages directly. All other users were restricted to paying for telegraph services that were relatively expensive.

*Information Storage*
- Telegraph messages could be prerecorded by punching holes into paper tapes. At some other time, these tapes could be read and transmitted as electrical impulses by automatic devices that translated the hole punches into Morse code.
- Paper tapes were intended only for short-term storage and were generally limited to small amounts of information written in cryptic style to minimize expense.
- Chemically treated paper that reacted to electrical impulses was developed for recording incoming coded messages that could then be translated at a later time. Like the prerecorded message tapes, these precursors to the electronic facsimiles were intended only for short-term storage and were limited to small amounts of information written in a cryptic style to minimize expense.

*Information Retrieval*
- Immediacy was of primary importance to users of the telegraph, and storage and retrieval systems served only to ensure the quickest possible routing and successful delivery of telegrams. Consequently, long-term storage and retrieval systems were not developed.

## IA AND THE TELEGRAPH

Some innovations in information and communication technologies (ICT) have a direct historical relevance to the IA profession, while the relevance of others has more to do with the facilitation of the IA process. The information organization, navigation, interaction, and flow characteristics of ICT innovations (ancient and modern) influence the shape of today's information spaces and therefore are also relevant to understanding information architecture.

### The Information Space: Organization, Navigation, Interaction, and Flows

The telegraph extended all the communication capacities of the written word and was the first networked global information space. All the organizational conventions used in writing apply to telegrams. However, because message senders were charged by the word, telegrams tended to be

"Thanks to the relentless pace of technological change, telegraphy was changing from a high-skill to a low-skill occupation: from a carefully learned craft to something anyone can pick up."

*Irving Fang*

This is a phenomenon that has been seen time and again with many new information and communication technologies. As they move from the domain of technicians to use in everyday life they become socialized.

"Time traveling Victorians arriving in the late twentieth century would, no doubt, be unimpressed by the Internet. They would surely find space flight and routine intercontinental air travel far more impressive technological achievements than [today's] global communications network. Heavier-than-air flying machines were, after all, thought to be totally impossible. But as for the Internet—well, they had one of their own [a global telegraph network]."

*Tom Standage*

cryptic. Navigation in the telegraph information space was mediated by specialized operators using technologies to which users of telegraph services did not have access or know how to operate. Interaction in the telegraph information space was a public communications activity involving the message sender, telegraph operator, and recipient. The telegraph information space enabled both one-way and conversational information flows.

## Direct Historical Significance

The relevance of the telegraph to IA is primarily technical, representing the dawn of the modern global network of information and communication technologies powering today's information economy. However, understanding the social impact of the telegraph (in some ways very similar to the Internet) is valuable to the field of IA. It reminds practitioners that there are many issues that continue to arise (and be considered) whenever a new information and communications technology is introduced, such as its influence on the location, character, and organization of human activity.

## CHAPTER 6

# Just Call Me
## The Telephone

"With it, man, instead of being able to make himself heard a few hundred yards away with a shout, can make himself heard and understood around the world with a whisper."

John Brooks

## HISTORY: A.D. 1875–Present

Constant improvement to telegraph technology quadrupled the capacity of a single telegraph wire, but as industry and commerce came to depend on the telegraph more and more, the demand grew. Increasing the capacity of an existing telegraph wire was the most effective way for telegraph companies to meet demand as it eliminated the cost of labor, materials, and maintenance associated with installing new lines, saving hundreds of thousands of dollars. Consequently, anyone who could come up with an invention that would enable telegraph wires to carry even more messages would have a ready market.

One new approach called the *harmonic telegraph concept* was based on the observation that humans are capable of separating individual notes (of different pitches) playing separate rhythms. The idea was to combine and transmit the electrical signals generated by a set of vibrating reeds and then separate them on the receiving end, where each reed in an identical set would respond only to the signal sent by its counterpart. By stopping and starting the vibration of each reed for varying lengths of time (dots and dashes), Morse telegraphy would be possible.

In 1875 many inventors were working on harmonic telegraphs, one of whom was Alexander Graham Bell. On June 2, Bell was testing an early prototype when a reed got stuck. His assistant, Thomas Watson, attempting to free it, apparently plucked it unusually hard. On the receiving apparatus, Bell then heard a reproduction of the twanging sound the plucked reed made that was far more complete than he expected to hear. Consequently, he concluded that his device might be capable of

"Inexpensive, simple to operate, and offering its user a personal type of communication that cannot be obtained through the written word, the telephone has become the most widely used telecommunications device. Hundreds of millions of telephone sets are in use throughout the world."

*Brittanica.com*

**KEYWORDS**
Alexander Graham Bell
harmonic telegraph
invention of the
   telephone
speaking telegraph

transmitting sounds as complex as the human voice rather than the simple, pure musical tones he originally intended to transmit. After improving his prototype, he filed for a patent on February 14, 1876. It was entitled, "Improvements In Telegraphy." He was granted the patent on March 3, and on March 10 he demonstrated that intelligible speech could be transmitted electrically. For some time thereafter, what we now know as the telephone would be referred to as a "speaking telegraph" (Winston, 1998).

The telephone had some distinct advantages over the telegraph. In an advertisement for telephone service in May 1877, the Bell Telephone Company articulated them:

> No skilled operator is required [and] direct conversation may be had by speech without the intervention of a third person. The communication is more rapid, the average number of words being transmitted by Morse Sounder being from fifteen to twenty per minute, by telephone from one to two hundred. No expense is required either for its operation, maintenance, or repair. It needs no battery and has not complicated machinery. It is unsurpassed for economy and simplicity.

Much like the telegraph, the telephone was immediately popular with the business community and readily became a tool integral to conducting business. It would be almost 50 years from the time of its invention before it became commonplace in the household.

Based upon the immediate popularity of the telephone, these advantages must have been obvious to many people. By the end of June 1877, 230 telephones were in use. Within two more months, over a 1,000 more phones were in service. Three years later, 30,000 phones were being used around the world and 10 years later, 250,000. By the turn of the century, nearly two million phones would be in use (Standage, 1998). Today, the telephone has become the predominant telecommunications technology with hundreds of millions of telephone devices in use worldwide. In the United States alone, over two billion telephone calls are placed each business day. Since the year 1896, advances in electronics have improved phone performance. Telephone devices are now smaller, lightweight, and portable, but the basic design remains unchanged.

## CULTURAL NOTES

The invention of the telephone took place along with many other new technologies at the end of the 19th century. Within a 35-year period the lightbulb, the refrigerator, the typewriter, electric streetcars, and the horseless carriage would all appear on the American scene. But it was the popularity of the telephone that set it apart from the others.

The growth from one device in Boston to eleven million nationwide within 40 years led Thomas Edison to observe that the telephone had "annihilated time and space, and brought the human family in closer touch." A very similar claim had been made about the telegraph. However, unlike the telegraph, eventually anyone could own and operate a telephone in their own home. For 50 years it was primarily a business tool.

| **TABLE 6–1   About Telephones** |
| :--- |
| The following milestones in the history of the telephone illustrate the remarkable diffusion of this technology into every corner of our lives. In any public place today, the probability is very high that you will see someone engaged in conversation on a cell phone. |

| | |
| :--- | :--- |
| 1877 | First permanent outdoor telephone wire was strung. |
| 1878 | Manual phone exchange enabled calls to be switched eliminating need for direct connections. |
| 1879 | Numbers began to be used to designate telephone subscribers rather than names. |
| 1880's | Long distance service was established. |
| 1891 | First automatic dial system was patented. |
| 1900 | First coin telephone was installed. |
| 1927 | New York to London service became operational using radio waves. |
| 1946 | Mobile telephone service established using radio waves. |
| 1955 | Transatlantic phone cables were laid. |
| 1962 | Telstar, the first international communications satellite, was orbited. |
| 1983 | Cellular phone network started in United States. |
| 1985 | Cellular telephones used in cars. |
| 1989 | Pacific Link fiber-optic cable handled 40,000 simultaneous calls. |
| 1996 | Pocket telephone/computer was marketed. |

And, for the first time in history, communication between individuals hundreds of miles apart (or one mile), could take place almost instantly and with a high degree of privacy. The telegraph may have first contributed to the world seeming "smaller" by enabling the rapid distribution of news via newspapers, but it was the telephone that personalized electronic communications. With the telephone, information could now flow from one individual to another without any intermediaries.

> "Lifeline of the lonely and lifeblood of the busy, the telephone is taken for granted, and for good reason—it comes as near as any invention to being an extension of the human body."
>
> *John Brooks*

## IA AND THE TELEPHONE

Some innovations in information and communication technologies (ICT) have a direct historical relevance to the IA profession, while the relevance of others has more to do with the facilitation of the IA process. The information organization, navigation, interaction, and flow characteristics of ICT innovations (ancient and modern) influence the shape of today's information spaces and are therefore also relevant to understanding information architecture.

### The Information Space: Organization, Navigation, Interaction, and Flows

The telephone extended all the communication capacities of the spoken word and is a networked global information space. The same organizational conventions used in conversation apply to the telephone information

---

**TABLE 6–2   Information Processing—Telephones**

Communication systems and technologies have various capacities for communicating, storing, and retrieving information. The telephone has the following information-processing capacities:

*Information Communication*
- The telephone, which simply extends the range of human speech, has almost unlimited capacity for communicating human experience. Unlike the telegraph, with which the fastest operators could transmit 30 words per minute, the telephone offered greater utility because of the higher rates (100+ words per minute) at which information could be transmitted.
- The phonetic qualities of speech enable the communication of subtle meanings that telegraph codes cannot communicate.
- Like the telegraph, the telephone is capable of transmitting information over long distances, and telephone lines can be interconnected to form worldwide communication networks.

*Information Storage*
- Initially, unless recorded in writing, storage was limited to the capacity of an individual's memory.
- Storing speech (and telephone transmissions) became possible with the invention of sound recorders.

*Information Retrieval*
- Initially, unless recorded in writing, storage was limited to an individual's ability to recall from memory.
- Indexing early sound recordings was limited to manually locating a specific part of the recording on the recording medium or timing the recording and assigning a time code to specific parts of the recording for future reference.
- Digital sound recording enabled highly specific indexing techniques and very fast and precise location and retrieval mechanisms.

---

space. Conversationalists can organize and reorganize the information they are attempting to communicate depending upon direct and indirect feedback received in the course of a conversation. Navigation decisions in conversations are negotiable. The potential for interaction in any conversation is very high. Conversation flows are nonlinear and two way; the potential for branching is unlimited.

Telephones and telephone systems were originally wire-based networks until the advent of radio technology that enabled wireless telephony. In the digital age, the telephone information space is being expanded to include text messaging, audio storage and playback, and Internet access capabilities. This expanded capability integrates the characteristics of the written word and the spoken word information space into a single, more complex information space.

## Facilitation of the IA Process

The telephone is an important communications device that extends the utility of conversation to every aspect in which it is used in the IA process (as it does in all of today's business enterprises). Telephone systems also support the transmission of facsimiles of text and graphic documents (faxes) and access to the Internet via dial-up connections—capabilities that are used in support of the IA process.

Like the telegraph, the relevance of the telephone to IA is technical and represents the introduction of personal, real-time (live), global, networked, electronic media. The invention of telephone technology also coincides with the development of the capability to reproduce sound electronically, leading to the capability to capture (record) sound electronically. This recording capability improved upon earlier technologies for recording sound and furthered the documentation of sound and the development of audio archives (voice, music, ambient sounds), changing what had always been temporal to the status of artifact. Now, documents could be created not only in textual and visual formats (including photographs), but also in audio formats challenging information management specialists of the day to develop new systems for the organization, description, storage, and retrieval of information. Audio recordings can be both entertaining and informative. The relevance of the ability to record audio lies in the power of audio as a storytelling medium and as a tool for the documentation of human activity. As such, it is useful as a research tool in the IA process and as a dynamic medium for supporting the dramatization or documentation of processes, experiences, or events in electronic information environments.

## Direct Historical Significance

The telephone's relevance to IA is also very important in terms of the history of IA research and design theory. In the 1920s and 30s, the first attempts to apply knowledge of human behavior and physical attributes to the design of products, equipment, machines, and large-scale systems for the purpose of optimizing human use (human factors) began in private industry at the American Telegraph and Telephone Company (AT&T). These human-factor concerns are highly relevant to the field of IA today, and numerous IAs come from this field (also known as *engineering psychology*) or the more recent and specialized extension of human factors called *human-computer interaction (HCI)*.

"It is conceivable that cables of telephone wires could be laid underground or suspended overhead, communicating by branch wires with private dwellings, country homes, shops, manufacturers, etc., uniting them through the main cable with a central office where the wires could be connected as desired, establishing direct communication between any two places in the city. Not only so, but I believe that in the future, wires will unite the head offices of the telephone company in different cities, and a man in one part of the country may communicate by word of mouth with another in a distant place."

*A.G. Bell*

# 7 | CHAPTER

# Wireless
## The Radio

"Radio has kept the wanderer home at nights, it has brightened the gloom of separation and shortened the long hours of loneliness. It is a comforting companion to the shut-in; it soothes the pain of suffering. It brings counsel to the housewife, information to the farmer, entertainment and gaiety to the young. On silent wings it flies to the forgotten corners where mails are uncertain and few, where the cheer of kindly voices comes only through the head-phones, where music is never heard. . . ."

Lee De Forest

## HISTORY: A.D. 1894–Present

When broadcasting became popular, it was observed that what had once been perceived as one of radio's biggest flaws—that it lacked privacy because anyone could tune into an openly broadcast signal—was actually its greatest strength.

### KEYWORDS
Guglielmo Marconi
radio history
invention of radio
*War of the Worlds*
   broadcast
wireless telegraphy

Another outcome of 19th-century research into the nature of electricity and electromagnetism was a theory by James Clerk Maxwell. A Scottish physicist, Maxwell claimed the existence of invisible electromagnetic waves. By both design and by accident, researchers proved Maxwell's theory correct when they observed that an electrical spark generated by one electrical device could induce a sympathetic spark in another.

In one notable instance around 1880, David Hughes (the creator of the microphone) was testing an electrical apparatus that had a faulty contact in its circuitry and noticed that when the faulty contact sparked, a microphone on the other side of the laboratory would emit a noise. Having a very inquisitive mind, Hughes continued to experiment. Eventually, he duplicated the same effect over a distance of 500 feet but did not consider that the electromagnetic radiation phenomena he was demonstrating could be used for sending signals.

In 1894 Sir Oliver Lodge used the idea of wireless telegraphy to demonstrate to an audience at Oxford University that electromagnetic waves were detectable. He transmitted signals from a "spark gap" device in a laboratory to a receiving device 150 yards away in the university museum. Since his primary interest was researching electric phenomena, he did not consider that wireless telegraphy could have any value outside his laboratory.

It was Guglielmo Marconi who would eventually be credited with inventing the radio. Having read the findings of Lodge and other physicists, Marconi, a businessman, was confident that money was to be made with a device that was capable of sending signals without wires. Assisted by friend and physics professor Auguste Righi, Marconi began studying and conducting wireless signal transmission experiments of his own. Succeeding in sending signals over 30 feet indoors, he moved outdoors where he theorized signals could be sent farther if the point from which they were transmitted was elevated. Constructing an antenna, he proved his theory correct and was soon successfully sending signals over a distance of two miles. With more improvements, Marconi was ready to demonstrate his wireless telegraph.

Traveling to Great Britain, Marconi demonstrated his apparatus to representatives of the British Post Office (BPO). Having witnessed signals being sent without wires over a distance of 9 miles, the British immediately determined that Marconi's invention would be very useful in communicating with ships at sea. In 1897, after turning down an offer from the BPO, Marconi founded the Wireless Telegraph and Signal Company and began selling radio equipment to the British Army and Navy as well as to commercial shipping companies. As a consequence, wireless telegraphy was used primarily at sea for communicating weather conditions and for emergencies.

Using a recently developed amplification tube called the *Fleming valve,* Canadian experimenter Reginald Fessenden transmitted speech and music from a wireless station in Massachusetts (Winston, 1998). "On Christmas Eve 1906, ship wireless operators over a wide area of the Atlantic, sitting with earphones to head, alert to the crackling of distant dots and dashes, were startled to hear a woman singing" (Barnouw, 1975). Fessenden had conceived of a new use for the wireless telegraph, but only wireless operators on ships were listening.

It would be six years later, on April 14, 1912, that a famous distress call would help publicize the wonder of the wireless around the world. It was an SOS signal from the *Titanic.* Through his imagination fired by the dramatic distress call of the *Titanic,* David Sarnoff saw the commercial potential of sending a radio signal to many unknown receivers—broadcasting (an old term for sowing seeds)—and envisioned a "music box" in every home. His idea would gain popularity quickly. By November 2, 1920, America's first radio station, KDKA, was on the air. A few thousand people listened in to the returns of the Harding-Cox presidential election. By 1925 radios were in two million households (Fang, 1997).

Over time, continuous improvements in both radio transmitting and receiving technology would extend the reach of radio as well as raise the

"The history of radio went through two distinct periods of social use, point-to-point communication and broadcasting. Point-to-point communication began as wireless telegraphy and became wireless telephony. Each period led into the next. Each had its own technology, purpose, economic underpinning, and sound. Telegraphy was the sound of dots and dashes. Telephony was the sound of voices, and broadcasting carried voices, music, and many other sounds."

*Irving Fang*

Like television and the Internet, radio was originally seen as a noncommercial public service holding great promise for the future of education. "Its potential seemed limitless as people speculated about radio's teaching potential. It seemed that as of now, through the connectivity of radio, a single dazzling teacher could inspire thousands of bored students to learn and become educated.

*Susan Douglas*

quality of the sound. Radio programming remained primarily live until the 1950s when the broadcast of recorded music became very popular. Today, music dominates commercial radio programming.

## CULTURAL NOTES

With the introduction of advertising, radio became a real moneymaker, networks were formed, and radio programming for a broad range of listeners was being broadcast: morning soap operas, children's adventure programs, news analysis, dramas, comedies, live music, and game shows, to name but a few. But radio in early days was more than just an entertainment medium. It was a connection to the rest of the world and an escape from the hard times of the Great Depression. Each radio station had loyal followers who would schedule their days around their favorite programs. Receivers were inexpensive, programming was free, everyone was listening and, consequently, radio had a strong cultural influence.

The broadcast of the Harding-Cox election results marked the beginning of major changes in political campaign strategy. Politicians capitalized on the fact that more and more people were staying home to listen to political events on the radio and shifted from giving long "platform" speeches in town squares to more concise radio addresses delivered to an unseen audience. Also, knowing that huge audiences were listening in to political events as they happened rather than reading about them later in the newspaper, speech writers began drafting speeches for listening audiences rather than reading audiences. It soon became apparent that the candidate who had a command of the "art of radio oratory" had a distinct competitive advantage (Vorisek, 1997).

Parents began to take advantage of the magical qualities of radio. Noticing that radio programs captivated not only them but their children, radio was often used to "baby-sit" children. Networks capitalized on this fact by promising to "free parents from the confines of parenting while simultaneously allowing them to share time listening to a favorite radio show" (Vorisek, 1997).

Believing that radio had great potential for communicating with and educating the public, educators spoke of radio as the "people's university." As a consequence, schools and universities owned 13 percent of all broadcast licenses issued by 1923. It seemed that now thousands of students could be motivated by and learn from one inspired instructor (Vorisek, 1997).

But, even before the end of the 1920s, the majority of broadcast programming entertained people in the comfort of their homes with music, drama, comedy, and sporting events, providing them alternatives for entertainment that they never had before (Vorisek, 1997). One famous demonstration of the emotional power of radio occurred on October 30,

Like previous communication technologies in their infancy and those to come, early radio receivers were difficult to use, or, in today's parlance, they weren't very user friendly. "They were large, clunky, temperamental boxes with lots of knobs, tubes, wires, and a large messy, smelly battery filled with acid, not unlike the storage battery of an automobile."

*Irving Fang*

Across the 150-year history of the rise of mass culture, communication products have become more and more standardized. The news gathering and distribution power of the telegraph led to both mass circulation and local newspapers featuring the same stories. So it was with radio networks, that transmitted into every home equally homogenized news and entertainment.

---

**TABLE 7–1 About Radio**

Radio proved to be a very versatile and powerful communications medium. It was like the printing press in that the same information was being disseminated to large numbers of people. However, unlike books, radio could reach illiterate adults or preliterate children.

1. Early radio was a point-to-point wireless telegraph communication technology used primarily for military and commercial maritime purposes.
2. Radio was later used as a one-point-to-many wireless telephony communication technology to broadcast entertainment and news programming to large numbers of listeners in their homes.
3. Early radio sets did not have amplifiers or loudspeakers and listening could be done only with headphones, one person at a time.
4. The addition of amplifiers and loudspeakers allowed multiple individuals to listen at one time, and gathering around the radio became a common family activity.
5. The addition of amplifiers and loudspeakers also allowed listeners to be able to engage in other activities anywhere within earshot of the receiver (Rhoads, 1993).
6. Six percent of all adults in the United States could not read in 1920, and radio gave advertisers a medium for reaching illiterate adults and preliterate children (Rhoads, 1993).
7. Radio commercials could not be disregarded as could ads in newspapers and magazines (Rhoads, 1993).
8. Opposed by most newspaper publishers, President Franklin Roosevelt used radio broadcasts to bypass them and communicate directly with the voters.
9. Before World War II, broadcasting was a very formal production. Even though no studio audiences were present, announcers, musicians, and performers often were elegantly dressed.
10. Before broadcasting recorded music became popular, many local stations had their own staff orchestras.

---

1938. Orson Welles' popular Mercury Theater broadcast a reading of H.G. Well's novel *War of the Worlds* in such a convincing manner that an estimated six million Americans believed that Martians had invaded Earth and were killing thousands with death rays. Many ran screaming into the streets fearing that the world was coming to an end.

With the growth of radio networks, the broad reach of increasingly powerful transmitters, and the standardization of programming shared in common by huge audiences, many experts believe that radio contributed to the rise of a more homogeneous or "mass" culture.

## IA AND THE RADIO

Some innovations in information and communication technologies (ICT) have a direct historical relevance to the IA profession, while the relevance of others has more to do with the facilitation of the IA process. The information organization, navigation, interaction, and flow characteristics of ICT innovations (ancient and modern) influence the shape of

"By the end of WWII, 95% of all homes had radios, but by the early 1950s television already had begun to erode its popularity. Radio stations began to shift their programming focus from news and story segments to mostly music. The introduction of the transistor radio was able to positively impact radio growth in the face of the threat of television by allowing for the production of cheap, portable radios that could be used in cars and outdoors."

*Duke University*

**TABLE 7–2    Information Processing—Radio**

Communication systems and technologies have various capacities for communicating, storing, and retrieving information. The radio has the following information-processing capacities:

*Information Communication*
- The radio extends the range of all sound and has almost unlimited capacity for communicating human experience.
- Radio, like the telegraph and the telephone, enables almost instantaneous communication over long distances.
- Radio is a versatile technology and can be used for point-to-point communication or for mass communication.

*Information Storage*
- Initially, unless recorded in writing, storage was limited to the capacity of an individual's memory.
- Storing radio programs became possible with the invention of sound recorders.

*Information Retrieval*
- Initially, unless recorded in writing, storage was limited to an individual's ability to recall from memory.
- Indexing early sound recordings was limited to manually locating a specific part of the recording on the recording medium or timing the recording and assigning a time code to specific parts of the recording for future reference.
- Today, digital sound recording enables highly specific indexing techniques and very fast and precise location and retrieval mechanisms.

today's information spaces and are therefore also relevant to understanding information architecture.

## The Information Space: Organization, Navigation, Interaction, and Flows

"The growth of networked and high-powered [radio] stations established national and regional audiences encouraging the rise of a national culture."

*A. M. Vorisek*

Radio extended all the communication capacities of the spoken word and was the first electronic broadcast medium. In the radio information space, information is organized into story form, and the storyteller controls the experience. Listeners' interaction levels with the information resource, the storyteller, are generally low. Interaction with the information embedded in stories is an internalized personal activity. The flow of information in storytelling is primarily one way: from the storyteller to the listener(s).

## Direct Historical Significance

The relevance of radio to IA is what it represents for the future of the Web. The infrastructure for a wireless Web is in the process of being constructed. The wireless Web information space will be accessible by a variety of mobile devices including cell phones and handheld computers that will support Web browsing, email, text messaging, and playing music, and will have color displays for the presentation of high-resolution graphics and video. These devices will be part of a collection of software and hardware that use the Internet's networked connections for personal and institutional purposes. With the growth of a more mobile information environment will come many new market possibilities. Along with these new possibilities will arise a demand for IAs who can leverage those possibilities with effective and efficient information environment designs.

# The Tube
## Television

"I believe television is going to be the test of the modern world and that in this new opportunity to see beyond the range of our vision, we shall discover either a new and unbearable disturbance of the general peace, or a saving radiance from the sky. We shall stand or fall by television—of that I am quite sure."

E. B. White

Television means "seeing at a distance," and its roots go back as far as 1807 with the discovery of selenium. Selenium turned out to be photoemissive; that is, when selenium is struck by light it releases electrons—it produces electricity. Early electron beam tubes (now known as *cathode ray tubes*) that used selenium because of its photoemissive qualities were developed for photo-electric emissions research. It was not imagined at the time that these tubes would have any commercial application.

**KEYWORDS**

cathode ray tube, tv
effects of television
television history
invention of television
telephonoscope

## HISTORY: A.D. 1923–PRESENT

The idea of television was fairly popular many years before television sets were actually manufactured. As early as 1879, a British cartoonist depicted a large screen over a fireplace mantle where, while speaking over the telephone, one could see the person to whom he or she was talking. The cartoonist's name for the device was the "telephonoscope."

By 1907 all of the scientific principles that would make possible the technological development of television were known. In 1908 Campbell Swinton (the man who introduced Marconi to the British Post Office) outlined a scheme for an all-electric television system that would lay the foundation for modern television. He then declared that it would be too expensive to build. It was three years later, in 1911, when the British patent office filed a patent entitled "A Method of Transmitting Images Over a Distance" submitted by a young Russian, Boris Rozing. The patent was filed in the "facsimile transmission" category under a recently created new subcategory labeled, "television." Rozing's design never left the laboratory, and he later disappeared during the Russian Revolution. However, Vladimir Zworykin, Rozing's assistant, would immigrate to the United States and eventually work for Westinghouse where he would construct and demonstrate a working prototype. It was 1923 when he gave his demonstration, and this is the date that is most often cited as the year television was invented (Winston, 1998).

After 15 years of further development and refinement, the first all-electronic television sets would be marketed for the first time. In 1939 at the New York World's Fair, whose theme was "The World of Tomorrow," RCA created a great deal of excitement with demonstrations of television in their pavilion. But convincing Americans to buy a television would prove difficult. Early television sets were big and bulky, had very small screens, poor-quality black-and-white images, and there were few programs to watch. With the advent of World War II, television development was halted in the United States with only six experimental stations broadcasting to 10,000 receivers.

However, news stories about television continued throughout the war, and the public was ready to be entertained in their homes by the time peace was declared. Production of television sets soared between 1946 to 1948 going from 6,000 sets to 1,160,000. By 1950, almost 10 million sets would be in use in the United States and by 1968, 200 million worldwide (78 million in the United States). Today there are over 100 million TV sets in the United States alone (Fang, 1997).

Television's early developments are linked to attempts to send images over a telegraph wire. One of the first devices that was successful was called a *scanning telegraph.* Not finding any ready market, the idea was abandoned only to be resurrected years later for the purpose of sending electronic facsimiles of paper documents over telephone lines—the fax machine.

---

**TABLE 8–1   About Television**

The printing press, telegraph, telephone, and radio all changed the way we communicate and get information. Just on the basis of how much time is devoted to watching television, it is safe to say that television has changed how we live.

1. Early thinkers envisioned television as a technology for transferring single images onto paper. This idea was closer to what we now call the fax machine.
2. The electron beam tube, now more commonly known as the *Cathode Ray Tube (CRT),* was introduced in 1897 and used to study photoelectric emissions. It was not imagined at the time that it would ever have any commercial application.
3. Some of radio's best reporters, among them Edward R. Murrow, were highly critical of early television programming and refused to attend press conferences if television cameras were present. Others went as far as to try to sabotage the efforts of television reporters by pulling out camera power cords and making obscene gestures during broadcasts (Fang, 1997).
4. The television set is on in the average U.S. home for over seven hours a day.
5. During the coverage of the Kennedy assassination in 1963, as many as 9 out of 10 Americans were watching and an estimated 600 million viewers in 23 other countries (Fang, 1997).
6. Recent findings indicate that the average adult [American] male and female watches television over three hours a day.
7. Almost 80 percent of Americans consider watching TV with their children a family activity (Mediascope, 2000).
8. American children spend 22–28 hours per week watching TV—more than any other activity except sleeping.
9. By the age of 18, American children will have watched an average of 25,000 hours of television (Fang, 1997).
10. By the time today's children reach age 70, they will have spent 7 to 10 years of their lives watching TV (Mediascope, 2000).

When in its infancy, many saw television as a powerful educational tool and were greatly disappointed that it became primarily a news and entertainment medium, much as radio did before it.

## CULTURAL NOTES

"Television has gone further than [the telegraph, the telephone, movies, and the radio] in affecting how we spend our hours and our money, how we relate to others, and what we talk about and think about" (Fang, 1997). Never in human history have so many people been so enthralled with any single communications medium or form of entertainment. According to Neil Postman, the reason is "[that television] encompasses all forms of discourse. From what other single source can one access national and international political news, sports, weather, the most recent scientific discoveries, moving human interest stories, home improvement tips, self-improvement advice; enjoy classic, popular, and made-for-television movies; learn-at-home educational programming; and hundreds upon hundreds of other subjects. Everyone goes to television for all these things and more, which is why television resonates so powerfully throughout [all] cultures" (Postman, 1985).

By virtue of the fact that television is so remarkably popular and people spend large percentages of each day in front of a televison set (an average of four hours for American adults), television's influence on culture is a controversial topic, and numerous studies have been conducted on its effects. In its October 17,1984 issue, *Newsweek* reported that some experts view televison as

For many years three major broadcast networks would serve over 90 percent of the total American television audience. With the introduction of a new communication technology, cable television, they would lose a significant percentage of what primarily had been a captive audience. It is the opinion of many media experts that this was the beginning of the fragmentation of mass media brought on by the introduction of television spin-off technologies (cable, direct TV, VCRs, DVDs) and new information and communication technologies that compete for the attention of media-saturated audiences.

> "… a fatal attraction, a sort of cultural death wish" and that, "It stands accused of weakening our social institutions, driving up our crime rate, [shortening] our attention spans, distorting our perceptions of reality and illusion, eroding our regional distinctions in speech and dress, [displacing] our games of childhood, encouraging illiteracy, pregnancy and even obesity in adolescents and reducing all it touches—politics, education, economics, religion—to 525 lines of phosphor-dot frivolousness."

Research has also shown that television is used primarily as a form of relaxation, as a distraction, and that just watching is more important to the viewer than any specific programming (Fang, 1997). Regardless of how they judge televison's effects, experts all seem to agree that television has a powerful influence.

## IA AND TELEVISION

Some innovations in information and communication technologies (ICT) have a direct historical relevance to the IA profession, while the relevance of others has more to do with the facilitation of the IA process. The information organization, navigation, interaction, and flow characteristics of ICT innovations (ancient and modern) influence the shape of today's information spaces and are therefore also relevant to understanding information architecture.

| **TABLE 8–2  Information Processing—Television** |
|---|
| Communication systems and technologies have various capacities for communicating, storing, and retrieving information. Television has the following information-processing capacities. |

*Information Communication*
- Combining both sound and image, television comes closer to replicating "natural" human communication than any other medium.
- Like the telegraph, the telephone, and radio, television also enables almost instantaneous communication over long distances. Live news coverage of events of global importance often attracts audiences numbering in the hundreds of millions.
- Unlike the telegraph, telephone, and radio, for most of its history television has been primarily a one-to-many mass communication device. However, it is likely that one-to-one television communication will become commonplace in the 21$^{st}$ century.

*Information Storage*
- Initially, unless the audio portion was recorded in writing, storage was limited to the capacity of an individual's memory.
- Storing television programs became possible with the invention of video recorders.

*Information Retrieval*
- Initially, unless recorded in writing, storage was limited to an individual's ability to recall from memory.
- Indexing early television tape recordings was limited to manually locating a specific part of the recording on the recording medium or timing the recording and assigning a time code to specific parts of the recording for future reference.
- Today, digital video recording enables highly specific indexing techniques and very fast and precise location and retrieval mechanisms.

## The Information Space: Organization, Navigation, Interaction, and Flows

The introduction of television represents the first time information and communications technology closely replicated natural human experience. The television information space is both a storytelling information space and a conversational information space. Television programs are broadcast both over the air and through coaxial cable systems. Live one-to-one, one-to-many, and many-to-one interactive television transmissions through the telephone system are used regularly to conduct business transactions. The Web currently supports low-quality video "streams," "movies," and live one-to-one two-way video. It is assumed that, as Internet bandwidth increases, Web-based video of all types will be of a higher quality, and two-way video communication will become ubiquitous.

Early television cameras were quite primitive, and actors had to wear black lipstick and green makeup because the cameras had trouble with the color white.

"At first it wasn't clear where the market for television was. Movies were shown in theaters, so perhaps television would replace film there."

*Irving Fang*

Television eventually found its place in the home, and the networks, hungry for programming, would turn to the movie industry to satisfy their rapidly growing audiences.

The television information space is primarily a storytelling information space. The storyteller controls the experience, and the listeners' interaction levels with the information resource, the storyteller, are generally low. Interaction with the information embedded in stories is an internalized personal activity. The flow of information in storytelling is primarily one way: from the storyteller to the listener(s).

Two-way television (teleconferencing) is a conversational information space in which information organizational and navigational schemes, interaction levels, and flows of information are controlled by more than one individual. Consequently, the television conversational information space is much more dynamic and adaptive than the storytelling information space. Conversationalists can organize and reorganize the information they are attempting to communicate depending on direct and indirect feedback received in the course of a conversation. Navigation decisions that determine the course of a conversation are negotiable. The potential for interaction in any conversation is very high. Conversation flows in the conversational television information space are nonlinear and two way; the potential for branching is unlimited.

## Facilitation of the IA Process

Television can be both very entertaining and informative, and its relevance to IA lies in its power as a storytelling medium and as a tool for the documentation of human activity. As such it is useful as a research tool in the IA process and as a dynamic medium for creating, capturing, and presenting the dramatization or documentation of processes, experiences, or events in electronic information environments. Eventually, it will also be an important two-way communication device supporting every aspect of the IA process.

The ability to record human activities on film and videotape added yet another document type to be archived and managed along with text, photos, and sound recordings. The introduction of this new document type once again challenged information management specialists of the day to develop new systems for the organization, description, storage, and retrieval of information.

## PART 3

# HUMAN AND COMPUTER INTERACTIONS
## The Evolution of Computing Systems

"When we approach the history of computing, we frequently think of it as the history of machines. The mainframe generation, the minicomputer era, the PC revolution. We look at the significance in the changes in processor development, in memory capacity, in networking. . . ."

"These are important subjects. But often lost among them is a more important story: the story of the relationships between the computer and its users, and how that relationship has evolved."

David K. Allison

## CHAPTER 9

# ENIAC
## Computational Solutions for Scientific Problems

"Often the computer is thought of as a twentieth-century phenomenon, but its genealogy is sprinkled within three hundred years of scientific advancement. [Its] development is intertwined with the quest for understanding, [and a ] search for order. The [computer] was designed to sort and organize information and solve problems."

Scott McCartney

## HISTORY: 1943–1955

By 1820 the Industrial Revolution was well under way, and mass-production manufacturing was becoming commonplace as more and more machines were being designed to automate mindless, repetitive, and labor-intensive processes. It is therefore not surprising that someone, Charles Babbage, would conceive of a machine to automate long computational operations—a way to mechanize mathematics. Babbage was also motivated by his realization that with the rise of industrialized society would also come a demand for better, faster, and more accurate methods of calculating.

Beginning in 1823 and with funding from the British government, Babbage worked for 10 years to try to develop a working prototype of a machine that could generate mathematical tables by comparing differences in numbers. He called it a *Difference Engine*. Unfortunately, the tools of the day were still too crude to build such a machine, and the project was abandoned as Babbage turned his attention to a new idea for a computing machine: the Analytical Engine.

His design for this new device was very similar to modern computers. The Analytical Engine would be capable of any kind of calculation (not

"People have long realized the competitive advantages that could be realized by having available more efficient data storage and computational ability. From counting on the fingers, to making marks on the walls of caves, to the invention of picture numbers, to the modern check or banknote, there has been a steady progression away from directly manipulating the objects that computations describe and toward the use of abstractions for the originals. Mechanical [computational] devices have played an important part in this sequence."

*Richard Sutcliffe*

**KEYWORDS**
Analytical Engine
history of computing,
    ENIAC
history of ENIAC
invention of ENIAC
vacuum tubes for
    calculation

just tables), "programmable," able to store information, and, most importantly, able to take a different path in a computation based upon conditional values. When Babbage turned to the British government again for money, they refused to fund his "radical contraption." Regardless, Babbage's brilliant design would eventually become a reality as industrial society sought solutions to larger and more complex computational problems.

One such problem in search of a solution was the processing of American census data. Data from the 1880 census had taken the U.S. Census Bureau nearly seven years to count, and they feared that the 1890 census might take them 10 years, making the whole effort worthless. Herman Hollerith of the Massachusetts Institute of Technology would have the answer, inspired by a train conductor. He watched the conductor punch holes in a passenger ticket so as to record a "punch photograph" of each passenger. Each hole represented a specific physical characteristic such as hair color, eye color, distinctive facial features, etc. Hollerith then built a punch-card reader and tabulator for the census. Instead of 10 years, the 1890 census data was tabulated in six weeks. However, the population total of just over 65 million was almost 10 million short of the figure that had been projected, and the disparity was blamed on Hollerith's device. Eventually, he was vindicated, and punch-card technology became the standard. His company, the Tabulating Machines Company founded in 1896, would ultimately become the International Business Machines Corporation (IBM).

Through the early 1900s more and more refinements were made to electro-mechanical calculating machines. However, such devices either were not very precise or required constant recalibration because the moving parts would wear or slip. And, although faster than previous counting devices, a demand for even faster machines was building. In fact, doing things faster in general was becoming part of the American way of life. It was in August 1942 that John Mauchly, a physics researcher and instructor, presented a proposal to the University of Pennsylvania for funding the development of a completely electronic machine. He entitled his proposal, "The Use of High-Speed Vacuum Tube Devices for Calculation." In it he stated that his machine would be not only more accurate than any existing calculating devices but that it would also be much, much faster. "Mauchly's [proposal] was ignored by Penn's deans, dismissed as the unsophisticated musings of a man known to have pipe dreams."

As with many innovative technological developments throughout history, it would be the military that would see value in Mauchly's proposal. In 1943 World War II was not going well for the Allies. One particular problem had to do with producing firing tables for big artillery pieces that were rapidly being manufactured and deployed in Europe. To fire the big guns with any degree of accuracy required the consideration of a number of variables: muzzle velocity, air density, wind speed,

> "The idea [of stored programs] arose in conjunction with the development of automatic looms by the French inventor Joseph Marie Jacquard (1752–1854). First shown at the 1801 Paris Exhibition, the looms used a collection of punched metal cards to control the weaving process."
>
> *Richard Sutcliffe*

> "Each firing table for every new weapon required the tabulation of dozens of factors across the thousands of possible trajectories, any one of which required a half of a day's work for a human computer with a desk calculator."
>
> *Brian Winston*

and so on. Tables considering these variables in every possible combination were being calculated by teams of women called "computers" using mechanical desk calculators, and they were falling further and further behind. A quicker way was needed. Dr. Herman Goldstine, a lieutenant assigned to the U.S. Army's Ballistics Research Laboratory, was charged with finding a quicker way. In the course of his search, Goldstine was asked by a graduate student at the University of Pennsylvania if he had heard of Mauchly's proposal. He had not and quickly sought out Mauchly. Enthusiastic about what he saw, Lieutenant Goldstine assisted in securing the funding from his department for the design and development of the Electronic Numerical Integrator and Computer (ENIAC).

On February 16, 1946, after years of intensive work, a press release from the U.S. government began with, "A new machine that is expected to revolutionize the mathematics of engineering and change many of our industrial design methods was announced today by the War Department." It went on to state, "The ENIAC is capable of computing 1000 times faster than the most advanced general-purpose calculating machine previously built. The electronic methods of computing used in the ENIAC make it possible to solve in hours problems which take years on a mechanical machine—a time so long as to make such work impractical." The computer industry in America was born (McCartney, 2001).

> "The war department today unveiled the world's fastest calculating machine and said the robot possibly opened the mathematical way to better living for every man."
> *The Associated Press, February 14, 1946*

## CULTURAL NOTES

Just as with many other technological innovations of the past, the first electronic computer was used for very specialized purposes by small groups of users in a highly controlled context before being used by the general population. ENIAC was initially developed to address national security problems and was used by scientists. And, because ENIAC was an experimental machine, its operators had to be engineers.

Consequently, the most immediate cultural effect of ENIAC would be felt in the scientific community. With a computer capable of automating what were once considered calculations too large and time consuming to be considered practical to compute by existing methods, scientific users began to use numerical solutions more and more to solve scientific problems. ENIAC forever changed the way scientists approached research.

In spite of ENIAC's highly specialized purpose, while in development its designers were also considering possible peacetime applications. Some of those potential applications, such as nuclear physics (for the generation of power), aerodynamics, and scientific weather prediction, would ultimately have an influence, although indirectly, on individual Americans' quality of life (Allision, 1996). However, ENIAC was a new technology that would change the world.

> "The computer age was off to a blazing start. ENIAC quickly showed that it was not just a demonstration project but a useful, long-lived tool, a true workhorse. Even more than that, it was an instant inspiration to the world of computing."
> *Scott McCartney*

**TABLE 9–1  About ENIAC**

ENIAC was the first digital electronic computer. Consisting of 49-feet-tall cabinets, early press accounts referred to is as a "Giant Brain."

1. ENIAC was a big improvement over human computers. Calculations that could take an individual two days to perform could now be done in 20 seconds.
2. The first computational problem ENIAC worked on was completed in two hours, a task that would have taken 100 man-years of trained human computers' work.
3. The Army and Navy believed ENIAC would have a tremendous impact in the science of weather forecasting. It was used to predict Russian weather patterns (to determine the spread of nuclear fallout in the event of war) but also to develop thermonuclear weapons, to design wind tunnels, and, as originally intended, to calculate ballistics tables.
4. ENIAC had 18,000 vacuum tubes, 6,000 switches, 500,000 soldered joints, 70,000 resistors, and 10,000 capacitors.
5. As compared to a modern computer with a 150-MHz Pentium microprocessor:

    Speed:      ENIAC was capable of 5,000 additions per second.
    A 150-MHz Pentium processor can calculate 300 million additions per second—60,000 times faster than ENIAC.

    Memory:     ENIAC could store 200 digits.
    A modern computer with 16 megabytes of RAM stores 16 million digits—80,000 times the memory capacity of ENIAC.

    Size/Weight ENIAC was 10 feet tall, required 1,800 square feet of floor space, and weighed 30 tons.
    A modern laptop can measure 11.5 inches by 8 inches and weigh 6 pounds or less. The microprocessor itself can be the size of a lapel pin (*Times,* 1996).

6. Because ENIAC had so many tubes, there were always a few burning out, and it was not operational more than 70 percent of the time.
7. Two days before the public unveiling of ENIAC, the ballistics program to be demonstrated was not working. The solution to the problem came to an ENIAC programmer in the middle of the night. One of its 6,000 switches was off by one place. ENIAC then performed flawlessly.
8. The Electronic Discrete Variable Calculator (EDVAC), the second-generation ENIAC, would be simpler, faster, and smaller, have more memory (requiring one-tenth as much hardware as ENIAC). Today, over 50 years later, this trend in computer technology continues.

"We've seen the black-and-white newsreels of the crew-cut fathers of the computing revolution in their white shirts and pocket protectors standing proudly in front of their huge, blinking baby [ENIAC]. But how many knew that the revolution had mothers? That the huge hulking machine couldn't do a thing until it was programmed by a half-dozen women."

*Kathleen Melymuka*

## IA AND ENIAC

Some innovations in information and communication technologies (ICT) have a direct historical relevance to the IA profession, while the relevance of others has more to do with the facilitation of the IA process. The information organization, navigation, interaction, and flow characteristics of ICT innovations (ancient and modern) influence the shape of today's information spaces and therefore are also relevant to understanding information architecture.

| **TABLE 9–2**   Information Processing—ENIAC |
|---|
| Communication systems and technologies have various capacities for communicating, storing, and retrieving information. ENIAC had the following information-processing capacities: |
| *Information Communication* <br> ENIAC was programmed solely for performing numerical calculations and not for communication purposes. |
| *Information Storage* <br> ENIAC was capable of storing only 200 digits at a time. Numbers were loaded into ENIAC either from punch cards, stored mechanically using electrical switches, or stored electronically in accumulators during computations. |
| *Information Retrieval* <br> Only one 10-digit number could be transmitted at a time. |

## Direct Historical Significance

ENIAC represents the birth of the computer age. During the same period that ENIAC was in development (1945), Vannevar Bush, now recognized as a prophet of the computer age, urged scientists to turn their energies to the task of making the vast store of human knowledge accessible and useful. He proposed the development of an "infostructure" that would be realized in what we now know as the Internet. He also proposed the development of the "memex." He described it as "a device in which an individual stores all his books, records, communications, and which is mechanized so that it may be consulted with exceeding speed and flexibility. It is an enlarged intimate supplement to his memory." He imagined "translucent screens on which material can be projected for convenient reading," a keyboard, and buttons and levers. He also imagined that "wholly new forms of encyclopedias will appear, ready made by associative trails running through them, ready to be dropped into the memex." He even described how the memex would be used in certain scenarios such as: "The physician, puzzled by a patient's reactions, strikes the trail established in studying an earlier case, and runs rapidly through analogous case histories, with side references to the classics for the patient anatomy and histology" (Vannevar Bush, 1945). All this he imagined one year before one of the world's first electronic computers—ENIAC—was operational and 27 years before the first computer that began to resemble his memex, both in appearance and functionality, was developed—the Alto.

Vannevar Bush's vision was for a machine that would boost the powers of the human mind rather than his physical powers. It was also a call to the scientific community "for a new *relationship* [emphasis added] between thinking man and the sum of [humankind's] knowledge" (*The Atlantic Monthly*, 1945). In doing so, Bush defined a new type of context for human intellectual activity, a computer-mediated information space within which all the tools and resources necessary to support "the logical

"The women [who programmed ENIAC] were part of a pool of about 80 female mathematicians who, with most men tied up in the war effort, had been hired by the U.S. Army to manually compute ballistics trajectories at the Moore School of the University of Pennsylvania. Because no one had ever programmed a computer before, the women had to wing it. Programming for them didn't mean writing; it meant physically routing data and electronic pulses through the 80-foot-long behemoth using 3,000 switches, 18,000 vacuum tubes, and dozens of cables."

*Kathleen Melymuka*

processes of thought" were at users' fingertips. His premonition inspired and guided many pioneers, and pioneering organizations, in the early days of computing technology and the Internet. Among these was another visionary concerned with the *synergistic relationship* between the human intellect and computerized information handling—Douglas Engelbart.

Douglas Engelbart was a prolific inventor (the mouse, hypermedia, windows, and many more) and was also instrumental in formulating the theoretical framework for a new discipline that came to be called human computer interaction (HCI). He was motivated by the recognition that with the advent of digital technology there was a danger that technological evolution would speed ahead of the nontechnical and automate the capabilities that humans have developed over hundreds of years to boost their intellect, rather than "augment" the human intellect. By augmenting the human intellect, he meant "using modern technology to give direct aid to an individual in comprehending complex situations, isolating the significant factors, and solving problems" (Engelbart, *Augmenting Human Intellect: A Conceptual Framework,* 1962).

His primary research and development goals were to "find the factors that limit the effectiveness of the individual's basic information-handling capabilities in meeting the various needs of society for problem solving in its most general sense, and to develop new techniques, procedures, and systems that will better match these basic capabilities to the needs, problems, and progress of society." He recognized that meeting these goals would require a systematic approach and include the contributions of dozens of disciplines. The significance of Engelbart's conceptual framework is that it is still very relevant to the practice of IA today and encompasses numerous IA concerns that are now characterized as human-computer interaction and usability concerns. In fact, many IA practitioners come from the HCI field, a field that began with the pioneering efforts of Douglas Engelbart.

## CHAPTER 10

# ERMA
## Automated Computing Solutions for Business Problems

"[Designing computers for business] would be a very different proposition from designing ENIAC, and not just because the technology was now advanced. The characteristics of the users would also be very different. For successful operation, computer designs need to be as sensitive to the nature of the people who use them as they do to the technical state of the art."

David K. Allison

"ERMA, developed in the 1950s, is one of the earliest use-directed centralized application [computer] systems."

*Charles Babbage Institute*

ERMA has also been credited with being the biggest single advance in banking history. It not only allowed banking to explode in the 50s and 60s, but it also eventually transformed banking operations and services.

## HISTORY: 1953–1963

First-generation computers, like ENIAC, were extremely complicated to program, used thousands of vacuum tubes (that generated tremendous amounts of heat), had the energy requirements of a small town, were extremely large, and could be operated only by engineers. The invention of the transistor would replace the vacuum tube, and, along with advances in memory storage, second-generation computer technology would become smaller, faster, more energy efficient, and more reliable than experimental first-generation computers like ENIAC. Eventually, the customized machine language coding used to instruct first-generation computers would be replaced by abbreviated programming codes called *assembly language* that made programming far easier than before.

Coupled with demands from the business community, these new developments would lead to the creation of mainframe computers specifically designed for commercial applications. One such demand was reaching crisis proportions in the banking industry. Check use in

**KEYWORDS**

history of computing, ERMA

history of computing, big iron

history of computing, giant brains

history of computing, MICR

Stanford Research Institute, ERMA

the United States had doubled from four billion to eight billion checks per year in the nine years between 1943 and 1952. Considering that the writer of a check and the receiver often did not bank at the same institution, in 1952 as many as 69 million checks may have had to be sorted, proofed, and accounted for on any given day. Consequently, bank employees were overwhelmed by the increasing volume, and the number of bank employees required just to process checks was rising rapidly. Banks were even closing in the middle of the afternoon in an attempt to process and proof the day's transactions. Data processing was becoming a bottleneck that was affecting the future growth of the banking industry.

The creation of bank branch offices and the rapidly increasing number of checks used by a growing clientele threatened to overwhelm the existing manual processing and record-keeping system of the banking industry. This led the Bank of America to contract with the Stanford Research Institute to design an automated check processing system.

The industry was in need of a system that would lower labor costs, reduce the high error rate associated with manually processing billions of checks, and speed up the entire process. All of these factors led S. Clark Beise, the senior vice president of the Bank of America (BOA), to contract with the Stanford Research Institute (SRI) to design an automated check processing system. SRI was a nonprofit research center dedicated to applied research in physics, economics, and engineering. Their agreed-upon goal was to develop a computing system that would accomplish the following:

1. Credit and debit all accounts,
2. Maintain a record of all transactions,
3. Retain a constant record of customer balances for printing,
4. Respond to stop-payment and hold orders, and
5. Notify the operator if a check caused the account in question to be overdrawn. (Allision, 1996)

The Stanford Research Institute (SRI) was recognized in March 2001 as a pioneer in computerized banking. It was acknowledged that SRI's contribution constituted the first successful use of computers in business operations in the world.

Also, because the principal users were to be data clerks, it was important that the system be easy enough to use so that they could focus on the information they were processing rather than the machine. It was equally important that the look and feel of BOA checks remain unchanged to avoid any possibility of upsetting its customers. This requirement symbolized a new generation in computing defined in terms of users, not just in terms of the technology itself.

In 1955, after several years in development, SRI produced a successful prototype system, the Electronic Recording Machine—Accounting (ERMA). Critical to the success of the system was the innovative use of magnetic ink so that accounting numbers (coded in unique Arabic font symbols) could be recorded on checks and then read automatically by electronic readers. Having worked closely with other banking institutions and the American Banking Association, the Bank of America's standards would quickly be adopted throughout the United States (Allision, 1996). The magnetic ink character recognition (MICR) system is still used worldwide today. After a series of production machines were manufactured, ERMA went into operation in late 1959.

| TABLE 10–1    About ERMA |
|---|
| ERMA gave the Bank of America a competitive edge by enabling them to provide faster, more efficient, and less-expensive services—all of which consumers would quickly come to expect from other banking institutions. Although not yet in the hands of the general population many people were beginning to enjoy the benefits of computing power in a very direct way. |

1. Unlike ENIAC, ERMA was developed for a practical business application, not scientific research.
2. Data clerks, not engineers, were trained to operate ERMA. However, engineers were still required to program ERMA.
3. ERMA used an innovative form of input device, the recordable magnetic ink stripe.
4. The production version of ERMA used transistors rather than vacuum tubes.
5. ERMA had all the components associated with modern-day computers: printers, tape storage, memory, operating systems, and the ability to store programs.
6. Experience with emerging information technologies (IT) allowed Bank of America not only to reduce its costs but to expand its markets and implement more control throughout the BOA organization.
7. Recognizing the value of IT, BOA became a pioneer in developing new career paths for computer system managers.
8. BOA IT's newly acquired knowledge of applications and mainframes allowed it to provide data processing services to small businesses that could not afford the price of a mainframe and expensive business applications. By 1973 BOA was conducting almost 70 percent of all computer service business in southern California.

## CULTURAL NOTES

Although ERMA was as specialized in its original application as ENIAC, the advent of flexible programming languages and ERMA's ability to store programs meant that new instructions for different applications could be installed quickly. This capability allowed these very expensive computer systems to be more cost effective and productive. As a consequence, more data processing applications were developed, marking the beginning of new types of careers (programmers and computer systems experts) as well as the beginning of the software industry.

The most immediate cultural effect of ERMA would be felt within the banking industry, but ERMA was developed for business use. Before long, computers in America would be used predominately for business applications rather than for scientific purposes. Consequently, more and more people began to have day-to-day contact with computers, and a general awareness of their presence in the workplace began to build. The notion of computers as "Giant Brains" used for secretive and esoteric purposes was giving way to the idea that computers were sophisticated business tools.

Among the many challenges designers faced when designing ERMA was enabling the machine to read information from checks, deposit slips, and other banking documents. Adding to the challenge was the Bank of America's (BOA) stipulation that the look and feel of their current banking materials remain the same. It was feared that any radical changes would undermine customers' confidence. The solution settled upon—using magnetic character recognition ink to print unique Arabic symbols on existing materials—ultimately proved to feel completely natural to the BOA's customers.

| TABLE 10–2    Information Processing—ERMA |
|---|
| Communication systems and technologies have various capacities for communicating, storing, and retrieving information. ERMA had the following information-processing capacities: |
| *Information Communication* <br>     ERMA was originally developed to process checks but eventually evolved into a fully integrated system with internal communications (distributed access to centralized information) that made possible the ability to provide customers with up-to-date information regarding their accounts. Information communication was limited to numerical financial information. However, such information was highly confidential, and access to it was controlled. <br><br> *Information Storage* <br>     ERMA used magnetic tape for loading programming information, storing current account and transaction data, and archiving dated accounts and transactions. <br><br> *Information Retrieval* <br>     ERMA was the first computer to enable multiple workers within a banking environment to determine an account's status and to validate inputs electronically. |

## IA AND ERMA

"The ERMA system was designed for innovative forms of input. In earlier computers, innovation was primarily in processing and storage of information. Input and output was done in a basic and routine fashion, usually via punched cards. But as computers were integrated in different settings [other than for scientific purposes] innovation was also needed in input and output. The most important innovation in input in ERMA was the magnetic character recognition code (MICR)."

*David Allision*

Some innovations in information and communication technologies (ICT) have a direct historical relevance to the IA profession, while the relevance of others has more to do with the facilitation of the IA process. The information organization, navigation, interaction, and flow characteristics of ICT innovations (ancient and modern) influence the shape of today's information spaces and therefore are also relevant to understanding information architecture.

### Direct Historical Significance

ERMA's relevance to IA is primarily technical. It represents the early application of computerized information technologies for business purposes and the introduction of computers into everyday life. That ERMA revolutionized the banking industry is a reminder of the powerful influence the introduction of new information and communication technologies can have on the location, character, and organization of human activities. Banking and finance transactions were once entirely face-to-face and paper-based activities that took place in the space of a typical working day (8 A.M. to 5:00 P.M.), five days a week. Now, most banking and financial transactions are electronic, online, and take place 24 hours a day, seven days a week. ERMA also represents one of the first examples of user-centered design in the computer industry. The user populations for which ERMA was designed included banking customers and data clerks to operate ERMA.

## CHAPTER 11

# The Alto
## Computing Gets Personal

"Consider a future device for individual use, which is a sort of mechanized private file and library … a device in which an individual stores all his books, records, and communications and which is mechanized so that it may be consulted with exceeding speed and flexibility. It is an enlarged intimate supplement to his memory."

Vannevar Bush

## HISTORY: 1972–1979

Like ERMA, computers built between 1959 and 1965 are often referred to as "second-generation computers." Although smaller and faster than first-generation giants like ENIAC, they were very expensive, costing from hundreds of thousands to millions of dollars. Consequently, they were generally used only by banking institutions, governments, or large research organizations. The invention of integrated circuits would dramatically change all that and lead to even smaller, but more importantly, less-expensive computers that were immediately very popular with large businesses and universities. This further miniaturization also led to the development of the first "pocket" calculators.

Possessing more computing power than the original Univac, pocket calculators were also extremely popular, and manufacturers rapidly introduced new models with more functionality to improve their marketability. Wanting to reduce the time necessary to bring a new model to market, one company conceived of integrating a programmable microprocessor, referred to as a "chip," in their calculators. With such a chip, new functions could now be added without manufacturing an entirely new device. It would be a descendant of this first chip, the 4004, that would handle the processing requirements of the first "personal" computer, Alto.

Many of the features we take for granted in today's personal computers can be traced to one device designed almost 30 years ago—the Alto. The ideas behind the Alto weren't new; rather, their time had come. Technology had advanced to the point where they were viable.

**KEYWORDS**

graphical user interface, Engelbart

history of computing, Xerox PARC

history of computing, Xerox Alto

history of computing, Xerox Star

invention of the mouse

However, chip technology was not the only innovation that would lead to the development of Alto. Focused on innovative input devices for manipulating information, Ivan Sutherland in 1968 built one of the first graphical user interfaces, a system he called *Sketchpad*. Using a light pen, a user could draw graphical figures on a CRT (cathode ray tube) display which could then be moved, copied, reduced, enlarged, and rotated. Around the same period, Douglas Engelbart and a team of researchers who were experimenting with different types of computer displays and input devices at the Stanford Research Institute (SRI) developed a system known as NLS (*On-line System*). They were exploring ways of using computers "to augment the knowledge worker." The NLS also used a CRT to display information (other computers used teletype) and a unique input device they invented called an "X-Y position indicator." It would later be nicknamed the "mouse."

In 1970 Xerox founded a research center in Palo Alto to develop the "architecture of information." The Palo Alto Research Center's (PARC) mission was to establish the technical foundation for electronic office systems that Xerox intended to take to market in the 1980s. To this end they began searching for a new approach to computing. Alan Kay, one of the founders of Xerox PARC, was familiar with the work done at SRI (also located in Palo Alto) on the NLS and soon hired a number of people who had worked on the NLS project. They all shared his dream of developing what they later coined a "personal computer" capable of providing an individual user with the ability to capture information, view it, store and retrieve it, process it, and communicate it to others. This design concept in 1975 was significantly different from anything else at the time or that came before it, and many people has a hard time accepting it (Roberts, 1989).

The head of the Xerox team that developed the Alto, Bob Taylor, has been credited with saying that, "Computers should be devices for communicating with others, not engines for making calculations; that everyone should have one; and that all computers should be networked to one another." It took a while for his team to accept his vision of individual, interactive computing.

Their first prototype was named Alto. It was designed to fit in an office comfortably yet was powerful enough to support a reliable, high-quality operating system and graphical display. It consisted of four major parts: a graphics display, a keyboard, a mouse, and a disk storage/processor box. Software was also developed for Alto to extend its capabilities as well as support peripheral devices such as a laser printer. Systems software and applications developed for Alto included standardized communications protocols (Ethernet) so that Altos could be networked, a What-You-See-Is-What-You-Get (WYSIWYG) text editor, a graphic editing (drawing) program, a page-description program for laser printing, shared file storage protocols, and a local network email program (Lampson, 1988).

Alto was introduced in 1972. Initially, only a few were built but, after software was developed, demand for them within PARC and Xerox grew rapidly. Eventually, over 1,000 Altos were built. Purely experimental, the Alto was not intended to be manufactured for commercial purposes. A commercialized version of Alto, named Star, was built at the end of the 1970s but was not marketed very successfully. Xerox eventually discon-

> **TABLE 11–1   About Alto**
>
> The focus of Xerox PARC's researchers on the user to improve usability resulted in a range of features and functions that are commonplace today: windows, What-You-See-Is-What-You-Get displays, the mouse, graphical user interfaces, and the desktop metaphor. All were designed to make the distribution, storage, retrieval, and manipulation of information easy and ultimately to increase intellectual effectiveness.
>
> 1. Alto was the first workstation that used a mouse.
> 2. Alto could display several documents simultaneously in individual windows.
> 3. Alto had a graphics display that featured menus and icons as navigational aids.
> 4. Alto users could link to a local area network.
> 5. Alto users could communicate via email within a local area network.
> 6. Alto users could share a printer on a local area network.
> 7. Alto users could share files on a local area network.
> 8. Alto's graphical user interface (GUI) predated by 10 years the use of a GUI by the Macintosh in 1984.
> 9. Alto was one of the best funded and largest computer prototyping efforts in the history of computer technology.
> 10. Many of the innovations pioneered in Alto's development were later adopted by other developers including Atari, Apple, and Microsoft.

tinued manufacturing it. However, according to Len Shustek of The Computer Museum, it was while visiting Xerox PARC in 1979 that Steve Jobs saw Alto, the prototype for Star. Realizing that if a personal computer were correctly built and marketed, Lens claims that Jobs stated, "it could blow the competition away." Inspired by what he saw, Jobs would later build the Macintosh.

## CULTURAL NOTES

With few exceptions, Alto was never used by anyone but Xerox employees. It did lead to the development and marketing of the Xerox "Star" which, although ahead of its time, was never a commercial success. However, the concept of a personal computing device would become immensely popular and lead to the phenomenal success stories of many who jumped on the bandwagon early—pioneers like Steve Jobs and Bill Gates. Instrumental to this success was all the effort invested in designing a computer that was easy to use.

From their beginnings, calculators and computers were tools developed primarily to solve government, military, and business problems. Although originally conceived of as an office tool, the Alto represented a move toward a new direction in computing—a device for processing information and for solving a range of problem types in a more personalized way. This innovative approach to computing set the stage for the widespread diffusion of computer technology into a broad range of contexts, including the home.

Two innovative concepts led to the development of the Alto: Alan Kay's idea for a small, cheap, and easy-to-use computer for nonprofessionals that he called a "dynabook" and Xerox Corporation's vision for the office of the future—the electronic office. Kay wanted to make the computer a "personal and dynamic medium for handling information, which can model the world and make the world visible." The electronic office idea was based on using electronic media to do all the work of an office: capturing information, viewing it, storing and retrieving it, communicating it to others, and processing it.

*Butler Lampson*

> **TABLE 11–2 Information Processing—Alto**
>
> Communication systems and technologies have various capacities for communicating, storing, and retrieving information. Alto had the following information processing capacities:
>
> *Information Communication*
> Alto was designed as a communications device and its features included the ability to share text documents, accessible on a local area network server, as well as exchange internal electronic mail. Alto could not process any dynamic data such as audio or video.
>
> *Information Storage*
> Alto could store documents locally on magnetic disks or on a local area network server.
>
> *Information Retrieval*
> To facilitate quick and easy retrieval of information, Alto was among the first computers to use a hierarchal filing system for organizing and managing documents.

The prevailing attitude in 1975 was that computers were fast and people were slow. The designers of the Alto believed that this relationship was true only when people had to play on the machine's terms. However, they stated, "When the [computer] is required to play the game in humans' terms, presenting a page full of attractively formatted text, graphs, or pictures in a fraction of a second in which the human can pick out a significant pattern, it is the other way around—people are fast, and [computers] are slow."

*Butler Lampson*

## IA AND THE ALTO

Some innovations in information and communication technologies (ICT) have a direct historical relevance to the IA profession, while the relevance of others has more to do with the facilitation of the IA process. The information organization, navigation, interaction, and flow characteristics of ICT innovations (ancient and modern) influence the shape of today's information spaces and therefore are also relevant to understanding information architecture.

### Direct Historical Significance

The Alto represents the early manifestation of the visions Vannevar Bush and Douglas Engelbart had for a device that would augment the human intellect. Engelbart's research laboratory developed a prototype personal computer, but it was the Xerox Palo Alto Research Center (PARC) that would systematically apply Engelbart's ideas to the development of a commercial personal computer designed for office workers. The Alto and the subsequent production version called the Star had a profound effect on the computer industry.

The process by which the Alto became a reality also has historical relevance. Today, like previous pioneers and visionaries, professionals from multiple disciplines (information architects) are developing an orienting vision that is inclusive of new computing technologies, the individual human intellect, the conceptual structures humanity has collectively developed for managing information over many centuries, and the unique and pragmatic needs of clients and users.

## CHAPTER 12

# The PC Evolution
## From Mainframes to Minis to Micros

"Where the original software patriarchs solved various problems in the creation of the first computers, the personal computer pioneers struggled with equally vexing problems involved in using computers to create leverage for human intellect, the way wheels and dynamos create leverage for human muscles. Where the patriarchs were out to *create* computation, the pioneers sought to *transform* it."

Howard Rheingold

## HISTORY: 1975–PRESENT

Although developed by Xerox researchers, when the Alto was introduced in 1972, many within Xerox were skeptical about the usefulness of a personal computer. They could not imagine for what purpose an individual would need an entire computer. This was still the era of the mainframe, and as late as 1965 there were only about 30,000 computers in the world—all large mainframes. Capitalizing on the invention of the integrated circuit, some mainframe companies eventually did manufacture and market computers that were smaller in size and capacity, called "minis." The smallest minis were still the size of a large filing cabinet and ranged in price between $150,000 and $200,000. They were used for very specialized applications and proved to be popular with businesses that could not afford "big iron." However, as late as 1975 the computer industry had not considered the possibility that there was a consumer market for even smaller and less-expensive computers—micros.

It was the development of useful software applications that eventually changed the minds of skeptics in Xerox about the Alto, and its popularity grew. Although Alto was intended to be only a prototype, demand in Xerox led to the production of almost 1,000 Altos before Xerox introduced the commercial version of the Alto, the Star system. Eventually, the graphical user interface, mouse, and utilitarian software that Alto's

The world has never had any problem using the constant stream of innovation offered by the computer industry. With very few exceptions, every time hardware or software has become smaller (or more efficient), cheaper, faster, and more powerful, new groups of users have presented themselves or existing users have upgraded.

**KEYWORDS**

history of computing, Apple

history of computing, Microsoft

history of computing, microcomputers

history of computing, minicomputers

history of computing, personal computers

In the late 1950s, plans to sell computers to individuals were occasionally proposed, but the minicomputer manufacturers, whose machines could be operated by an individual, were not interested. However, minicomputer prices started at $30,000 and would have been unaffordable to the majority of consumers any day. It was therefore destined that PCs would come from outside the established computer industry.

designers pioneered, in combination with an affordable central processing unit, would make the prospect of purchasing a personal computer for the home attractive to millions of people around the world. However, when early PCs appeared, the computer industry ignored them. The revolution would begin with two college dropouts on a workbench in the garage of a suburban home in California.

*Radio-Electronics* magazine ran a story in July 1974 featuring the design of a machine they described as a personal minicomputer. It was called the Mark 8. For $5.50 readers would receive an instruction manual on how to build it, and for $48 they would receive the manual and circuit boards. All other components to complete the kit, including an Intel 8008 chip, would have to be purchased separately from other vendors. The magazine sold 10,000 copies of the manual and around 2,500 circuit boards. It is estimated that just over a thousand were ever actually assembled, but the Mark 8 and another more complete microcomputer kit named Altair generated a lot of interest among hobbyists, even spawning computer clubs. It would be at an Altair club named "Homebrew" that Steve Jobs and Steve Wozniak, who once attended the same high school, would meet again. Together they developed their own version of a microcomputer, with the intent of selling it preassembled rather than in a kit form, and called it the Apple I.

Working out of Jobs' garage, they eventually sold 175 in and around the area that would become known as Silicon Valley. The Apple I had no keyboard, no power supply, and no case. It sold for about $666. Encouraged by their success, Wozinak designed and built an improved version, the Apple II, and Jobs solicited financial backing to manufacture it. The Apple II more closely resembled PCs as we know them today and featured a keyboard, power supply, and plug-in slots for peripherals. In April 1977, along with two other "packaged" systems, the Apple II was announced. Delivery started in the fall of the same year. When Apple went public as a company in December 1980, it was valued at $1.2 billion. With that valuation, the mainstream computer industry began to pay attention. In 1981 IBM entered the market with the PC.

There were only a few hundred computers in homes in 1975, the first year that microcomputers were offered completely assembled. By 1982 a million had been sold and by 1984 almost ten million. Within 10 years the number grew to thirty-five million and in 1995 alone an additional five million computers were purchased. Rapidly increasing computing power and decreasing cost contributed to this growth. For example, in 1983 IBM's first personal computer, the PC/XT, shipped with 10 megabytes of memory. An additional 10 megabytes of memory could be purchased for $3,000—$300 per megabyte. A little over 10 years later a 1.6 gigabyte personal computer hard drive could be purchased for $225—$0.14 per megabyte (Gates, 1996).

Today it is difficult to imagine any area of human activity, whether at home, at work, or at play, in which a computer is not involved. Since originally envisioned nearly 50 years earlier as a purely computational device for scientific applications, a broad range of other fields including business, entertainment, journalism, and academia could now not function without computers. Computers are integral to almost every facet of everyday life in the new millennium, and new applications continue to arise. With the advent of networked computing in the 1980s came the merging of computing and communication that within a decade led to the development of the Internet and the emergence of the World Wide Web. With the Web, a new era in the history of computing began—the era of the information marketplace.

## CULTURAL NOTES

The personal computer represents a phase in the evolution of computing technology during which the computer made its way out of corporate and government institutions and into the daily lives of millions of people. Early computers were difficult to reprogram and generally were dedicated to running highly specialized applications. Modern personal computers are able to run, with little or no reconfiguration, a broad range of software applications to accomplish an equally broad range of tasks. This is where the true power of the PC lies and has had the most influence on contemporary life. Capitalizing on the raw computational power provided by phenomenally fast microprocessors, software developers offer tools for every conceivable task at home, the office, and in the marketplace.

Well-designed applications are easy to use and highly effective. In one example, a new software product actually led to dramatic changes in an entire industry—the printing industry. Desktop publishing software enabled individuals who were not expert typesetters or layout artists to produce "camera-ready" products of equal or better quality than those produced by professional printing firms. Ultimately, desktop publishing software became sophisticated enough to level the playing field in the industry, enabling smaller printers who couldn't afford costly typographic composition equipment to compete with larger printing companies. In the telecommunications industry a similar effect was felt with the introduction of desktop, all-digital, nonlinear video and audio editing systems.

A host of other software applications such as spreadsheets, database, and computer-aided drawing programs put into the hands of small businesses and families "tools" to perform complex tasks that previously only highly trained specialists could do. In 1983, David Rodman, a programmer and pioneer in the development of database management software said:

> A really good program designer makes an artist out of the person who uses the keyboard, by creating a world that puts them in the position of, "Here's the keyboard, and here's the screen. Now once you learn a few rudimentary communication skills, you can be a superstar." (Rheingold, 2000)

Early computer tasks were highly specialized and centered on number "crunching." Reprogramming to perform different operations meant hours of resetting wires and switches. Today, PCs can perform a wide range of tasks and are able to switch from one application to another with little or no reconfiguration.

In the late 1970s, IBM noticed the success that Apple was having selling personal computers. IBM did not consider Apple to be a threat to its huge mainframe business but wanted in on the market. The success of the IBM PC took everyone by surprise. By 1984 three out of every four personal computers were IBM PCs. Because IBM used Microsoft's operating system and Intel's microprocessor [chip] in the PC, they both profited greatly from the PC's success.

---

**TABLE 12–1 About the PC**

We take for granted many of the different applications for which PCs are used today. Although the PC is a relatively recent technological innovation, it was certainly not ever imagined that it would be used as a communications device or for sharing document files across a global network. As the printing press, telegraph, telephone, and television were either unique combinations of previous inventions assembled to perform a new function or spin-offs from research into new technologies intended for wholly different purposes, so it was with the PC.

1. The microprocessor that eventually became the heart of early PCs was designed specifically for handheld calculators. By 1975, when the first PCs were introduced, 750,000 already had been sold.
2. Much of the research that led to dramatic advances in improving human-computer interaction was first implemented in personal computing devices and contributed to the early popularity of PCs. The mouse, a graphical user interface, and windows were all first introduced to consumers by PC manufacturers. Although not always as "user-friendly" as advertised, these developments did give users more interaction options than inputting commands from a keyboard. It is widely accepted that these features contributed to the spectacular growth of the PC industry.
3. The software applications most important to early PC users were gaming, text editing (word processing), spreadsheet, database, and graphics programs. With the arrival of the Internet and modems, communication applications became highly popular.
4. The PC led to the integration of multiple media into one application and the development of interactive "multimedia" programs. Using either a variety of input and navigation devices, such programs allowed the users control of what they could hear and see as well as the ability to gather, process, and communicate their own ideas. Early multimedia audio, graphic, and video resources were stored on laser discs controlled by a PC. CD-ROM technology would later dominate as the preferred multimedia storage and distribution medium. CD-ROM players soon became an integral feature of PCs.
5. The easy-to-use World Wide Web browser application, Netscape Navigator, was at first given away to PC users as a strategy to build quickly a large base of users that businesses could target with advertising. Netscape's owners became wealthy in the process.
6. With the successful development of Web browser applications and the phenomenal growth of the Web, the PC became a tool for gathering information from a global network of information resources as well as a global communications device for conducting both personal and business transactions.

---

Improvements in human-computer interaction research have been spectacular and, more than any other factors, have triggered the explosive growth in computing. One example is the now ubiquitous graphical interface which is based on the Xerox PARC work done during the development of the Alto.

Although his claim may have been overstated, useful software applications continue to fuel the PC industry.

One software application in the history of the PC stands out among the rest in terms of its popularity and its influence on American culture. In the late 1960s another development in computing technology paralleled the development of the PC. It focused on the possibility of interconnecting computers for the purpose of allowing groups of individuals to "time-share" a single "multiaccess" computer. The idea was based on the fact that computers performed operations much faster than the rate at which a human could communicate programming instructions to them. Consequently, many large and expensive mainframes sat idle. Once time-sharing applications were working, researchers began looking for ways to interconnect numerous time-sharing "communities" across the United States. Out of this research a unique way of communicating evolved. Over a decade after the first time-sharing communities were formed, a commercial version of this communication tool would be marketed as "electronic mail." It would become known among software developers as the first "killer app."

## IA AND THE PC

Some innovations in information and communication technologies (ICT) have a direct historical relevance to the IA profession, while the relevance of others has more to do with the facilitation of the IA process. The information organization, navigation, interaction, and flow characteristics of ICT innovations (ancient and modern) influence the shape of today's information spaces and therefore are also relevant to understanding information architecture.

### The Information Space: Organization, Navigation, Interaction, and Flows

Faster and more powerful personal computers led to the integration of text, graphics, and dynamic media such as audio and video into one digital domain. Although the organization, navigation, interaction, and flow characteristics unique to each medium remained the same in a multimedia information space, new organization, navigation, interaction, and flow issues were introduced. The multimedia information space was made more complex than traditional information spaces not only by virtue of the number of different types of media used but also by the fact that they could be linked together and new relationships constructed between them that had not been possible before. This new kind of information space was complicated, confusing, undefined, and defied the traditional conceptual models used by information designers to design usable and coherent information environments. Consequently, graphical user interfaces were developed to assist in mediating navigation within software application environments, a computer's operating system environment, and interaction with content resources and application tools.

### Direct Historical Significance

The era of the PC represents the diffusion of computing technology into everyday life and the personalization of computing. Since the introduction of the first personal computers, great improvements have been made in their usability. Contributing to these improvements has been the

While mainframe computers had been around for a long time, the average hobbyist interested in computers or programming had no computer resources available for a reasonable price or size for home use. During the early days before 1970, hobbyists borrowed time on mainframe computers owned by educational institutions or research facilities. One of these hobbyists was Bill Gates.

In 1982, one year after IBM introduced the PC, *Time* magazine departed from its tradition of naming a "man of the year," choosing instead to name the computer as the "machine of the year." *Time's* publisher, Hone Meyers, wrote of the decision, "Several human candidates might have represented 1982, but none symbolized the past year more richly, or will be viewed by history as more significant, than a machine—the computer."

### TABLE 12–2 Information Processing—PC

Communication systems and technologies have various capacities for communicating, storing, and retrieving information. PCs have the following information-processing capacities:

*Information Communication*

Early commercial PCs were not designed as communications devices. Eventually, with the introduction of local area networks (LANS) and electronic mail applications, individual PCs began to function as network "nodes" between which a variety of document types could be shared including text, database, and spreadsheet files. Later, improved networks with greater bandwidth enabled the sharing of large dynamic data files such as audio and video. This integration of multiple media types into a "digital domain" was referred to as an electronic convergence and greatly expanded the ability for humans to document and communicate the human experience.

*Information Storage*

For the first time in history, humans could record and store speech, writing, and imagery all within a single context. However, how to archive digitized information is still a source of controversy. One important issue is related to the rapid rate of obsolescence for computer hardware and software. Even if digitized information is stored on an archival-quality medium, there is also a high probability that computer hardware and software in the future will not be "backward" compatible with today's hardware and software. It is ironic that manuscript paper made from rags hundreds of years ago is still very stable today.

*Information Retrieval*

PCs enable extremely quick retrieval of information and commonly use a variety of information management schemes for organizing and filing documents including: alphabetical indexes, time and date "stamping," hierarchal systems, and a variety of search "engines."

"By the end of the 1990s, the PC had [changed] the lives of most people. Many could not perform their jobs without a PC. Other functions [that the PC enabled] would be so labor intensive that it would be economically unfeasible to perform them without a PC. Becoming computer literate is now a goal in elementary schools today, and colleges offer courses [that require] using computers and the Internet."

*C. T. Evans*

power of microprocessors (almost doubling every 18 months), and software programmers and interface designers taking advantage of greater computing power to support more sophisticated interface designs. Another contributing factor has been the efforts of practitioners in the field of human-computer interaction who, through the application of carefully considered theories and practices, have made significant strides in making computers easier to use. However, designers are facing new usability challenges presented by the advent of new types of information spaces on the Web and in distributed computing environments. Traditional HCI design situated the user outside of the computer, looking at a monitor upon which information was displayed. Now, designers from multiple disciplines are beginning to consider an alternative view that situates the user within a computer-mediated information space. Among these designers are information architects from the fields of library science and information science, disciplines that have historically been concerned with the form and organization of information and information spaces.

## PART 4

# COMPUTER NETWORKS
## Communication and Computing Systems Converge

"When people do their informational work 'at the [computer] console' and 'through the network,' telecommunication will be as natural an extension of individual work as face-to-face communication is now. The impact of that fact, and of the marked facilitation of the communicative process, will be very great—both on the individual and on society."

J.C.R. Licklider

## CHAPTER 13

# Internauts
## Architects of the Intergalactic Network

"The world of information and communication technology that influences so much of our lives today was not created by the existing computer industry, nor was it championed by the orthodoxy of computer science. Rather, it was built by a handful of rebels who weren't seeking fame or fortune, but spent their lives creating a new tool for enhancing human thought. They created it because they wanted it for their personal use, because it was a cool thing to do, and because they thought it would improve the human lot."

Howard Rheingold

## HISTORY: 1962–PRESENT

The notion of using computers as a communication medium among people was an important conceptual shift in the history of computing machines. In fact, the work of scores of researchers in the early 60s was influenced by this vision, and their collective efforts eventually resulted in what we now know as the Internet. Many agree that this vision originated with one individual—Vannevar Bush.

## VANNEVAR BUSH (1890–1974)

In July 1945 near the end of WWII, the *Atlantic Monthly* published a paper authored by the director of the Office of Scientific Research and Development, Dr. Vannevar Bush. The article, "As We May Think," urged scientists, who up until that time had been focused on supporting the war effort, to turn their efforts to "the massive task of making more accessible our bewildering store of knowledge." He added that "instruments are at hand which, if properly developed, will give access to and command over the inherited knowledge of the ages."

Vannevar Bush was never directly involved with the Internet and died before the invention of the World Wide Web. However, his innovative ideas for automating human memory, as described in his famous essay, "As We May Think," (see *Appendix A*), influenced many of those who did contribute to the creation of the Internet. More importantly, his work to create a strong relationship between government and the scientific community during WWII changed the way scientific research was conducted in the United States and fostered the environment in which the Internet was later created.

**KEYWORDS**

ARPA, *Sputnik*
history of computing, cyberspace
Intergalactic Network, Licklider
Vannevar Bush, memex
thinking centers, Licklider

After elaborating on the need for such an instrument, he described his vision of such a machine in some detail, writing, "Consider a future device for individual use, which is a sort of mechanized file and library. It needs a name, and, to coin one at random, "memex" will do. A memex is a device in which an individual stores all his books, records, and communications and which is mechanized so that it may be consulted with exceeding speed and flexibility. It is an enlarged supplement to his memory. It consists of a desk, and while it presumably can be operated from a distance, it is primarily the piece of furniture at which he works. On the top are slanting translucent screens, on which material can be projected for convenient reading. There is a keyboard and sets of buttons and levers. Otherwise it looks like an ordinary desk." He even alludes to what we now know as hypertext or linking when he says that the machine is capable of "associative indexing." He describes associative indexing as the "basic idea. … a provision whereby any item [projected on the translucent screen] may be caused at will to select immediately and automatically another. This is the essential feature of the memex. The process of tying two items together is the important thing" (Bush, 1945).

Many computer scientists were heavily influenced by Bush's vision and were early believers in the idea that a machine could aid human cognition. Among them was J. C. R. Licklider who would later influence Robert Taylor and Larry Roberts with his own vision of the future of computing. All would be influential in the design, design development, and innovative use of computing devices for human communication.

## J. C. R. "LICK" LICKLIDER (1915–1990)

Like Vannevar Bush, Licklider was a scientist and a visionary. In 1960 he published a paper, "Man Computer Symbiosis," proposing that computers could augment the human intellect by freeing it from mundane tasks. His hope was that "the resulting partnership will think as no human brain has ever thought and process data in a way not approached by the information-handling machines we know today." To that end he gave a great deal of thought to better ways humans and computers could interact, imagining a device very similar to today's personal computers. He also considered how information could be stored and retrieved describing his vision of networks of "thinking centers" that incorporated the function of libraries, interconnected by wideband communication lines (Waldrop, 2000).

Envisioning the future was one of Lick's great joys, and equal to it was his passion for sharing his visions. In 1962, while serving as the director of the Department of Defense's Advanced Research Projects Agency (ARPA), Licklider found fertile ground upon which to grow many of his ideas. ARPA had been established in 1957 in reaction to the surprise launching of *Sputnik*. Its charge was to fund basic research for the purpose of reestablishing the United States' leadership role in science and

In 1968 in a paper entitled, "The Computer as Communication Device," Licklider stressed, "Our emphasis on people [rather than technology] is deliberate. A communications engineer thinks of communicating as transferring information from one point to another in codes and signals. We believe that communicators have to do something nontrivial with the information they send and receive. And we believe we are entering a technological age in which we will be able to interact with the richness of living information not merely in the passive way we have become accustomed to using books and libraries, but as active participants in an ongoing process, bringing something to it through our interaction with it, and not simply receiving something from it by our connection to it."
*Science and Technology,*
*April 1968*

technology. One area of research concerned how to best use the substantial investment the military had made in computers. These computers were being used to do research related to making timely military decisions and having forces carry them out in the field—Command and Control Research (CCR). Realizing that improvements in CCR could be made only by advancing computing technology, Lick pushed his division of ARPA in that direction and succeeded.

As a consequence, the Information Processing Techniques Office (IPTO) was established. Its charge was to do far-reaching research in advanced technology. Licklider moved quickly to establish research contracts with a number of leading computer research institutions to address this area of concern. He nicknamed the group the Intergalactic Network (ICN)—an early reflection of his interest in the interconnection of on-line communities. From the ICN would come the key individuals who would design and build the ARPAnet, the original Internet. In 1964 Licklider left ARPA. His successor, Ivan Sutherland now known as the "father of computer graphics," would lead the IPTO for two years—funding most of the academic research in advanced computer science in the United States.

## ROBERT TAYLOR

In 1966 Robert Taylor assumed the directorship of IPTO. Although Taylor would only be with ARPA for 11 months, the role he would play in the development of large-scale computer networks would prove to be critical. Taylor noticed that there was duplication of research among ITPO's various ARPA-funded research institutions and proposed networking the computers of a number of them for the purpose of sharing resources and reducing expenses. His vision was undoubtedly influenced by Licklider's interest in having computers help people communicate with each other—Licklider's intergalactic network. The proposal was funded, and Taylor immediately sought out Larry Roberts, a computer scientist who had experimented with small-scale networks and had good management skills. Roberts, who knew of and believed in Licklider's ideas, would lead the engineers who designed and implemented the first ARPAnet connections. Shortly after the successful launch of ARPAnet, Taylor would leave ARPA to join Xerox's Palo Alto Research Center (Xerox PARC).

## LARRY ROBERTS

In 1967, soon after accepting the position of manager of IPTO, Roberts attended a meeting of all of the scientists leading ARPA-funded projects. In this meeting he laid out his plans for connecting all ARPA-sponsored computers over dial-up phone lines—ARPAnet. Although Roberts' proposal was intriguing to the scientists, they were reluctant to give up any of their

"Taylor was convinced of the technical feasibility of sharing resources over a computer network, though it had never been done.... Licklider's ideas about [computer] time-sharing were already bearing fruit at universities all over the country. But the networking idea marked a significant departure from time-sharing. In a resource-sharing network, many machines would serve many different users, and a researcher interested in using, say, a particular graphics program on a machine 2000 miles away would simply log on to that machine. The idea of one computer reaching out to tap the resources inside another, as peers in a collaborative organization, represented the most advanced conception yet to emerge from Licklider's vision [to amplify human intellectual power]."

*Kathie Hafner*

"Interconnecting a matrix of machines, each with distinct characteristics, would be exceedingly complicated. To pull it off was probably going to require calling on every expert Roberts knew in every area of computing and communications."

*Kathie Hafner*

computing resources. With some guidance on how to reconfigure his plan, Roberts later modified his plan to include additional computers to mediate communication between the host computers. With the prospect of getting additional computing power, scientists warmed to his idea, and he prevailed. Recalling this experience years later, he commented,

> Although they knew in the back of their minds that it was a good idea and were supportive on a philosophical front, from a practical point of view ... everybody with their own machine [computer] wanted [to continue having] their own machine. It was only a couple of years later that they started raving about how they could now share research, and jointly publish papers, and do other things that they could never do before. (Abbate, 1999)

J. C. R. Licklider's vision of the future was becoming a reality.

## IA AND THE INTERNAUTS

"The inexorably rising share of the nation's output that is [intellectual content] appears to have accelerated following WWII with the insights that led to the development of the transistor, microprocessor, laser, and fiber optic technologies. By the 1990s, these and other critical innovations had fostered an enormous capacity to capture, analyze, and disseminate information and had begun to alter significantly how we do business and create economic value, often in ways that were not foreseeable even a decade ago. Indeed, it is the proliferation of information technology throughout the economy that makes the current period so special."

*Alan Greenspan, 2001*

Some innovations in information and communication technologies (ICT) have a direct historical relevance to the IA profession, while the relevance of others has more to do with the facilitation of the IA process. The information organization, navigation, interaction, and flow characteristics of ICT innovations (ancient and modern) influence the shape of today's information spaces and therefore are also relevant to understanding information architecture.

### Direct Historical Significance

The Internauts are representative of a larger community of researchers and developers whose primary focus was on people (rather than technology) and who envisioned the computer as a networked communication device with which people interacted with information. This emphasis was a major departure from a traditional communications-engineering point of view and the first step toward an information-centric rather than computer-centric point of view. From this conceptual shift emerged the notion of cyberspace, an information space that exists apart from, rather than stored in, any single or multiple computing device. In this new conceptual framework, information was no longer seen as being contained in a machine and allowed for a new focus that emphasized interacting with information and the design of information within computer-mediated information environments. Another outcome of this conceptual shift was the eventual emergence of the field of IA.

## CHAPTER 14

# ARPAnet
## The Birth of the Internet

"The ARPA theme is that the promise offered by the computer as a communication medium between people dwarfs into relative insignificance the historical beginnings of the computer as an arithmetic engine."

ARPA Completion Report

## HISTORY: 1969–1990

While working at Lincoln Laboratory, a few years before arriving at ARPA in December 1966, Larry Roberts had become very interested in communications between computers. When the laboratory became involved in conducting an ambitious networking experiment linking two different computers on opposite sides of the United States over dial-up telephone lines, Larry Roberts was charged with overseeing the project. Although only two computers were involved, the result of the experiment was the first ever wide-area computer network. It was deemed a successful experiment, demonstrating that the time-shared computers could operate well together. However, the existing telephone circuit switching system proved to be problematic. Any improvement in networking computers via phone lines would require advances in how messages were switched (relayed from one circuit to another) through the lines.

As the APRAnet program director, Roberts would have to overcome not only the phone system challenge but also the problem of interconnecting many computers—each incapable, without modification, of communicating with the other. To succeed would require drawing upon the expertise of numerous computing and communication pioneers to solve the technological challenges. Once operational, an organization to manage the system would also have to be established. But first, Roberts would have to sell the idea.

Early in 1967, Roberts presented his idea of connecting all of the ARPA-funded time-sharing computers over dial-up phone lines to ARPA's

"The Internet has revolutionized the computer and communications world like nothing before. The invention of the telegraph, telephone, radio, and computer set the stage for this unprecedented integration of capabilities. The Internet is at once a world-wide broadcasting capability, a mechanism for information dissemination, and a medium for collaboration and interaction between individuals and their computers without regard for geographic location."

*Barry M. Leiner*

**KEYWORDS**

Internet history, ARPA
Internet history, TCP/IP
Internet history, packet switching
Internet history, Paul Baran
Internet history, IMPS

During the late 1960s, ARPA was funding computer research at several U.S. universities and research laboratories. The decision was made to include these research contractors in an experimental network, eventually called the ARPAnet. A plan was created for a working network to link 16 research groups. This plan for ARPAnet was made available at the October 1967 ACM (Association for Computing Machinery) Symposium in Gatlinburg, Tennessee.

In 1965 experiments with getting computers to talk to each other over a low-speed dial-up telephone proved the concept that computers could be networked, and, indeed, resources on one computer could be accessed and used from another at great distances. However, these experiments also established that the existing schemes for routing data through the telephone network were totally inadequate and that a new scheme was needed. Packet switching was that scheme.

principal investigators. They had gathered in Ann Arbor, Michigan, for a regularly scheduled meeting. His plan called for using research computers at ARPA sites to handle the network functions of the experimental network he was proposing, plus their existing computing tasks. Not wanting to give up any of their computing resources, the principal investigators were not enthusiastic about Roberts' idea. Adding to their skepticism was the fact that each of their computers "spoke" languages significantly different from the others. Roberts' attempt to sell the idea on the basis of the value of resource-sharing was also met with skepticism. It seemed that his idea was going to die an early death.

As the meeting concluded, however, Wes Clark of Washington University in St. Louis privately proposed a different networking scheme. Clark suggested using smaller computers to manage the network functions and leaving each "host" computer alone. Clark's idea also simplified the problem of how to get the host computers to talk to each other. With the smaller computers all speaking the same language, researchers at each ARPA host computer site would have to write software for their local host only in order to connect it to the standardized smaller computer. Management of the network would also be simplified because the subnetwork of smaller computers would remain under ARPA's direct control. Roberts' enthusiasm was renewed by Clark's idea. He called the subnetwork of small computers that would control the network Interface Message Processors (IMPS). They would function to interconnect the network, send and receive data, check for transmission errors, route data, and verify that messages arrived at their destinations.

Adding more detail and revising his plan, Roberts presented his first paper on the ARPAnet at an Association for Computing Machinery (ACM) conference in Gatlinburg, Tennessee, in 1967. It was entitled, "Multiple Computer Networks and Intercomputer Communication," and it summarized the standards for the ARPAnet network design. This time his idea was well received. At this conference he would also have the good fortune to learn of research done by Paul Baran and Donald Davies that would be critical to the success of the ARPAnet.

In the early 1960s, Paul Baran and Donald Davies in different parts of the world, unknown to each other and for different reasons, were researching new ideas for improving communication networks. In the United States, Baran was focused on developing a communications system that would survive nuclear war. In the United Kingdom, Davies wanted to capitalize on new technologies—digital computers and switches—for the purpose of creating a new public network. He was motivated by his belief that the existing phone system was not well suited to support data exchanges between computers. Both Baran and Davies proposed breaking messages into small "packets," each carrying instructions for reassembling the original message once they reached their destination.

This concept, labeled *packet switching*, allowed for more efficient allocation of bandwidth and for each packet to be sent out over a distributed network. Unlike the phone networks that used central relay switches, a distributed network used multiple decentralized switches or nodes. Based on a packet's set of instructions, each node would have the ability to calculate the best way to route the message on to its destinations. With this design if one node or even multiple nodes were destroyed, the system would still function. Having not yet figured out how to support communication between computers, Roberts was delighted to discover that many of the design details for networking computers had already been worked out by Baran and Davies. He would draw heavily upon their work and collaborated with both of them throughout the assembly of the ARPAnet.

Based on ARPA-sponsored research that would support the project, Roberts selected four sites to form the core from which the network would grow: the University of California Los Angeles UCLA, the Stanford Research Institute (SRI), the University of Utah (UU), and the University of California Santa Barbara (UCSB). In mid-1968 Roberts released a request for bid to build the IMPS. At the end of the year, he selected a contractor. The first IMP was to be delivered to UCLA in August of 1969 with SRI, UCSB, and UU receiving their IMPS in October, November, and December, respectively. By the end of 1969, the four sites were connected. ARPAnet and the budding Internet were becoming a reality.

Representatives from the four sites soon gathered to begin working on the problem of getting the hosts to interact with each other. The subnetwork of IMPS would get the messages to the hosts, but the basic rules for host-to-host communication had not been developed. These rules would become known as *protocols*. Eventually this group of representatives would become known as the *Network Working Group* (NWG). The NWG was breaking new ground, and their pioneering eventually led to the development of the Transport Control Protocol and the Internet Protocol, now commonly known as TCP/IP. In December 1970 an early version of the Network Control Protocol (NCP) was completed, allowing the users of the network to begin developing applications. Eventually, in 1983, ARPAnet dropped NCP and adopted TCP/IP. TCP/IP was relatively simple and very easy to use over a broad variety of computer platforms—factors that permitted the interconnection of networks and contributed to the rapid growth of the Internet.

In 1972 at an International Computer Communication Conference in Washington, D.C., a demonstration of ARPAnet was held. Until this moment, APRAnet was unknown to the public. However, Larry Roberts knew that if the network were to be anything other than a fabulous experiment, the world needed to become aware of its incredible potential. The demonstration drew a tremendous amount of interest and was considered to be very successful. Many representatives from the telecommunications and computer industries were excited by what they saw, sensing they were witnessing the birth of a new market. Within 15 years, ARPAnet would be only one of hundreds of ARPA networks.

A Request for Proposal (RFP) set out specifications for the ARPAnet project and asked for bids. The proposal invited bidders to create an operational network consisting of four sites and to provide a design for a network of up to 16 sites. The contract was awarded in January 1969. The planned network would make use of minicomputers to serve as switching nodes for the host computers at the four sites to be connected to the network. In 1972, the first public demonstration of ARPAnet was held at an International Computer Communication Conference in Washington, D.C.

It was October 1972, when ARPAnet first went public. ARPA scientists demonstrated a fully operational node with 40 terminals at the First International Conference on Computers and Communication. The demonstration stimulated further research in the scientific community throughout the Western world and soon other networks appeared. Another important outcome of the conference was the establishment of an Internet Working Group (IWG) to coordinate relevant research taking place. Encouraged by the successful debut of ARPAnet, ARPA scientists continued to refine the system and expand its capabilities.

| **TABLE 14–1   About APRAnet and the Internet** |
|---|
| The ARPAnet was not just the first network of many that would become part of the Internet; its development shaped the technological and philosophical foundation upon which the Internet was built and thrived. William Stewart describes some of the Internet's most important features. |
| 1. The Internet reaches around the world, and once you have connected to any part of it, you can communicate with all of it. |
| 2. The Internet is a very robust network and is able to adapt almost instantaneously to damage and outages of its individual parts. |
| 3. The Internet has no irreplaceable central control, administration, or authority and therefore cannot be bought, hijacked, or monopolized. |
| 4. The Internet is very fast and operates at near real-time speed. Two computers would have to be over 6,000 miles apart before experiencing a 1/10-second communications delay. |
| 5. Because the Internet is based on a common standard, the TCP/IP protocol, all computers on the Internet have the same capabilities to access the network. |
| 6. The Internet is growing extremely fast in terms of its size, processing power, and software sophistication (Stewart, 1997–2001). |

"The computer will become the hub of a vast network of remote data stations and information banks feeding into the machine at a transmission rate of a billion or more bits of information a second. Laser channels will vastly increase both capacity and the speeds with which it will be transmitted. Eventually, a global communications network handling voice, data, and facsimile will instantly link man to machine—or machine to machine—by land, air, underwater, and space circuits. [The computer] will affect man's ways of thinking, his means of education, his relationship to his physical and social environment, and it will alter his ways of living .... [Before the end of the century, these forces] will coalesce into what unquestionably will become the greatest adventure of the human mind."

*David Sarnoff, 1964*

In 1990 the aging ARPAnet would be phased out by the Department of Defense and replaced by a National Science Foundation–funded network, NSFnet. In a Department of Defense ARPAnet completion report drafted in 1978, ARPAnet was considered by its authors to have "created no less than a revolution." "There is little doubt that the techniques of network mail developed in connection with the ARPAnet program are going to sweep the country and drastically change the techniques used for intercommunication in the public and private sectors" (Hafner, 1996).

## CULTURAL NOTES

ARPAnet scientists were certainly aware that what they were building would eventually surpass the needs of ARPA and the Department of Defense. No one, however, could have predicted the phenomenal growth and popularity of the Internet that would lead to claims such as the following:

> The promise is that this constellation of networks will promote an information society that benefits all: peace, friendship, and cooperation through improved interpersonal communications; empowerment through access to information for education, business, and social good; more productive labor through technology-enriched work environments; and stronger economies through open competition in global markets. (Borgman, 2000)

Other voices warn, "Communication technologies often increase, rather than decrease inequities, and we should be wary of the promises of a global information infrastructure" (Borgman, 2000). Regardless of which

| TABLE 14–2    Information Processing—The Internet |
| --- |
| Communication systems and technologies have various capacities for communicating, storing, and retrieving information. The Internet has the following information-processing capacities: |

*Information Communication*
- The Internet has an almost unlimited capacity for processing and communicating human experience. It is capable of supporting one-to-one, one-to-many, and many-to-one communication using multiple media types including text, graphic, audio, and video. Asynchronous and synchronous delivery of each type is possible.
- When adequate bandwidth is available, the Internet will support interactive multimedia programs that integrate text, graphic, audio, and video resources in a hyperlinked environment.

*Information Storage*
- The Internet is a computer-based communication medium, and messages may be stored in electronic filing systems or printed and stored in filing cabinets.
- Because it is computer-based, all resources on the Internet are subject to the same issues related to the long-term storage of electronic files—the rapid rate of obsolescence for computer hardware and software. Even if digitized information is stored on an archival quality medium, there is a high probability that computer hardware and software in the future will not be "backward" compatible with today's hardware and software.

*Information Retrieval*
- Because the Internet is a computer-based communication medium, extremely quick retrieval of information is possible using a variety of information management schemes for organizing, filing, and locating documents.

scenario the future favors, the fact remains that this new technology in its early years changed our communication habits and later, with the advent of the World Wide Web, how we accessed and used information resources.

## IA AND ARPANET

Some innovations in information and communication technologies (ICT) have a direct historical relevance to the IA profession, while the relevance of others has more to do with the facilitation of the IA process. The information organization, navigation, interaction, and flow characteristics of ICT innovations (ancient and modern) influence the shape of today's information spaces and therefore are also relevant to understanding information architecture.

### Direct Historical Significance

The development of ARPAnet represents the convergence of computing and communication technologies and the birth of the first global, computer-based, and networked information and communication system—the

ARPA continued to grow and expand. When commenting on the success of ARPAnet the authors of the Department of Defense's project *Completion Report* stated, "Just as the telephone, the telegraph, and the printing press had far-reaching effects on human intercommunication, the widespread utilization of computer networks which has been catalyzed by the ARPAnet project represents a similarly far-reaching change in the use of computers by mankind."

*ARPAnet Completion Report*

Internet. The Internet is a collection of interconnecting commercial and noncommercial computer networks used primarily to support information and commercial applications. It is the infrastructure that made possible the convergence of personal computing systems and a global information and communications network.

The development of the Internet opened access to oceans of information that were previously inaccessible to multitudes of people and also coincides with the dawning of the information age. Like other powerful new information and communication technologies, the introduction of the Internet has affected the location, character, and organization of human activities, including traditional information design practices. Richard Saul Wurman, a highly successful information designer and author, acknowledges these effects when he states, "Living in an Information Age has profoundly altered our lives, and those who fail to recognize that the rules of information design are changing will find themselves left behind" (Wurman, *Information Anxiety* 2, 2001). It is not surprising that a new profession concerned with the design of digital information environments (information architecture) began to emerge along with the maturing of the Internet.

## CHAPTER 15

# Email
## The First Killer "App"

> "Bob Kahn had just devoted a year of his life demonstrating that resource-sharing over a network (APRAnet) could really work. But at some point in the course of the event (the 1972 International Conference on Computer Communication), he turned to a colleague and remarked, 'You know, everyone really uses this thing for electronic mail.' "

> Katie Hafner

## HISTORY: 1971–PRESENT

In the early 1960s before ARPAnet (a network of multiple computers for the purpose of time-sharing computing resources and reducing expenses), the practice of creating a specific file where different users could leave messages for each other was popular on single-computer time-sharing systems. One program developed at MIT for this purpose was actually called MAILBOX. However, although these "internal" mail programs continued to grow in popularity, they were limited to groups of users using the same computer. In 1969 when ARPAnet became operational and multiple computers began "talking" to each other, ARPA researchers familiar with internal mail programs began to consider the possibility of sending messages among themselves over the transcontinental ARPA network.

In 1971 Ray Tomlinson adapted an existing internal mail program to work with ARPAnet's network communication protocols. He sent his first message to himself to test his mail program. Succeeding, his second message was sent to all ARPAnet users, and it included instructions on how to address mail. The addressing convention he developed (user's log-in name@host computer name) is still in use today. Although crude by today's email standards, his program was an immediate success, and innovations that improved its functionality were quickly developed. Within 12

Concurring about the importance of email, the authors of the Department of Defense's ARPAnet *Completion Report* published in 1978 wrote, "The largest single surprise of the ARPAnet program has been the incredible popularity and success of network mail. There is little doubt that the techniques of network mail developed in connection with the ARPAnet program are going to sweep the country and drastically change the techniques used for intercommunication in the public and private sectors."
*ARPAnet Completion Report*

**KEYWORDS**

ARPAnet history, email
history of email
first killer application, email
Ray Tomlinson, email
Stephen Lukasik, email

months of Tomlinson's first message, most of the email functions we take for granted today had been added:

- The ability to list messages by subject and date
- The ability to selectively delete messages
- The ability to send and receive mail from the same program (Tomlinson's program required separate send and receive programs)
- The ability to forward messages
- The ability to file and save messages

Stephen Lukasik, ARPA's director from 1971 to 1975, was a great fan of network mail. Lukasik was a physicist; at the time it was considered unusual for someone other than a computer scientist to have such a high interest in network mail. Lukasik regarded email as a management tool, and he encouraged everyone in ARPA to use it. Even while traveling, he checked his messages frequently, just like today's business travelers. Curious as to how the ARPAnet was being used, he commissioned a study in 1973. The results revealed that almost 75 percent of all traffic at that time was attributed to email. That trend would continue throughout the history of the ARPAnet.

## ABOUT EMAIL

In 1968 J. C. R. Licklider published his visionary paper entitled, "The Computer as a Communication Device." What he envisioned 33 years ago has come to pass today: "When people do their informational work at the [computer] console and through the network, telecommunication will be as natural an extension of individual work as face-to-face communication is now. The impact of that fact, and of the marked facilitation of the communicative process, will be very great—both on the individual and the society."

The remarkable popularity of email has been the subject of a great deal of research. In an online history of the Internet entitled "LivingInternet.com," William Stewart came to the conclusion that there are four primary reasons why email has become important to so many people:

1. Email is a push technology—it comes to you.
2. Email waits for you—it is asynchronous.
3. Email is one-to-many—it lets you communicate with many people at once.
4. Email is almost free—text-based communication is very inexpensive.

### Email Is a Push Technology

Communication technologies are often described as either being a "pull" technology or a "push" technology. A pull technology requires that a user actively seeks and retrieves information. Examples of pull technologies include a book library and the Web. On the other hand, a push technology delivers information to the user without any active participation on the part of the user. Ease of use of any technology improves the possibility that people will use it. This fact gives push technologies an advantage over pull technologies. Examples of push technologies include radio and television. That email is a push technology has been an important factor in its widespread use.

## Email Waits for You

Email waits for you, instead of demanding that you structure your activities to be present at the same time as others you communicate with. For example, the recipient doesn't have to be available when you compose and send email to them. You can send email at a time that is convenient for you. And, you don't have to be available when someone else sends you email. Your email waits on your email server until you log in and download it at a time of your convenience. (Stewart, 1997–2001)

## Email Is One-to-Many

"Interactions are sometimes divided into four types—one-to-one, one-to-many, many-to-one, and many-to-many—each with its own attributes and strengths. For example, the typical phone call is one-to-one, and the typical teleconference is many-to-many. Email is the most successful one-to-many technology" (Stewart, 1997–2001). You can send email to more than one person at a time, and you can receive email that has been mailed to more than one person. This attribute of email contributes to more efficient communication between individuals and groups, making it the communications technology of choice for many organizations.

## Email Is Almost Free

Text-based electronic communication requires very little bandwidth. Based on a cost of $10 per gigabyte for bandwidth (a conservative estimate), it would take 50,000 email messages to accumulate $1 in bandwidth expenses. This factor is the reason that email-only accounts are often so inexpensive, or free, and it removes most of the expense normally associated with global communication technologies.

# CULTURAL NOTES

It soon became obvious to others outside of the ARPA community that email was going to become a very important communication medium. The private sector began to develop and sell commercial email software applications to large private and public institutions for use over local area networks. Along with the growth of the Internet and the booming personal computer industry, email's popularity continued to eclipse all other network applications. In 1996 more email than postal mail was sent for the first time. By the end of 2000, the number of computer hosts worldwide on the Internet had grown from the original four ARPAnet hosts to over 90 million. In the same period, the number of Internet users expanded from just over 100 to over 400 million. From the beginning, email has been the most commonly used Internet application.

"There is evidence that email is rearranging communication patterns within families. Not only does the volume of communication grow inside families where email is used, but it might be the case that email is used in those families as substitutes for conversations. [Many family members] who email relatives say that because of email they can stay in touch with family without having to spend as much time talking to family members."

*Pew Research Center*

| TABLE 15–1 Information Processing—Email |
| --- |
| Communication systems and technologies have various capacities for communicating, storing, and retrieving information. Email has the following information-processing capacities: |

*Information Communication*
- Email is much like the telephone in that it is a networked communication medium that enables direct one-to-one communication.
- Unlike the telephone, the written word lacks the phonetic qualities of speech (tones that inform us that the speaker is excited, angry, etc.), and punctuation (that signals tone in writing) is minimal.
- When using email, the writer must compensate for a lack of gesture, tone, or facial expression in order to make written words clear all by themselves.
- One unique characteristic of email is that it is technically possible for a single original message, without duplication, to be distributed to millions of recipients. Typically this is not ever done, but a mailing to multiple thousands of individuals is not uncommon.

*Information Storage*
- Email is a computer-based communication medium, and messages may be stored in electronic filing systems or printed and stored in filing cabinets.
- Because it is computer based, email is subject to the same issues related to the long-term storage of electronic files—the rapid rate of obsolescence for computer hardware and software. And, even if digitized information is stored on an archival-quality medium, there is a high probability that computer hardware and software in the future will not be "backward" compatible with today's hardware and software.

*Information Retrieval*
- Again, because email is a computer-based communication medium, fast retrieval of information is possible using a variety of information management schemes for organizing, filing, and locating documents.

"An ever-growing media palette has failed to dislodge the centrality of the written word from our lives. In fact, the written word doesn't just remain; it is flourishing like kudzu vines at the boundaries of the digital revolution. The explosion of email traffic on the Internet represents the largest boom in letter writing since the 18th century. Today's cutting-edge infonauts are flooding cyberspace with gigabyte upon gigabyte of ASCII musings."
*Paul Saffo*

## IA AND EMAIL

Some innovations in information and communication technologies (ICT) have a direct historical relevance to the IA profession, while the relevance of others has more to do with the facilitation of the IA process. The information organization, navigation, interaction, and flow characteristics of ICT innovations (ancient and modern) influence the shape of today's information spaces and therefore are also relevant to understanding information architecture.

### The Information Space: Organization, Navigation, Interaction, and Flows

Email has extended all the communication capacities of the written word and is a networked global information space. The email information space has all the same information organization and navigation characteristics as the written word information space. However, because it is also a computer-mediated and networked information space, it shares interaction and flow characteristics with the following:

- *Spoken word's storytelling information spaces:* Author controls the content of the message and the reader's interaction levels with the author, and the flow of information is primarily one way: from author to reader.
- *Spoken word's conversational information space:* Conversationalists organize and reorganize the information they are attempting to communicate depending on direct and indirect feedback received in the course of a conversation. Navigation decisions in conversations are negotiable. The potential for interaction in any conversation is very high. Conversation flows are nonlinear and two way: the potential for branching is unlimited.
- *Telegraph information space:* Globally networked communications system that extended all the communication capacities of the written word in which navigation was mediated by specialized operators.
- *Telephone information space:* Globally networked communications system that extended all the communication capacities of the spoken word in which navigation was mediated initially by specialized operators and later by mechanical and digital switching technologies.
- *Personal computer information space:* Virtual space within which a graphical user interface mediates navigation within software application environments, mediates navigation in a computer's operating system environment, and also mediates interaction with content resources and software application tools.

## Direct Historical Significance

Email represents how powerful and pervasive the unintended consequences of a new technology can be. From its inception as a simple communications application developed by the engineers of the ARPAnet for their own convenience, email is now used by millions of Americans who send over two billion messages each day, and it is a cornerstone of corporate business.

## Facilitation of the IA Process

For many organizations, email has practically replaced written documents, faxes, and even the telephone as the primary communication conduit, as Kevin Crane points out when he states, "The importance of and complexity of email has evolved from a few simple text messages into a multitude of mission-critical documents. Negotiations, bids, proposals, contracts, legal agreements, regulatory forms, and a host of other vital correspondences now find form in email" (Kevin Crane, 2001). As it is for most businesses today, email is an important communication and management tool that is critical to the successful practice of IA.

"Potentially, email allows individuals to be their own publishers and reach as many people as their creations merit. As a form of two-way communications, email favors active thought over passive reception. Because email does not require immediate response, it can allow time for study, analysis, contemplation, and deliberation. And because email involves reading and writing, it gives strong incentive to acquire these vital cultural skills. The technologies of freedom will be greatly strengthened as computer communications and email join the more established communications technologies and become universally available."

*Lloyd N. Morrisett*

# 16 CHAPTER

# WWW
# The World Wide Web

**KEYWORDS**

hypertext, Ted Berners-Lee

Marc Andreessen, Netscape

Marc Andreessen, Mosaic

Tim Berners-Lee

World Wide Web history

"Despite its spectacular growth and usefulness, the Internet did not become a widespread cultural phenomenon until the Web—and the browsers like Mosaic and Netscape needed to navigate it—hit the streets."

Michael Dertouzous

## HISTORY: 1989–PRESENT

It all started with a proposal drafted by Tim Berners-Lee, a researcher at the Conseil Europeen pour la Recherche Nucleaire (CERN), a European physics laboratory. When first working as a consultant at CERN in 1980, Berners-Lee found understanding CERN's large, complex, and rapidly changing research environment to be a daunting task. CERN employed thousands of researchers around the world who worked on many different projects and used a variety of information-processing systems to support both their research and project administration. To help keep track of who was working on what project, the software used to support each one, and the relationships of various projects to each other, Berners-Lee developed a simple hypertext program for his personal use. He called it Enquire.

Completing his consultancy, Berners-Lee left CERN in 1981. He returned in 1984 with the conviction that the utility his hypertext program offered him for managing information would also be highly useful for supporting information-sharing among researchers in CERN's High Energy Physics department. Between the time Berners-Lee developed his hypertext "notebook" (Enquire) and his return to CERN, the Internet was well established and was supporting a broad community of researchers. Attracted to the potential the Internet offered to connect CERN researchers and collaborators around the world, he began an effort within CERN to put the power of Enquire in everyone's hands—a global hypertext system. In 1989 he completed a project proposal to

CERN's administrators simply entitled, "Information Management: A Proposal." The overview read:

> Many of the discussions of the future at CERN end with the question, "Yes, but how will we ever keep track of such a large project?" This proposal provides an answer to such questions. Firstly, it discusses the problem of information access at CERN. Then, it introduces the idea of linked information systems and compares them with less flexible ways of finding information. It then summarizes my short experience with non-linear text systems know as "hypertext," describes what CERN needs from such a system, and what industry may provide. Finally, it suggests steps we should take to involve ourselves with hypertext now, so that individually and collectively we may understand what we are creating. (Berners-Lee, 1999)

The proposal then presented the problem of information loss at CERN, a description of the "linked information system" he envisioned, and the technical and functional requirements for such a system. He noted that the information resources to be linked could be text, graphics, video, anything—a "hypermedia" system. With some changes, his proposal would be accepted. In the fall of 1990, Berners-Lee developed the first hypertext "browser" and editor. It featured a graphical user interface. By the end of the year, it was deployed within CERN. He debated with himself over what to call it. Two names came to mind: "Infomesh" and "The Information Mine." Discarding those, he settled on a third—World Wide Web (WWW). In 1991, to encourage widespread dissemination, Berners-Lee insisted that the WWW program code be put in the public domain where anyone could download it for free to use or improve upon it.

Other browser applications would soon follow. In 1993 Marc Andreessen of the National Center for Supercomputing Applications, Illinois (NCSA), introduced Mosaic X. It was easy to install, easy to use, and, unlike WWW, offered 24-hour customer support. Mosaic X also had improved graphic capabilities over WWW. Part of NCSA's mission is to support scientific research through the development of noncommercial software. Like WWW, Mosaic was offered free to the public. It quickly became the most popular Web browser. In 1994 NCSA licensed all commercial rights to Mosaic to a number of different companies. Among them was Microsoft. Microsoft's commercial version of Mosaic would be called Internet Explorer.

Also recognizing the great commercial potential of Web browser software, in 1994 members of the Mosaic development team (including Marc Andreessen) formed a private company to develop a commercial Web browser. They named their new company Netscape. In his online history of the Internet entitled "LivingInternet.com," William Stewart observes,

> Netscape quickly provided many powerful new browser features and conveniently integrated three Internet technologies in one application—Web

"The dream behind the Web is of a common information space in which we communicate by sharing information. Its universality is essential: the fact that a hypertext link can point to anything, be it personal, local, or global, be it draft or highly polished. There was a second part of the dream, too, dependent on the Web's being so generally used that it became a realistic mirror of the ways in which we work, play, and socialize."

*Tim Berners-Lee*

"Browsers made possible a quantum leap in the simplicity both of hypertext and the Web. Marc Andreessen's Mosaic software, now commercialized as Netscape Navigator, allows users simply to point a mouse at a hypertext word or picture and to click on it, thus opening up a new file. With the creation of Mosaic, the Internet completed its migration from a computer scientist's research tool to something that a toddler could use. By January 1997—fewer than four years after the birth of Mosaic—more than a quarter of a million Web sites were available for browsing. So popular has the Web become that many people now talk of it as synonymous with the Internet itself."

*Frances Cairncross*

"One of the most striking pieces of evidence of how the Web has become woven into people's everyday lives is the amount of time people spend on the Internet and the frequency with which they go online. The timescape looks like this: Every day 60% of those who have Internet access, some 55 million Americans, go online. Of those who go online on an average day, 56% logged on exclusively from home, 21% logged on exclusively from work, and 20% logged on from work and home. Half of the Internet users (56%) spend an hour or more online during all their online sessions, 36% said they had spent a half hour to an hour, and about a quarter said they had spent less than a half hour."

*Pew Internet & American Life Project*

"The Web is an abstract (imaginary) space of information. On the Net [Internet], you find computers—on the Web you find documents, sounds, videos, . . . information. On the Net, the connections are cables between computers; on the Web, connections are hypertext links. The Web exists because of programs which communicate between computers on the Net. The Web could not be without the Net. The Web made the Net useful because people are really interested in information and don't really want to know about computers and cables."

*R. T. Griffiths*

[Internet access], email, and newsgroups. Netscape also made a point of ensuring that their browser was designed to run on all three major computer types [operating systems]—Windows, Macintosh, and Unix. (Stewart, 1997–2001)

In 1995 with the introduction of online services provided by Internet Service Providers (ISPs), millions of new users would have the capability of accessing the Internet. Three of the major ISPs were Compuserve, American Online, and Prodigy. Once primarily the domain of relatively small research communities, the Internet was now open to the entire world. There were 100,000 Internet computer hosts worldwide when Tim Berners-Lee first proposed his global hypertext program. By 1995 the number of Internet hosts exceeded four million.

William Stewart describes two significant effects of this "democratization:" (1)

It added millions of new users, many now accessing the net from their homes, and showing it to their friends and neighbors. This greatly increased general knowledge of the net's capabilities, and further spurred its growth. (2) It legitimized the Web, and by extension the Internet. (Stewart, 1997–2001)

Large amounts of capital from a wide variety of sources began to be invested in the net after the online services connected, further expanding its growth. Broad coverage by the popular press also generated interest in this "new" technological wonder.

Since its inception, the growth in the usage and size of the Internet has increased exponentially due in part to advances in networking technologies, programming languages, user interfaces, and cheaper large-scale information-storage media. When combined, two old ideas, hypertext and networking, would lead to the introduction of Web browser applications and commercial online services in the 1990s. These technologies resulted in a dramatic increase in an already dramatic "adoption" rate fueled by the introduction of email applications in the 1970s.

## CULTURAL NOTES

In addition to communication technologies developed earlier in the 20th century, the advent of the Internet and the World Wide Web has led to a sense of consumers having worlds of information at their fingertips—scanning radio frequencies, dialing a telephone, surfing television channels or the WWW with a keypad or keyboard. It is easy to understand why this period is so often referred to as the information age.

In a culture driven by the commonly accepted notion that the more we know, the better off we are, it is also easy to understand why more information, and easier and quicker access to information, would be greatly valued. Another commonly held belief is that more information

---

**TABLE 16–1     About the World Wide Web**

The Web is a set of protocols (sets of rules that allow communication between Internet computer hosts) and a common set of services that makes use of the computers and networks that are the Internet. Originally, the WWW was developed to allow information sharing among internationally dispersed teams of physics researchers. Now, tens of millions of people use the Web for exchanging, buying, or selling a broad range of services, goods, and information. Its success has been attributed to a number of factors:

1. The Web's architecture is an "open" architecture: it was designed to accommodate advances in technology, including new networks, protocols, object types, and data formats.
2. Web sites all over the world can be accessed from a single desktop connection: Web servers are interconnected on the Internet and are not centrally controlled.
3. It is easy to use: graphical Web browser software applications simplified access to the Web for millions of people.
4. Many data types are available to users: text, images, audio, and video are all accessible on the Web.
5. It can be used for one-to-one or one-to-many communication: users can engage in both asynchronous and real-time text, audio, and video communication on the Web.
6. It is not limited to computer users: the Web's open architecture makes it easy to build Web browsers for different types of devices such as cell phones, personal digital assistants, and pagers.
7. It is easy to publish information: there is an ever-growing amount of information available on the Web on a broader and broader range of subjects.
8. It is searchable: search engines improve the usefulness of the Web by providing users with the capability to search through millions of Web pages in seconds.

---

is the only way to ease today's economic, social, and employment-related pressures. However, as a society we are suffering from "information anxiety," or an "information overload" resulting from an "information glut." Some are warning that one can have too much of a good thing, that too much information can actually reduce our quality of life. They foresee stress, confusion, and ignorance as possible by-products of an information "tidal wave" and, in the long term, that these effects will be destructive to our society as a whole.

Controversy and exaggerated claims, both positive and negative, have always surrounded the introduction of new communication technologies. As far back as the introduction of the electrical telegraph, futurists predicted the inevitability of world peace, believing that better communications would alleviate any misunderstanding that would lead to war. This same prediction was also made with the introduction of the radio, the telephone, the television, and more recently, the Internet. Conversely, in each case, skeptics have predicted disastrous dehumanizing effects and widespread moral decay.

The Internet and Web have given us the sense that a sea of information that once was not very accessible now is. However, these technologies have not yet matured. Finding relevant, accurate information

"The World Wide Web is the killer app of the 1990s, turbo-charging a communications revolution that is redefining the information-seeking habits of Western civilization. With capabilities that zoom past CDs, the Web offers users a plethora of changing information resources, widespread access and delivery through telephone lines at next-to-nothing costs, multimedia, interactivity, and transactional, and authoring capabilities."

*Alison Head*

| **TABLE 16–2 Information Processing—World Wide Web** |
| :--- |
| Communication systems and technologies have various capacities for communicating, storing, and retrieving information. The World Wide Web has the following information-processing capacities: |

*Information Communication*
- Web browsers made the Internet more usable for and accessible by millions of people—enhancing its almost unlimited capacity for processing and communicating human experience. Web browsers also make easier one-to-one, one-to-many, and many-to-one communication using multiple media types such as: text, graphic, audio, and video. Asynchronous and synchronous delivery of each type of media is possible with Web browsers.
- With adequate bandwidth, Web browsers support interactive multimedia programs that integrate text, graphic, audio, and video resources in a hyperlinked environment.

*Information Storage*
- Web-based software applications have been developed that are compatible with many types of computer-based electronic filing and storage systems.
- All Web-based resources are subject to the same issues related to the long-term storage of electronic files—the rapid rate of obsolescence for computer hardware and software. Even if digitized information is stored on an archival-quality medium, there is a high probability that computer hardware and software in the future will not be "backward" compatible with today's hardware and software.

*Information Retrieval*
- Because the Web is computer based, extremely quick retrieval of information is possible using a variety of information management schemes for organizing, filing, and locating documents.

"Trying to explain the Internet [and the WWW] recalls to mind the fable of the blind man describing an elephant. It is like the phone system, enabling anyone to reach anyone else with a private message. No, it is like radio, enabling one person instantly to reach millions. No, it is like a newspaper, reporting fresh information, plus features, advertising, and a public forum. No, it is like the postal service with its private mail and junk mail. No, it is like television, with an ability to add pictures and sound to words. It is a huge library. It is a huge soapbox. And on and on."

*Irving Fang*

can be confusing, complicated, and time consuming. But there are solutions evolving, both technological and human, for managing these new information-age disorders.

## IA AND THE WEB

Some innovations in information and communication technologies (ICT) have a direct historical relevance to the IA profession, while the relevance of others has more to do with the facilitation of the IA process. The information organization, navigation, interaction, and flow characteristics of ICT innovations (ancient and modern) influence the shape of today's information spaces and therefore are also relevant to understanding information architecture.

### The Information Space: Organization, Navigation, Interaction, and Flows

Because the Web is a networked, multiuser, multimedia environment where users communicate, collaborate, and interact with other users across immense distances and a surrounding virtual environment, it shares organization, navigation, interaction, and flow characteristics with all the information and communication technologies that predate it. All of these characteristics have yet to be fully synthesized in the Web information space. This monumental task is the focus of the emerging profession of information architecture.

## Direct Historical Significance

As a "place," the Web information space is beginning to mirror the American culture. Every day millions of people use the Web to shop, entertain themselves, look for information relevant to every aspect of their lives, communicate with each other, market services and goods, and manage their professional and personal lives. As a technology and a social system, the Web represents the continuation and aggregation, within a single digital system, of virtually all the information and communication technologies that predated it (and the respective institutions associated with them). This intertwining of information and communication systems also represents, to many, the foundation upon which will be built a new global information and communications infrastructure that is essential for sustaining a broad range of human affairs in an information-oriented society. Not unlike other infrastructures of the past such as power and telephone systems (that are usually invisible to us unless they are not working), the technologies and social systems necessary for forming a stable and ubiquitous global information and communications infrastructure will take many years to develop and be adopted. Just as new industries and fields of knowledge developed to meet the needs created by the establishment of new infrastructures in the past, so it is today. Information architecture is one such new field.

## PART 5

# INFO AILMENTS
## Unintended Consequences of the Information Age

"[The invention of the printing press] increased the availability of desirable classics and lowered the costs of spreading new knowledge, but the unscrupulous used it to publish scurrilous, heretical, pornographic, or simply inaccurate works. Access to information created its own problems. Sorting through from falsehood could be a full-time activity, and savants worried about spending a lifetime with information overload. It's a lament that would fit all too comfortably in the pages of *Wired* or *Fast Company* [today]."

The Los Angeles Times

## CHAPTER 17

# Info Glut, Info Trash, Info Hype, and Info Stress

"Our ability to create information has far outpaced our ability to search, organize, and publish it. Information management—at the individual, organizational, and even societal level—may turn out to be one of the key challenges we face. It is the next stage of literacy."

Peter Lyman

## INTRODUCTION

In the past, new technological development has generally been associated with the promise of a better life for all. Today we continue to be optimistic about the promise of new technologies and are looking for electronic answers to many of the questions we are wrestling with in our modern world. However, we have learned that sometimes technological progress can have unintended and problematic consequences. Consideration of the paradox this presents for users (that new information and communication technologies can have positive and negative effects) is important for minimizing the obstacles that hinder the realization of their potential. A user-focused design discipline such as information architecture can help maximize the value of these new technologies and minimize the negative effects.

## INFO GLUT: TOO MUCH INFORMATION

The industrial age was an age of machines, many of which were designed to retrieve and record data and to produce, reproduce, process, transfer, and distribute information. Machines of this type include: the telegraph, telephone, fax machine, radio, television, and computer. Collectively, all of these technologies, and their information-age extensions, like computer networks, constitute a pervasive global information infrastructure supported by an information-oriented society. Today, whether we are

"Physiologically, people have tolerance levels or thresholds for information which are determined by the quantity and structure of information. Comprehension and quantity of information are positively correlated only to a certain point. Beyond that point, comprehension declines. In addition, there can be a negative effect on what was learned before. Thus, when individuals are bombarded with more information than they need or can use, attentiveness declines, errors and frustration increase, and productivity suffers."
*Suzanne Watzman*

### KEYWORDS

information overload,
  information age
information literacy,
  information age
human-centered design,
  Donald Norman
social informatics,
  Rob Kling
usability, Jakob Nielsen

playing, working, learning, conducting business, or communicating, more and more of our daily activity involves the use of information technology. Not surprisingly, for the first time in human history, along with this profusion of new information technologies (and increased access to information), information is being generated at a rate that is exceeding our abilities to find, review, and understand it.

This is a relatively recent development (about 50 years old), and, until now, the idea of too much information was inconceivable. As David Shenk point outs, it was with good reason:

> Information and communications have made us steadily healthier, wealthier, and more tolerant. Because of information, we understand more about how to overcome the basic challenges of life. Food is more abundant. Our physical structures are sturdier, more reliable. Our societies are more stable, as we have learned to make political systems function. Our citizens are freer, thanks to a wide dissemination of information that has empowered the individual. (Shenk, 1997)

All of these benefits of information have remained unchanged. The problem is, however, too much information interferes with finding accurate information that is useful. Faced with a flood of information from multiple information channels, our personal strategies for managing information are becoming ineffectual. It was once simpler to quickly discern between useful and useless information. Now, faced with immense quantities of data, simple routines for managing information no longer work. Info Glut is an information overload problem that can be managed through increases in information systems literacy and improvements in the usability of information systems.

## Information Literacy

Information literacy is the human aspect of information management and is an important factor in information overload. Not understanding how to manage an information-seeking process through a sea of information contributes to a sense of information overload. Improving information literacy raises awareness levels of the information explosion and improves understanding of how information systems can help identify, access, and obtain data needed for problem solving and decision making. "Being able to understand what is required to find information is an important element in the process of overcoming information overload" (Horton, 1983). Developing and teaching more effective information-seeking strategies will help diminish the problem of information overload.

## Usability

Application usability focuses on designing information systems that are easily understandable. Jakob Nielsen states that all systems with which

---

"It's not more bandwidth we need. It's not faster computers. It's not more gigabytes. It's information literacy we need. We [do] need to create less information of higher quality. We need to be able to manage information much, much, better, getting rid of junk and out-of-date stuff. We need skills that help us search better, and to be able to judge better and faster the quality of the stuff we find."

*Gerry McGovern*

---

"Today's environment is one of accelerating change and increasing complexity. New technologies arrive every day creating new opportunities and new challenges, demanding new skills and processes. To develop communications that will be read [viewed, listened to], understood, and used, we must consider the environment of information overload within which we and our audiences work; and understand how this environment affects the development of these communications."

*Suzanne Watzman*

humans interact have five characteristics of usability, and all five need to be considered in any design project. They are:

- *Ease of learning:* How fast can a user who has never before seen the user interface learn it sufficiently well to accomplish basic tasks?
- *Efficiency of use:* Once an experienced user has learned to use the system, how fast can she accomplish tasks?
- *Memorability:* If a user has used the system at some earlier date, can she remember enough to use it more effectively next time?
- *Error frequency and severity:* How often do users make errors while using the system, how serious are the errors, and how easy is it to recover from using an error?
- *Subjective satisfaction:* How much does the user *like* using the system? (Nielsen, 1998)

Tools for identifying and locating relevant information resources have not increased in effectiveness at the same explosive rate as the quantity of available information. Consequently, our ability to find, review, and use information is limited and also contributes to feelings of information overload. Developing information management tools that are easier to use and are more sophisticated is an important factor in helping to alleviate the problem of information overload.

## INFO TRASH: POOR-QUALITY INFORMATION

Technological advances have made the retrieval, production, and distribution of information so much easier than in earlier periods. The result is an explosion in often irrelevant, unclear, and inaccurate data fragments, making it ever more difficult to see the forest through the trees. (Heylighen, 1999)

Publishing was once the domain of an elite few. Due to computer technology and the rise of the Internet, today almost everyone has the ability to generate and distribute appealing and authoritative-looking information. Put it on the Web, and it is literally accessible to millions. Unlike any previous technology in history, the Web democratizes information authorship, distribution, and retrieval.

In the past, much of the information that reached us passed through the hands of librarians, journalists, educators, or other experts who had carefully evaluated and organized it from credible sources. That, unfortunately, is no longer the case. Much of the information presented to us today through a variety of media, or that we access on the Web, is inaccurate, out-of-date, biased, or shallow. Info Trash is an information quality and accuracy problem that can be managed through improvements in critical-thinking skills and in scanning and filtering technologies.

"The net is like a huge vandalized library. Someone has destroyed the catalog and removed the front matter, indexes, etc. from hundreds and thousands of books and torn and scattered what remains. . . . 'Surfing' is the process of sifting through this disorganized mess in the hope of coming across some useful fragments of text and images that can be related to other fragments. The net is even worse than a vandalized library because thousands of unorganized fragments are added daily by the myriad cranks, sages, and persons with time on their hands who launch their unfiltered messages into cyberspace."

*Michael Gorman*

## Critical Thinking

Lida L. Larsen from the University of Maryland's Office of Information Technology asks, "Unless you already have a base knowledge of a particular field and its experts, how do you tell if information is 'good'?" She answers that it takes intellectual effort on the part of the information consumer to develop valuable critical-thinking skills necessary for evaluating information resources. She encourages keeping the following in mind when determining the value of an information resource:

- *Scope:* Identify the scope of material presented. Scope is the basic breadth and depth question of what's covered and in what detail.
- *Authority and bias:* Look for who provided the information and why, their credentials, their affiliations, their "pitch," and any explicit statement of authority.
- *Accuracy:* Look to see if the topic is appropriate for the publication's intended audience, if the source of the information is clearly posted, what credentials the author or publisher has, and if there are references from other sources on the same or related topics.
- *Timeliness:* Evaluate the timeliness of a resource. Some data gathered by electronic means can be displayed immediately on the Internet while other information translated from printed materials may already be out-of-date.
- *Permanence:* On the Internet, information resources may move, be edited online, or be deleted. Users may wish to download and file online resources for future reference.
- *Value-added features:* Anything that helps the users find the information they are looking for is considered value added. Look for Web sites moderated by trained professionals who receive and respond to feedback; evaluation or ratings of informational content or presentation; and text-only formats, search engines, and navigational and help tools.
- *Presentation:* Evaluate the page or site layout, clarity or intuitiveness of the site's organizational design, and help/example sections. (Larsen, 1999)

## "Intelligent" Technology

A number of software technologies are emerging to assist users in sorting and evaluating Web content: intelligent agents, "push" technology, and "repel technology." Intelligent agents assist the user in scanning and filtering information resources based upon preferences set by the user. Push technology actively seeks content from designated Web resources based upon user preferences and downloads it to the user's desktop. Repel technology is designed to prevent unwanted and unsolicited information (based upon user preferences) from reaching the user's desktop.

---

"Audio buffs have long been familiar with the phrase signal-to-noise ratio. It is engineering parlance for measuring the quality of a sound system by comparing the amount of desired audio signal to the amount of unwanted noise leaking through. In the information age, signal-to-noise has also become a useful way to think about social health and stability. How much of the information in our midst is useful, and how much of it gets in the way? What is our signal-to-noise ratio? We know that the ratio has diminished of late, and the character of information has changed: As we have accrued more and more of it, information has emerged not only as a currency, but also as a pollutant."

*David Shenk*

---

"The pace of technological change leaves us breathless, and the future promises to be more demanding than the present. Technology will be an increasingly important factor in change and will require numerous agonizing decisions. It will be used to address contradictions in the social order and will create new contradictions in its wake. It will continue to present us with the hope of utopia and the threat of devastation. As such, it demands our studied attention."

*Robert Lauer*

However, all are limited by existing data structures, such as HTML (Hypertext Markup Language) that simply define a document's visual characteristics. New "self-describing" data structures have been developed, such as XML (Extensible Markup Language), that enable layers of information to be embedded within documents. Such "metadata" will enable sorting and evaluation software technologies to function with greater precision (Kerka, 1997).

# INFO HYPE: UTOPIAN AND ANTI-UTOPIAN EXAGGERATIONS

> By focusing on new technologies as agents of social change and assuming that social systems will use them effectively, technological utopians ignore the social conditions for technologies to be effective. Consequently, they often overstate their social value. In contrast, technological anti-utopians often understate the social value of technological innovations and the way that all technologies pose problems. (Kling, 2000)

## Technological Utopianism and Anti-utopianism

Information technologies are powerful forces that are stimulating an explosion of hype. Utopians believe these technologies to have democratizing and humanizing effects leading to nothing less than an ideal society. Anti-utopians fear that the same technologies will have a fragmenting effect and will lead to social disorder. Utopians see technology as good and having only positive effects on existing social orders. They also see any problems caused by technological innovation as being solvable with new or improved technologies. Utopians assume that the skills or knowledge necessary for integrating new technologies into everyday life are easily accessible and that the benefits are obvious. Anti-utopians fear that new technologies will be used as instruments of oppression leading to the destruction of society. They believe that the skills and knowledge necessary for using new technologies are often unfairly distributed to the advantage of an elite class and to the disadvantage of the ignorant. Essentially, "utopian tales are devised to stimulate hope in future possibilities, while anti-utopian tales are devised to stimulate anger at horrible possibilities" (Kling, 1996).

Exaggeration and alarm about new technologies and their implications have been around since the beginnings of the Industrial Revolution. Tom Standage, author of *The Victorian Internet* (the telegraph), draws parallels between reactions of the Victorians to the telegraph and our own reactions to the Internet. He points out:

> The hype, skepticism, and bewilderment associated with the Internet—concerns about new forms of crime, adjustments in social mores, and

"By focusing on new technologies as agents of social change and assuming that social systems will use them effectively, technological utopians ignore the social conditions for technologies to be effective. Consequently, they often over-state their social value. In contrast, technological anti-utopians often understate the social value of technological innovations and the way that all technologies pose problems."

*Robert Kling*

redefinition of business practices—mirrors the hopes and fears and mis-understandings inspired by the telegraph. Indeed, they are only to be expected. We can expect the same reactions to whatever new inventions appear in the twenty-first century. (Standage, 1998)

Unfortunately, until a new technology is "socialized," such predictions can lead to unrealistic hopes and inordinate fears that ultimately disap-point and lead to feelings of disillusion and distrust. Examining such ex-aggerated claims, John Seely Brown and Paul Duguid state:

> The instability that rapidly changing technology brings often lies less in the technology itself than in the enthusiastic expectations that every-thing being "just a click away" or "at your fingertips" will make life easy. Battered by such hype, it's easy to believe that everyone except you knows how to use this stuff without a problem. (Brown & Duguid, 2000)

The danger of utopianism is that it can discourage healthy skepticism and lead to a lack of foresight. It also distorts people's expectations and consequently their vision of the future. Anti-utopianism can lead to cyn-icism and the danger that the real benefits of technology may be dis-counted and overlooked. Sorting through all this hype can be complex and confusing. Info Hype is a social problem that can be managed through careful analysis of new technologies and understanding the im-portance of socializing new technologies.

## Analyzing Technology

Utopian and anti-utopian visions are actually alike in some respects: they are usually future oriented, overestimate the influence of technology on society, oversimplify the complexities of society, and are extreme in their views. A more realistic view can be achieved from carefully observing how technologies are actually being used, that is, how they really work in spe-cific social settings. Analyzing data gathered during the observation process shapes the observer's point of view as opposed to a strong pre-existing positive or negative bias based on hope or fear.

## Socializing Technology

Many people have difficulty using new information technologies because a huge gap often exists between the hype surrounding them and what is actually required to use them effectively. For instance, the notion of a "plug and play" computer system suggests a simple (and consequently easy to use) technology that is actually very complex and sophisticated. Describing equally complex technologies as "appliances" is also mislead-ing. Designers also overestimate the technology literacy levels of the av-erage consumer that also can lead to usability problems.

The powerful information processing capabilities of information and communica-tion technologies are, more often than not, the focus of most stories about computer-ization and social change. Technologies "offer exciting possibilities for manipulating large amounts of information rapidly with little effort to enhance control, to create insights, to search for infor-mation, and to facilitate cooperative work between people."

Less frequently, "some authors examine a darker social vision in that any likely form of computerization will amplify human misery—people sacrificing their freedom and privacy to busi-nesses and government agencies, people becoming very dependent on complex technologies that they don't comprehend, and sometimes the image of entire social groups denied access to crucial, enabling information technologies. Both kinds of stories often reflect the conventions of utopian and anti-utopian writing."

*Robert Kling*

Realistically, learning how to use information technologies can take considerable time, effort, and support from technicians or user groups. Socializing technology means both understanding that new technologies go through a socialization process before they are seamlessly woven into everyday life and anticipating the social resource needs of new users. Such socialization efforts enable consumers to estimate more accurately their own skill levels, cut through marketing hype and oversimplified claims, and gain access to the social resources they need to integrate new information technologies into their lives successfully.

# INFO STRESS: A SOCIO-TECHNO SYNDROME

Much of the writing about the social changes [positive and negative] that these new information and communication technologies will or could catalyze has relied on over-simplified conceptions of the relationship between technologies and social change. (Kling, 2000)

## Technology and Social Change

The relationship between technology and social change is often oversimplified. Such oversimplifications are commonly made in an effort to entertain, popularize, or provoke. Some of the claims we have heard about computers are that they will increase productivity, augment the human intellect, and transform the way we learn. There may be a kernel of truth in these, but all are oversimplifications. In actuality, the relationship between technologies and society is complicated, and any analysis (and inference) based solely on technological considerations is most often inaccurate.

The same holds true of various ailments, such as stress, that are commonly associated with the information age. These ailments are also being oversimplified when they are attributed to technology alone. Info Stress is generally a socio-techno system disorder. Socio-techno systems are complex, interdependent systems comprised of people, hardware, software, support resources, information resources, and information infrastructures. The stressful effects of socio-techno systems may arise from a combination of poor-quality information, too much information (even if it is high-quality information), misinformation, the introduction of new "un-socialized" information technologies, use of poorly designed information technologies, inadequate information technology support resources, and unrealistic cultural expectations of what it means to be informed.

Info Stress is a mental and emotional syndrome. A syndrome is a cluster of symptoms, usually occurring together, that characterize a specific disorder. Both individuals and organizations can suffer from Info Stress. Symptoms of Info Stress include feelings of anxiety, frustration, confusion,

Knowledge workers, professionals whose jobs rely on their ability to find, synthesize, communicate, and apply their knowledge, are facing a number of problems that are generating considerable stress for them:

1. Coping with rapid social and technological change in the workplace.
2. Learning how to effectively use new and rapidly changing information and communication technologies.
3. Finding useful information when it is needed.
4. Assimilating new and greater quantities of information more quickly.
5. Communicating changing information to coworkers.

The problem of Info Stress has both technological and human aspects. All too often information and communication technology design is approached from a technology-centric perspective—seeing technology simply as a tool for solving a specific problem without consideration for users or the social setting in which they work. Reducing Info Stress requires examining both social and technical systems in the workplace and, based on that analysis, designing a more user-centered system.

anger, and inadequacy. Info Stress in private and public organizations can lead to mistakes, misunderstandings, flawed conclusions, foolish decisions, and, ultimately, inefficiencies and financial loss. Info Stress management requires the careful examination of socio-techno systems and, based upon those examinations, the design of more usable systems.

## Examining Stress-Producing Socio-Techno Systems

Examining a socio-techno system requires using various discovery processes to analyze the "design, uses, and consequences of information and communication technologies in ways that take into account their interaction with institutional and cultural contexts" (Kling, 2000). The discovery processes, which closely connect designers and users, help designers understand the users' goals, tasks, and the context within which they are using these systems. These same processes also identify problems within the socio-techno system that contribute to users' stress and inform the design of more effective socio-techno systems. Socio-techno systems with high usability levels help reduce Info Stress.

## Designing Usable Socio-Techno Systems

*"We have created a compli-
cated superhighway of information for very high-speed
travel, without training
drivers . . . or training them
how to use a roadmap."*

*Geert Hofstede*

Designers of information and communication technologies generally start with the idea that they are designing tools that will assist users in achieving a specific goal or in gaining greater efficiencies. This technology-centric perspective ignores consideration of the context in which the technology will be used, and with luck, sometimes it is actually workable for people. However, more often than not, it is difficult to use or it is unusable and is abandoned. Design that produces a positive experience for the user is not a matter of chance or intuition. It happens because of a systematic process that includes data gathering, high-level structure, detailed design specifications, task-flow parameters, and testing. In the data-gathering stage, a designer with a socio-techno systems orientation first analyzes user preferences and the context in which the technology will be used. The results of this analysis then shape the design of a socio-techno system (as opposed to a tool). Design that is informed by a socio-techno systems approach improves the probability that information and communication technologies will have high usability levels.

## PART 6

# TOWARD A NEW DISCIPLINE
## Information Architecture

"Information Architecture is a rapidly emerging field concerned with the art and science of applying formal and systematic approaches to the organization and presentation of information. It is being developed in several disciplines (computer science, cognitive science, human computer interaction, information science, and library science). It has emerged rapidly as a developing professional practice—more rapidly than university curricula have been able, for the most part, to develop coherent approaches either to its theory and practice or to the professional needs of practitioners."

Keith Belton

## CHAPTER 18

# IA
# The Process

"In the past, people have outlived and outwitted monumental media transformations, and we will survive this chaos [the Information Age] too. There are no quick answers, though, because the future is wrapped up in the design process, only to be unveiled by teams of people from multiple disciplines, all asking, 'What is valuable? What is usable? What is better?'"

Clement Mok

"Systems design is a multidimensional process that requires a new kind of project manager—the information architect—who has the knowledge and experience to develop information structures that account for the multiple levels and layers of interaction among humans, machine, and the physical environment."

Andrew Cohill

## A NEW DESIGN PROFESSION IS EMERGING

Throughout history, innovations in information and communication technologies have influenced societies. Generally, as these innovations were adopted and socialized, they came to be viewed as beneficial, that is, contributing to improved living standards. Many of these older technologies are now so seamlessly integrated into modern societies that individuals, businesses, and governments cannot function very well, if at all, without them. Now, seemingly everyday, newer, more sophisticated, and complex digital information and communication technologies are being introduced that are exerting a significant influence on how we work, learn, and play. However, it seems that instead of these new technologies simplifying or improving our lives, as it is often touted they will do, they are, in fact, making life more complicated—even chaotic—and our society is struggling to adapt.

"Information architecture has recently emerged as an important meta-discipline concerned with the design, implementation, and maintenance of digital information spaces for human access, navigation, and use.... The term has been used for several years to describe the mix of competencies required to produce information resources that enhance human abilities to locate information."

*Journal of the American Society for Information Science & Technology*

**KEYWORDS**

Argus Center for Information Architecture

information architecture defined

information architecture, information age

information architecture, Web design

In his book, *Designing Business,* Clement Mok when talking specifically about today's business communities adapting to new technologies points out: "The need of businesses to communicate about products or services hasn't changed, but business and design approaches do need to change in response to the technological environment." From Mok's point of view, design offers a possible antidote for the chaos in our technological environments when he states, "Design, in its broadest sense, is the enabler of the digital era—it's a process that creates order out of chaos, that renders technology usable to business."

Given that continuous advances in information and communication technologies have not only changed how information is accessed and organized but also the amount of information available, it is not surprising that a new design profession is emerging that is concerned with addressing these issues—information architecture. The focus of IA is the design of structures—information environments—that provide users seeking information with the necessary resources to translate successfully their information needs into actions that ultimately lead to the accomplishment of their goals.

## DEFINING INFORMATION

Information begins as data: facts, observations, imaginings (content). How data is organized and presented (its context) influences how it is interpreted. The same set of data organized in different ways can lead to different interpretations. The context from which it is being interpreted and the intent of the interpreter also influence the final interpretation. Ultimately, however, information is formed from data by our personal interpretations, that is, what it means to us as individuals. In common usage today, the term *information* is generally used in place of *data*. In this textbook, the term *information* is used in the place of *data* to avoid constantly redefining it. However, we need to remember that there *is* a difference between the two.

## DEFINING INFORMATION ENVIRONMENT

Acquiring information from an environment—information seeking—is an activity critical to fulfilling problem-solving goals. Information seeking begins when the information seeker realizes that she is lacking some knowledge to fulfill a goal. This recognition leads to the formation of a knowledge need which, in turn, leads to taking action to find the needed information.

All human activity occurs within and is bounded by a context. Context determines the availability of the tools and resources that enable or assist people in taking whatever actions are necessary for accomplishing their goals. In contemporary society, the tools for seeking, processing, and

"Information design is about the clear and effective presentation of information. It involves a multi- and inter-disciplinary approach to communication, combining skills from graphic design, technical and non-technical authoring, psychology, communication theory and cultural studies. In fact, wherever relatively complex information needs to be made easier to understand, or tailored to the needs of a specific specialist or cultural community, the user-oriented methods of information design can be employed."

*Information Design Network*

communicating information are found in both physical and computer-mediated information spaces. An information space is defined in this case as the location (physical or computer-mediated) where the human mind interacts with information or communicates it to another (Andrew Treloar, 1994).

An information environment(see Figure 18.1) is a physical and/or computer-mediated information space within which context is defined by real and conceptual structures. Information environments include users; the facilities and technologies that facilitate users' interactions and experiences with each other, with other information systems, and with content of information spaces; and the organizational and navigational schemes of information spaces. As such, designers of information environments are concerned with

- sponsors of information environments,
- users,
- form and functionality (of the information space defining the context within which information-seeking activity takes place),
- organization and presentation of content within the context, and
- information and communication technology infrastructure (that supports all user interactions with and within the information environment).

Accordingly, information architecture design problems are complex, and information architects must draw upon the expertise of multiple disciplines for the successful resolution of IA design problems. This fact complicates the IA design process. To understand more easily what influences are shaping the evolving IA design process, it is helpful first to know more about

- design,
- a structured design process (method),
- users,
- usability,
- user-centered design,
- the scope of the information environment design problem, and
- the importance of managing an IA design process.

## DEFINING DESIGN

Through trial and error methods over time, the knowledge gained regarding the organizing and presentation of information has been passed on by example, hands-on training, and rules of thumb—like all craft traditions. It was not until the early 1960s that several disciplines (architectural design, graphic and interior design, and industrial design among them) recognized the common elements of the phenomenon we now call design (Coplien, 1999). All designed products are the result of a

"The different forms of professional design practice require a process incorporating the strategic and managerial aspects of design as well as the hands-on developmental application of design. These move from thinking, researching, and planning at one end of the process to the physical manufacture, assembly, packaging, and presentation at the other."

*Ken Friedman*

**FIGURE 18.1**
Information
environments are
defined by real and
conceptual structures.

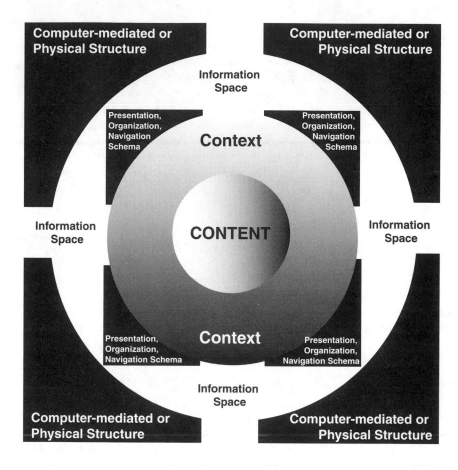

"Design is engaged for the
purpose of changing an
existing situation into a
preferred one. Whether that
change—that is, the goal of
designing—involves a new
computer system or an illustration, an automobile or a
building, a change in the skill
of an individual or a plan of
action, the designer focuses
his or her efforts toward
achieving a particular end for
the case at hand. Designing,
therefore, is a type of
planning and results in an
organized plan for achieving
a special purpose."

*Gordon Rowland*

process—a conscious, problem-solving process that begins with inquiry.
Design processes are knowledge intensive (requiring the use of intellectual tools like analysis and logic to conduct research), involve selecting
goals, and require developing strategies to meet those goals (planning
and management) (Friedman, 1997). Shaped by history and circumstances, design methodologies have evolved from skills-based craft traditions and are now moving toward more theoretical and scientific
inquiry-based design methods.

## DEFINING DESIGN METHODS

A structured design process—a method—introduces control or discipline into the design process. Design methods are concerned with principles and processes of design based on the nature of design and how
designers identify problems and generate and evaluate solutions. The
overarching goal of a design method is to improve the efficiency and effectiveness of design activities. Efficiency is a measure of the length of
time and the amount of resources used in completing a task. Effective-

ness is a measure of how well a task is completed. Generally, design methods include the following phases:

- Analysis
- Conceptual design
- Design and development
- Implementation

Differences in design methods vary from one knowledge field to another because of differences in their origins, underlying theoretical and philosophical assumptions, and differing histories of practice.

## DEFINING USERS

In speculating about where the information age may lead, James Dewar compares the impact of the printing press to the impact of networked computer communication systems. He points out that, with the introduction of the printing press, one structural change in how people learned [and interacted with information resources] is clear. "People shifted from being listeners to being readers," he states. He also notes that this transformation took place over a long period, and that it was a complex social and cultural phenomenon, and that learning is still primarily reading based today (despite the introduction of film, radio, and television). However, he states, "There are indications that [networked] computers will enable a fundamentally different kind of interaction [with information resources]. The first people to deal with computers were programmers," he says, and, "as libraries of programs became available and computers became more powerful, cheaper, and friendlier, the people who interacted with them came to be called 'users.'" They came to be called users, he believes, because of their ability to interact with the computer itself, with the information resources accessible via the computer and, with other users (James Dewar, 1998). Information architects believe that this interactive capability is unique in the history of communications and represents an important breakthrough in the ability of humans to communicate with each other.

## DEFINING USABILITY

The International Standards Organization (ISO) defines usability as "the extent to which a system supports users in completing their tasks efficiently, effectively, and satisfactorily." Well-designed information systems increase users' efficiency by enabling them to complete a task with few complications, without having to learn a lot of unnecessary techniques and with a minimal expenditure of energy. Well-designed information systems improve users' effectiveness by enabling them to complete their tasks at a high standard. Users of well-designed information systems are

"The new information age will require many information designers. They will have to be capable of taking information users into account as part of their professional activity. This will require a redefinition of their job, an acknowledgment of their own limitations, and an informed and sensitive awareness of the needs of the information user. The last of these can only be achieved by forming better theories about users, developing methods of design research that are not dependent on outside expertise, and acquiring a sense of the history of information design, combining all these to create new conventions to meet new communication needs and technologies."

*David Sless*

*"To make a design seem simple and clear to an end user, designers must do two things. First they have to make sure they don't let their own common sense slip in where it's not appropriate, and secondly they need to find out what, if anything, constitutes common sense to their target audience. Sometimes there may not be any common wisdom that can be depended on. At other times, there are rules-of-thumb and common knowledge, tacit and explicit, which everyone in that group knows. The only way to know this is to talk to and observe the end users."*

*Adam Smith*

satisfied with the usability of an information architecture when it supports their efforts in completing their tasks by providing useful assistance and saving them effort. In other words, a well-designed information system is easy to use and ultimately, as Arnie Lund points out, "Easy to use systems remove the barriers to accessing the underlying functionality that provides users' value."

## DEFINING USER-CENTERED DESIGN

User-centered design is a design methodology "based on the needs and interests of the user, with an emphasis on making products usable and understandable" (Norman, 1990). A user-centered design approach involves users throughout the design process. The growing popularity of user-centered design methods has now shifted designers' attention to the relationship between the user and information systems and recognizes the user as a participant in the construction of meaning.

Initially, most user-centered research was conducted in laboratory settings with the intention of gathering "objective" scientific evidence about users that could then be applied to design problems. Eventually, some researchers came to realize that, although analyzing the relationship between users and products was a step in the right direction to solving design problems, user-centered design methods needed to be even broader and inclusive of the relationships between users and their environments (homes, places of work, institutions).

Ben Schneiderman, a leading researcher in the field of human-computer interaction (HCI), comments on the limitations of controlled studies:

> The social and political environment surrounding the implementation of a complex information system is not amenable to study by controlled experiment. The experienced project leader knows that organizational politics and the preferences of individuals may be more important than the technical issues in governing the success of an interactive system. (Schneiderman, 1987)

Acknowledging the value of a systems view of design rather than a product view, information architects are gradually adopting a user-centered design philosophy that takes into account the "complex institutional and social frameworks within which [information systems] have to function ..." (Sless, 1996). However, this approach adds to the complexity of designing information systems that are truly usable. For instance, to create usable, effective designs, a designer must gather information regarding

- what the users' goals are (what they are trying to achieve),
- what users actually do to achieve those goals,
- what personal, social, and cultural characteristics the users bring to the tasks,

- how users are influenced by their physical environment,
- how users' previous knowledge and experience influence how they think about their work and the work flow they follow to perform their tasks; and
- what users value most that will make an [information product] be a delight for them. (Hackos, 1998)

All of the information gathered from each one of these areas of investigation needs to be understood as it relates to a whole functioning information system. Managing such an intensive data-gathering process requires the use of methods for managing a usability study process and techniques for capturing data.

## USABILITY STUDIES AND METHODOLOGIES

Usability studies are the mechanism that provides designers with crucial information central to a user-centered design process. "The recommendations arising from any usability study can only be as good as the information on which it is based. The quality of this information depends on the methods used to collect the data" (Norman, 2001). Although usability study methods vary, they all put users in the forefront of the design process, keeping designers focused on what users think, like, and need. Usability studies are generally conducted at three stages within the life cycle of a user-centered design process: The problem definition stage, design stage, and post-design stage.

### Problem Definition Stage

In the problem definition stage, designers analyze users' needs, define goals to meet their needs, and set objectives for meeting the goals defined. Techniques used to gather information at this stage include brainstorming and direct user research (user and task analysis based on direct observation or ethnographic studies). This stage can also include assessing the existing solution(s) for what works and does not work. Heuristic analyses and cognitive walkthroughs are two examples of inspection methods used to conduct such an assessment.

### Design Stage

In the design stage, designers are concerned with drafting a detailed specification for an information system. Developing prototypes from design specifications is an effective way to test whether or not design concepts are meeting the needs of users before implementation. Most techniques used at this stage are referred to as usability tests and are sometimes iterative (a repeated design and test cycle). Usability tests are important for studying the functionality of an information system and

*Usability studies and methodologies are tools used for the purpose of addressing the issue of usability in design. They can include a variety of data-gathering techniques and strategies for organizing and evaluating information gathered. The essence of any usability study or methodology is that it provides a structure for assisting designers in considering all the relevant design issues.*

the degree to which it satisfies the needs of users. Examples of usability tests are

- direct user research (observation of direct use of a prototype in a controlled or field test setting),
- questionnaires,
- interviews, and
- group discussions.

An additional goal in the design stage is ensuring the design maps to the users' representation of the domain, their expectations and the skills they bring to the interaction, and their projected needs and behavior.

## Postdesign Stage

Usability studies conducted in the postdesign phase are generally conducted to track the performance of an information system that has been implemented. Information gathered in the postdesign stage may be used for improving subsequent versions of the original information system. The same types of tests used in the design stage may also be used in the postdesign stage:

- Direct user research (observation of direct use of a prototype in a controlled or field test setting)
- Questionnaires
- Interviews
- Group discussions

An additional goal of the postdesign stage is demonstrating that not only does the application meet specified requirements but also delivers the expected value as measured by the return on the investment that justified the project in the first place.

## About Ethnographic Studies

The Ethnographic Point of View:

1. "You aren't your users; you aren't like your users.
2. It isn't possible to sit around a conference table and imagine correctly what people want and need.
3. The tools of understanding: immersion, observation, storytelling, a child-like ignorance."

*Marc Rettig*

Usability study methods are practical and systematic "tools" that user-centered designers employ to gather information for the purpose of designing information systems that work for users. At present, however, there is growing evidence that user-centered design methods (that depended on usability testing in controlled settings) may be too narrow in scope and do not adequately consider the social and political issues that are also important to successful design. As a consequence, design methods involving the study of users in a social context are developing—ethnographic studies. Ethnography is the practice of immersing oneself in a culture in order to describe that culture. The goal of ethnographic study is to achieve a richer understanding of the ways people work and the physical and cultural environments in which they work. While this broadening in scope of design methods improves the potential for developing effective design solutions, it also adds to the complexity of the information design process.

## IA DESIGN: DEFINING THE PROCESS

### The Scope of the IA Design Problem

Information architects are striving to determine how best to realize the potential of today's rapidly evolving information and communication technologies. Based upon their individual practices, principles, and values, they are working collectively to articulate their vision of an IA design process. They are also drawing upon multiple disciplines to develop a model of a such a process.

The primary goal of modeling is to facilitate the organization and visualization of the structure and components of a complex system or process, and predicting the impact of changes to the system or process. IA is concerned with how to improve the ability of users to generate, store, organize, locate, and communicate information using new information and communication technologies and, consequently, involves a variety of complex systems and processes including

- social systems,
- technical systems,
- design processes,
- programming and engineering processes, and
- management and implementation processes.

The following model is an informal model that attempts to diagram the scope of IA-related systems and processes and an integrated view of their relationships. Four primary activities are involved in this process:

- Identifying different viewpoints of IA-related systems and processes,
- Identifying the contexts within which these systems and processes are employed,
- Identifying what disciplines are involved in each context, and
- Identifying the relationships among the systems, processes, and disciplines.

### Identifying Viewpoints

Adopting the viewpoints of the major stakeholders involved in IA functions to bring into focus their primary concerns.

- *The sponsors' or clients' view:* Most projects require a business case to justify the expense. Sponsors or clients may need to increase their revenues or decrease their expenses. Changes in users' behavior are

> "Design management is a leadership activity focused on managing the creation of an entity." An entity can be an object, an event, a concept, or even a relationship. "The design manager's responsibilities include establishing a shared vision of the entity; defining, acquiring, and allocating the resources needed to create that entity; managing the effective use of those resources; and monitoring the design team's performance. The design manager is also responsible for establishing and maintaining standards for assessing the entity's overall quality."
>
> *William Miller*

the means to those goals. Other sponsor or client concerns may include promoting a brand image, building loyalty, or educating users.

- *The users' view:* At the heart of the IA model is concern for the user's experience when interacting with information and communication technologies (ICT)—the human component. The users' view informs the entire IA design and implementation process and is critical to the successful utilization and socialization of new information and communication technologies.
- *The designers' view:* Designers are concerned with developing "information structures that account for [and synthesize] the multiple levels and layers of interaction among humans, machines, and the physical environment"—the systems component (Cohill, 1991).
- *The programmers' and engineers' view:* Programmers and engineers are concerned with the physical storage and retrieval of data, the relationships and behaviors of data types, and the arrangement of structures in the software architecture that are utilized to display data—the technical component.
- *The production managers' view:* Production managers are concerned with the effective and efficient management of economic and human resources, scheduling, and quality control—the implementation component.

## Identifying Contexts and Related Disciplines

IA is an interdisciplinary field, involving disciplines that range from being primarily artistic in nature to others that are more scientific in their orientation. Professionals from these various fields participate within four major contexts. In the list below each context is followed by the disciplines associated with it.

- Usability: cognitive science, sociology, social informatics
- Information design: visual design, interface design, library and information science
- Interaction design: human–computer interaction, cognitive science, theater
- Programming and engineering: computer science, computer hardware and software engineering, network administration information and communication technology

## Identifying the Relationships

Figure 18.2 illustrates just how complex the design of information environments can become, involving a range of complex issues to be solved by teams of experts from multiple disciplines. This level of complexity and the high stakes often associated with information environment design projects can distract the designers of information environments from focusing on solving the design problem and, consequently, elevate the risk of failure. The management of the design process—which is concerned with reducing the risk of failure—is therefore becoming a critical component of the IA design process.

## THE NEED FOR IA DESIGN MANAGEMENT

If the process for managing the design of information environments is not explicit, the chances for failure increase. Therefore, information environment design management is most efficient and effective when it follows a method. Many design management methods follow a similar path:

1. An orientation stage where teams are formed and team briefings are held;
2. A vision statement stage where project goals and objectives are articulated, problems and opportunities are identified, and product features are broadly defined by the team;
3. A project specification stage where the outcomes of the vision stage are articulated in a rough form;
4. A project plan stage where roles, responsibilities, schedules, costs, and budgets are outlined;
5. A development stage, where the design, plan, and specifications are finalized into a development scheme; and
6. An implementation stage where the product is actually constructed and delivered. (Allinson, 1997)

The primary areas of responsibility of an information environment design manager can include

- planning (scheduling, budgeting),
- managing human and financial resources (hiring and estimating expenses),
- monitoring performance (constant assessment and refinement of human and financial resource applications), and
- monitoring quality (constant evaluation of the design's conceptual aspects and the functional and material characteristics of the product).

Some aspects of design management cannot be easily quantified, such as leadership skills, but can make a very real and qualitative difference in the final product. "Leadership is important for realizing the "beneficial 'capture' and effective utilization of the potential to be realized by design expertise and skill" (Allinson, 1997). As many information environment design projects exceed the expertise of an individual, teams of experts are often involved. This requires that an information architect also be sensitive to the human-relations aspect of management and be adept at facilitating the communication of design concepts among a design team (who represent various fields of knowledge).

> "Design management—a product of the development of design disciplines during the middle and later parts of the 20th century—has become headlined as a key to corporate innovation and business success in a post-modern era. [In design management] the emphasis is upon the project method, the importance of time management, and of realizing the potential of 'good' design in order to 'add value' within the context of the project process."
>
> *Kenneth Allinson*

**FIGURE 18.2**
Designing information
environments can be
a highly complex
activity, as this
diagram illustrates.

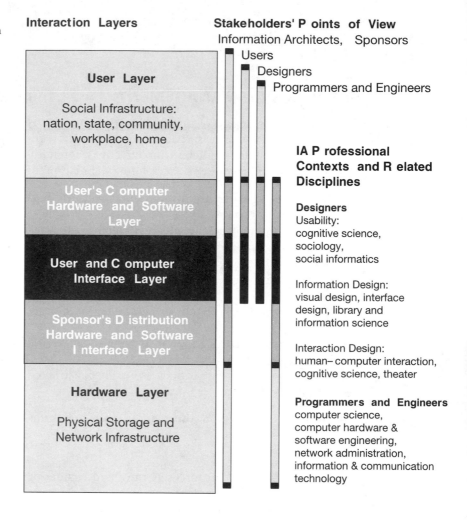

Managerial and design agenda can also be very different. Managerial
working methods are generally not very tolerant of ambiguity. On the
other hand, designers may purposely embrace ambiguity as part of their
design method. It is the responsibility of information architects to juggle
the imaginative practices of design with the more pragmatic concerns of
management—design management. Information architects must also balance the constraints that inevitably arise from clients, aesthetic and technical standards, and economics. Accordingly, to be successful, information
architects as leaders of the design management process must develop both
creative problem-solving skills and project management skills. Effective de-

sign methodologies reflect the value of both the "soft" imaginative practices and the "hard" pragmatic concerns related to time and money.

## IA DESIGN METHODS

Confronted with increasingly complex information environment design problems and a demand for design solutions that create new strategic opportunities for their clients, information architects are necessarily developing more comprehensive design methods that take into account the

- client's or sponsor's needs and goals,
- user's needs and goals,
- multidisciplinary nature of IA practice,
- collaborative nature of IA practice,
- affordances* of the conceptual structures of media and interfaces, and
- affordances of the physical structures of information and communication technologies.

Well-defined information environment design methodologies are tools for assisting IAs in systematically

- gathering and processing all of the design requirements gathered from the considerations listed above,
- translating the design requirements into a clear set of design parameters,
- articulating the design team's responsibilities and tasks,
- defining a design and implementation process, and
- effectively managing that process.

## AN EXAMPLE OF AN IA DESIGN METHOD

The following example of an information architecture design method is unique and interesting because it represents the fusion of the information design methods of three different companies. From 1998 to 1999, Sapient, a business and technology consulting firm, acquired Studio Archetype and Adjacency, two firms specializing in Internet design. In 1999, the following competencies of the three companies were merged into a single information architecture practice:

- A user-interface group that designed client-server applications,
- An information design practice that was oriented toward a "design for understanding approach," and
- An information architecture practice that was Web application-oriented.

> "Effective design requires appropriate methods and rooted understanding. Design in the industrial world is handicapped by outdated methods. The symptoms are rigid design thinking, the confusion of artistic solutions with design solutions, or— just as bad—the failure to understand the need for the union of grace and function in optimal design."
>
> *Ken Friedman*

---

*The properties of objects or concepts that influence a user's perception of how they are to be used or how they work.

Information design methods in each organization had evolved differently. Together, representatives from each organization synthesized their different methodologies into one "Process Framework for Information Architecture (PFIA)." The PFIA includes one pre-project phase and five major project phases.

### PFIA Phases

1. Discover (understand the context and scope),
2. Define (synthesize the variables and define the problem and opportunities),
3. Concept (explore the possibilities),
4. Design (architect and iterate the solution), and
5. Implement (validate and test the design and transfer knowledge).

Within each phase, multiple steps (following a process path) were defined. This type of path is also referred to as a *critical path*. The critical path is a linear progression of steps, each of which is wholly dependent on the completion of the previous step. This method is commonly used in the practice of architecture in the built environment. There are 21 steps in the process path. Associated with each step are specific "process activities" and "deliverables." Phases and Process Paths Steps are:

Pre-Project Phase
　Process Path Steps
　　Step A: Participate in client pitch
　　Step B: Inform proposal
Discover Phase
　Process Path Steps
　　Step C: Review proposal
　　Step D: Establish project context and focus
　　Step E: Plan process and revise scope
Define Phase
　Process Path Steps
　　Step F: Conduct focused research
　　Step G: Synthesize information
　　Step H: Define problem
Concept Phase
　Process Path Steps
　　Step I: Develop concepts
　　Step J: Evaluate concepts
　　Step K: Refine concepts
　　Step L: Choose concept

Design Phase
    Process Path Steps
        Step: M: Create site structure
        Step N: Model processes and activities
        Step O: Define detail
        Step P: Evaluate and validate architecture
        Step Q: Complete architecture documentation
        Step R: Review GUI design
Implement Phase—Part 1
    Process Path Steps
        Step S: Review site build
        Step T: Issue resolution
Implement Phase—Part 2
    Process Path Step
        Step U: Transfer knowledge

The foldout insert of figure 18–3 at the back of the book illustrates Sapient's entire Process for Information Architecture Framework as used in 2001 and includes itemizations of the tasks necessary for completing each step within all the phases of a project. It also illustrates the complexity of large-scale IA design problems and makes obvious the importance of documentation of this type. Well-articulated design methods lead to intelligent architectures, both physical and conceptual, that are needed in contemporary society. It should be noted that at Sapient, tasks that are sometimes associated with IAs were the responsibility of other specializations, namely content strategists and user researchers. Those tasks are not represented in the PFIA unless they were collaborative with the explicit IA role.

## ABOUT SAPIENT

Sapient provides a range of application design and integration services and is focused on building solutions that enable new processes, business models, and performance levels. Sapient is also concerned with generating a rapid return on their clients' investments through rigorous scope management and cost-effective implementation, reducing costs while improving service and performance through self-service and automated solutions, increasing usage and loyalty by providing audiences with experiences that are useful, usable, and desirable, and maximizing the use of technology without disrupting their clients' current operations.

# IA
# The Practitioner

"The IA must act as a mediator between client, user, business office, graphics team, and the programming department. [She] will be in charge of a wide variety of activities from content analysis to focus group research to web page framing. The effective IA has an arsenal of technical skills mixed with effective interpersonal communication, which puts [her] at the center of a complex web of communication between differing views and ideas. The IA plays the role of a diplomat by maintaining cohesion between team members and ensuring the project remains on schedule, meeting goals and deadlines."

Chris Ewing, 2002

"The single most important factor in the success of [information] architecture is the skill of its creator. This skill is applied through a combination of experienced professional judgment, thoughtful consideration of research findings, and disciplined creativity."

Jesse James Garrett

IA is an interdisciplinary field, involving disciplines that range from being primarily artistic in nature to others that are more scientific in their orientation.

**KEYWORDS**

information architect, Christina Wodtke

information architect, job description

information architecture, practice

information architect, responsibilities

information architect, skills

## A RAPIDLY DEVELOPING PROFESSIONAL PRACTICE

It has been estimated that, as early as January 30, 2001, there were between 2,000 and 3,000 individuals in the United States practicing information architecture. This growing group of practitioners is coming from a variety of disciplines, including library and information science, HCI, computer science, and visual design. Although professional associations representing professionals from each of these disciplines are currently sponsoring IA-related activities (SIGs, listservs, seminars, workshops, and conferences), as of March 2002 none has yet to develop an IA professional certification program. At a few major universities, IA graduate-level specializations are only beginning to be developed and offered.

Consequently, most IAs have no formal credentials and are self-identified as IAs. Regardless, IA is developing very rapidly as a professional practice and, although the specific job requirements for IAs vary from one organization to the other, basic sets of responsibilities and key knowledge and skills requirements are beginning to coalesce.

## RESPONSIBILITIES

Information architects are responsible for the design, development, and implementation of highly complex information environments that are easy to use yet provide satisfying experiences for users. As such, they are required to coordinate the efforts of multidisciplinary teams; facilitate communications within teams and between clients and teams; analyze, identify, and articulate design problems; and manage the design process, implementation, and evaluation of design solutions. Their primary responsibilities can be grouped under the following categories:

- Design and design management
- Project management
- Research
- Mediation

There are four major contexts within which information architecture professionals participate:
1. Usability
2. Information design
3. Interaction design
4. Programming and engineering

### Design and Design Management

IA design is a problem-solving activity requiring both analytical and creative skills. As designers, IAs are responsible for "designing solutions that reconcile user needs, business objectives, and the capabilities of technology" (Svec, 2000). To this end IAs may be responsible for an information environment's interaction design, navigation design, interface design, and information design. They may also be responsible for developing and articulating design processes as well as conceptualization and analysis tools that facilitate design processes. IAs are generally responsible for developing "blueprints" and other design-related documentation.

### Project Management

On large-scale IA projects, IAs have managed multidisciplinary teams charged with defining information environment design problems, designing the solutions, and implementing them. Consequently, IAs have had a broad set of project management and planning responsibilities, including providing leadership, defining and setting work flows and processes, defining quality standards, monitoring and evaluating the activities of team members, defining project tasks, scheduling project activities and deliverables, and budgeting financial and human resources.

The Alta Vista Information Architect is responsible for designing the structure and user experience of the Alta Vista Network. The IA translates business objectives, corporate strategy, and product marketing requirements into highly usable web projects and client-side applications.

*Erin Malone*

The role of the [Alta Vista] information architect is to organize information and to create a smooth path for the user to find what they are seeking. In addition, the information architect defines site interaction. They are responsible for defining the user flow with a decision making process.

*Erin Malone*

The [Alta Vista] information architect is responsible for designing from the user's perspective. They work closely with the software engineers and content producers to create the best user experience.

*Erin Malone*

## Research

At its core, IA is a user-centered design discipline intent on improving the usability of information environments. Therefore many IAs are strong advocates of user research. The responsibilities associated with such studies can be hands-on or more managerial in nature and may include conducting interviews, surveys, workshops, focus groups, ethnographic type studies, and usability tests.

## Mediation

IA is frequently a collaborative effort involving clients, users, and teams of people representing a diverse set of disciplines each with its own specialized languages and practices. IAs often find themselves "at the center of a complex web of communication between differing views and ideas." In this context "the IA plays the role of diplomat by maintaining cohesion between team members [and other stakeholders including clients and users] and ensuring the project remains on schedule, meeting goals and deadlines." As mediators, IAs are responsible for "educating, advocating, and translating the [project] requirements for all audiences involved" (Chris Ewing, 2002).

## IA KNOWLEDGE REQUIREMENT SUBJECT AREAS

Information architects must be knowledgeable, although not necessarily expert, in a variety of subject areas relevant to the design, development, and maintenance of information environments. These subject areas are

- Project planning and management
- Information systems and management
- Information searching and retrieval
- Information and communications technologies
- Human factors
- Research methods

## IA JOB REQUIREMENTS

The University of Texas at Austin's School of Library and Information Studies has compiled professional requirements from no fewer than 30 different IA-related job descriptions. The following selected requirements are representative of the complete listing. Some have been edited to improve readability and consistency. They are grouped under the categories of client interaction and management, discovery and analysis, IA design, production, and implementation.

## Client Interaction and Management

Applicants must be able to

- identify mission and target market
- review the competitive landscape
- lead client working sessions
- translate user needs to client

## Discovery and Analysis (Client and Production Research)

Applicants must be able to

- define, characterize, and prioritize the project's audiences
- identify and classify [information environment] content and types
- organize information in usable and meaningful ways
- assess and document information environment functionality and structure
- interpret client needs in a coherent and constructive form
- lead project team creative brainstorming sessions

## IA Design

Applicants must be able to

- design the navigation structure (hierarchy), system, and work flow (data flow)
- create user scenarios
- create user profiles
- conduct task flow analysis
- develop use cases
- create form, function, metaphor, interface, interaction, and visual design
- assist in the translation of business and user requirements into functional and design recommendations
- specify how users will find and interact with information by defining organization, labeling, and searching systems
- produce site maps, content maps, page schematics, and text-based outlines to communicate information structures and organization schemes
- develop storyboards
- develop wire frames
- develop controlled vocabularies and thesauri

## Production

Applicants must be able to

- act as a key advocate for users
- prototype site schematics for presentation to clients

> "From my own experience, I would say that the practitioners are professionals, versed in every aspect of web design, adept communicators, and gifted visualizers - they are people who eat, sleep and dream web design and structure. But you can't put that on the job description.
>
> Or - as I *Sing the Body Electronic* author Fred Moody observes: information architects are the sort of people who understand that the instructions on the shampoo bottle are just wrong: 'Lather. Rinse. Repeat.'"
>
> *Stephen Downes*

- conduct usability testing of proposed designs
- conduct user analysis
- conduct task flow analysis
- design [information environment] interfaces
- collaborate with designer, writer, project manager, and developer to identify and obtain client assets in all stages of design
- communicate with project manager and application architect to coordinate the [information environment] concept, visual design, writing, interface, and navigational structure of [information environment] with functional aspects
- advise designers on usability issues

## Implementation

Applicants must be able to

- conduct usability testing
- conduct paper prototyping (Chris Ewing, 2002)

# IA SKILL REQUIREMENTS

The University of Texas at Austin's School of Library and Information Studies has also compiled a list of skills needed to become an IA from IA-related job postings. The following selected skills are representative of the complete listing. Some have been edited to improve readability and consistency.

Applicants for this position must have the following skills (not all skills were required for each position advertised).

## Design and Design Management Skills

- Application interface design
- Information architecture design
- Navigation design
- Information structure design
- Work flow design
- Usability test design
- Critical thinking and problem solving
- Creation and documentation of design concepts and solutions using sketches, diagrams, maps, storyboards, rapid prototypes, and functional prototypes

## Project Management Skills

- Team leadership
- Lead clients through discovery, analysis, and design phases of project

- Interpersonal communication
- Verbal and written communication
- Coordinate organizational activities
- Time management and resource allocation

## Research Skills

- Design and conduct usability tests
- Conduct task analysis, task modeling, and usage scenarios

## Mediation Skills

- Customer service
- Collaboration (Chris Ewing, 2002)

Based upon the sets of responsibilities, and the key knowledge and skills requirements as they have been listed in IA job postings, we can begin to see that the marketplace is seeking a new kind of design professional. Sought is an individual who can "bridge the creative and technical elements of a project both for the project itself and for the production team, ensuring that the balance between the technical and creative elements remains stabilized so that the audience's [and the client's] needs are served" (Chris Ewing, 2002). The following example of an advertisement posted by one of the world's largest corporations for a senior manager of information architecture illustrates very well for what purpose corporate America is seeking information architects and the qualifications they believe these professionals need to satisfy their requirements.

## AN EXAMPLE OF AN IA JOB DESCRIPTION

The following ad was posted on the American Society of Information Science and Technology (ASIST) information architecture listserv on Thursday, August 16, 2001, by Lillian Svec of Walmart.com, a wholly owned subsidiary of Wal-Mart Stores, Inc.

> "Walmart.com is building a world-class User Experience team to continually enhance, improve, and expand the Walmart.com web site and to pioneer the design of a variety of new electronic retail delivery platforms, including in-store kiosks. We are deeply committed to customer-centered-design, online/offline integration, and proving that profitable consumer e-commerce is not a contradiction in terms."

As part of the User Experience Group, information architects (IAs) are responsible for determining how the interactive user interfaces we build should work. Employing user-centered design techniques and working on cross-functional teams, IAs create the plans that are used by other team members to develop the graphical user interface, content, and functionality. (At Walmart.com, the IA role includes what is called interaction design in some other organizations.)

## Senior Manager of Information Architecture Job Description

We are looking for a key individual who will be responsible for managing and providing leadership to the information architecture team responsible for the Walmart.com e-commerce web site.

Responsibilities:

- Provide strategy, direction, and oversight for all IA activities on the site's projects and manage a team of 2 to 5 IAs.
- Establish overall work processes, practices, and standards for the work done by the site's IA team, based on the overall IA group's practices.
- Work closely with other IA team members and the User Research Manager to plan and participate in user research activities.
- Foster a collaborative working environment between all disciplines working on the initiative.
- Act as a liaison between executives, merchants, store representatives, and the leaders of other development teams and the IA team.
- Occasionally, play a hands-on IA role on projects.
- Work with the Director of User Experience and other IA team members to establish work processes, practices, and standards for the IA team across all initiatives at Walmart.com.
- Work with the Director of User Experience and other IA team members to evangelize user-centered design and IA practices at Walmart.com and Wal-Mart Stores.

Requirements:

- 5+ years of Web-based information architecture or interaction design experience including designing the overall information architecture for multiple e-commerce web sites and extensive transactional design experience.
- 2+ years of experience managing IA or similar functional group.
- Demonstrated success in leading collaborative multi-functional project teams including project planning.
- Demonstrated client managerial experience (or equivalent for internal organization).
- Strong process skills and methodological orientation tempered by a willingness to be flexible and innovative in working approach.
- Strong business sense, excellent organizational and logical skills, and an eye for details.
- A broad understanding of the web and its associated technologies.
- Excellent oral, written, and visual communication skills.
- Knowledge of PC applications including: MS Office, Visio, Illustrator, Photoshop, Quark Express, and HTML page creation tools.
- Ability to travel occasionally.

# FROM PROFESSIONALS TO PROFESSION

Regardless of the fact that the emergence of a networked marketplace is generating a demand for the services of information architects, "the progress of the discipline [of information architecture] depends on the development and iteration of a body of knowledge. This body of knowledge, in turn, can only come about through deliberate consideration of a wide range of architectural problems and potential solutions" (Jesse James Garrett, 2002). Individual practitioners working alone cannot develop a body of knowledge. Such a professional activity requires the founding of a new professional organization for that explicit purpose or the endorsement and support of an existing professional organization or organizations, closely related to information architecture.

# 20 CHAPTER

# IA
# The Profession

Many organizations are recognizing the strategic and operational value of providing good information. Consequently, information specialists are increasingly seen as crucial to a growing diversity of markets, including publishing, multimedia, research, software development, and health, financial, and legal services. Additionally, the academic, public, and government sectors are striving to improve their information services and are seeking competent information specialists too.

Today's professions have three interrelated characteristics: "a group identity—those in the profession can easily identify one another; some shared or agreed-upon education, training, or certification—those in the profession generally agree upon and recognize certain requirements needed to practice their profession; and a special kind of knowledge—those who have the knowledge are able to perform services for others who do not."

Cynthia Brincat

"The professional practices of information architecture are being developed by a cohesive group of committed individuals. Its core practices of analyzing, designing, and building information structures are not only central to the present and future of the information sciences as a whole, but also central to the needs and concerns of society in an information economy."

Keith Belton

**KEYWORDS**

information architecture, ASIST

information architect, profession

information architecture, SIG

information architecture, summits

information architect, Lillian Svec

info-arch

## PROFESSIONS AND THE RISE OF CORPORATIONS

Before the Industrial Revolution, professions had a strong civic orientation. Along with the rise of a new type of business organization in the early 1900s—the corporation—professions began to place a new emphasis on science and efficiency rather than serving the public good. Corporations were "a form of organization designed to accumulate large amounts of capital, resources, and labor and apply them to the rational, planned conduct of economic activity through a division of labor and bureaucratic routine" (Williams, 1966). Wanting to benefit from the great success corporations were enjoying, professions quickly aligned their principles with those of emerging corporate America.

## TECHNICAL EXPERTISE AND PROFESSIONALISM

Being professional soon meant having technical expertise; that is, the capacity to use sophisticated techniques as a way to solve complex problems. This shift was very much needed by rapidly expanding industrial America and was highly valued. During this period many occupational groups, seeking greater economic stability and increased status, formed professional organizations. The professional authority these groups were seeking was reinforced by universities. "Possession of higher educational credentials gave the aspiring professional a kind of movable capital upon which to trade in the increasingly specialized marketplace" (Sullivan, 1995). The university and a formal professional educational experience were soon intertwined with professions and professionalism.

## NEW EXPERTISE IS NEEDED

With the passing of the industrial age and mass manufacturing, a new economy is emerging that places a high value on products, services, and distribution systems that meet "rapid and subtle differences in demand" (Sullivan, 1995). In such an economy, professional expertise and knowledge are critical for success. "[Professionals] provide specific skills that are basic to the operation of complex modern institutions in the spheres of industry, government, education, health care, and the law (Sullivan, 1995)." Along with new industries and new fields of knowledge developing to meet the needs of today's economy, new occupational groups are forming. Many of these are in fields related to information and communication technologies (ICTs) and services. Their emergence has coincided with the maturation of the Internet. Among them is information architecture.

## THE PROFESSIONALIZATION OF IA

Information architects are seeking to be recognized as professionals. At present, many IA practitioners are engaged in the process of identifying and defining the "unique, shared set of skills and knowledge" that distinguishes them as a clearly identifiable group. Most, if not all, of today's information architects were educated on the job or their formal educational experiences prepared them for occupations other than information architect. It has been through the collective efforts of individual IA practitioners that conferences and other organizational activities have been initiated for the purpose of professionalizing IA.

The primary sponsoring organization in these efforts has been the American Society of Information Science and Technology (ASIST). There are other professional organizations that have members who practice IA or whose activities are relevant to the practice of IA. Among them are:

- American Institute for Graphic Arts
- Association for Computing Machinery

> "An authentic profession can provide a strong sense of identity because, beyond providing a livelihood, it is a way of life with public value. It is the kind of thing one can build a life around. For the person possessing the requisite capacities and sufficient commitment, a profession can provide not only a career but a calling to useful work as well."
>
> *William Sullivan*

> "Standards of skills and training has [*sic*] become more and more a part of the character of professions. This is particularly evident when we think of groups that are seeking to be recognized as professionals...."
>
> *Cynthia Brincat*

- Human Factors and Ergonomics Society
- Society for Technical Communications
- Usability Professional's Association

Established in 1937, ASIST counts among its membership information specialists from the fields of computer science, linguistics, management, librarianship, engineering, law, medicine, chemistry, and education. The common denominator among its members is their interest in improving the way society stores, retrieves, analyzes, manages, archives, and disseminates information.

In a call for contributions to a "special topics" issue of its journal, ASIST invited contributions that "will help shape our understanding of IA, explore the role IA may play in information systems design, and even question the need of such a meta-discipline." The specific topics of interest listed were included:

- Information architecture as a new and original field
- Case studies of IA in practice
- The history, origins, and future of IA
- Techniques and methods for IA practitioners
- Empirical studies of the IA process or user-based analyses of information architectures
- Education and training of architects

ASIST has also sponsored three IA summits beginning in 2000 and a very active IA special interest group (SIG). The conference themes for each of these summits are a reflection of the professional evolution of IA.

- IA Summit 2000: Defining Information Architecture
- IA Summit 2001: Practicing Information Architecture
- IA Summit 2002: Refining Our Craft

Aside from the fact that the summits themselves are professionalization activities, each summit program included sessions devoted specifically to profession-building topics such as

- At the Crossroads: Information Architecture and the "Purpose Crisis"
- Defining Information Architecture
- Making the Case for Information Architecture
- Why, What, and When?
- New Roles in Information Architecture
- Education and Information Architecture

One panel discussion in the 2001 summit was entitled "Reflections and Projections" and was offered so that "investigators will mix it up with the audience on such controversial topics as where the field is headed, who should be an information architect, and whether we even need a field called information architecture" (ASIST, 2001).

All of the activities noted above are characteristic of a number of professionalization activities including establishing a group identity, identifying and agreeing upon the requirements needed to practice IA, and articulating a specialized body of knowledge. The professionalization of IA is still in its early stages, and its practitioners and sponsoring organizations have yet to move toward formalizing the professionalization process. However, examining the efforts of a more mature information-age occupation to establish itself as a profession can provide insight regarding the steps involved in professionalization.

## A MODEL FOR PROFESSIONALIZATION

Software engineering moved toward professionalization in the early 1990s and serves as an excellent example of the professionalization process. In 1993 a joint steering committee representing the Institute of Electronic and Electrical Engineers (IEEE) Computer Society and the Association of Computing Machinery (ACM) was formed for the purpose of "evaluating, planning, and coordinating actions related to establishing Software Engineering as a profession." The mission statement developed by this committee reads: "[Our mission is] to establish the appropriate set(s) of criteria and norms for professional practice of software engineering upon which industrial decisions, professional certification, and educational curricula can be based." Included in their rationale and approach to establishing software engineering as a profession were the following definitions taken from *Webster's New Collegiate Dictionary:*

Profession:

- A calling requiring specialized knowledge and often long and intensive academic preparation; a principal calling, vocation, or employment; the whole body of persons engaged in a calling.

Professional:

- Relating to or characteristic of a profession; engaged in one of the learned professions; characterized by or conforming to the technical or ethical standards of a profession.
- Participating for gain or livelihood in an activity or field of endeavor often engaged in by amateurs; engaged in by persons receiving financial returns.

Professionalism:

- The conduct, aims, or qualities that characterize or mark a profession or a professional person.
- The following of a profession (as athletics) for gain or livelihood.

The initial recommendations of the steering committee were to

- define ethical standards,

"There is an appreciation that the ability to conceive of a system that is practical and usable is a missing skill set with the IT [information technology] development team. At the same time, it is recognized that this missing skill set is quite different in nature to other skills found with the team. Business savvy and the ability to communicate are examples of such missing skills, and are traditionally seen unlikely to be capabilities of 'hard core' technologists. Thus there is this recognition that a new type individual must be included in the team. From this need, the emergence of the IA profession has taken root."

*Anne South*

- define the required body of knowledge and recommended practices, and
- define the appropriate curricula to acquire the body of knowledge.

A task force for each of these three tasks was assembled, and their respective purposes were defined:

- The purpose of the Ethics and Professional Practices task force was "to develop the ethical and professional responsibilities and obligations of software engineers."
- The purpose of the Body of Knowledge and Recommended Practices task force was "to define the body of knowledge and practices at different levels of knowledge/skill needed at different points in the career of a Software Engineer."
- The purpose of the task force on Education was to "develop a model undergraduate curriculum once there was agreement on accreditation criteria."

The final product of these task forces was a publication entitled "Software Engineering Code of Ethics and Professional Practice." See Appendix C for an unedited version of this document.

## A 21st CENTURY PROFESSION

Like new professionals in the early 20th century "sought to establish themselves by bringing new techniques for coping with the challenges presented by urban, industrial disorder" (Sullivan, 1995), information architects at the beginning of the 21st century are seeking to do the same for coping with challenges presented by the information age. And, just as many occupational groups did the same during the industrial age, IAs are also recognizing that forming organizations for the purpose of professionalizing their occupations can be of great benefit to them.

"The professional practices of information architecture are being developed by a cohesive group of committed individuals. Its core practices of analyzing, designing, and building information structures are not only central to the present and future needs and concerns of the information sciences as a whole, but also central to the needs and concerns of society in an information economy."

*Keith Belton*

## CHAPTER 21

# IA
# Educating Information Architects

"The educational structure supporting such an activity [a design-oriented approach to information architecture] would not only include the general problem-solving skills provided for by a design education, but also the specific development of design skills for information architecture. The challenge is to develop interdisciplinary languages and skills for design practice while also developing the methods and skills appropriate to information architecture."

Keith Belton

## DEMAND FOR A NEW INFORMATION PROFESSIONAL

"Information architecture is headed straight toward the heart of business strategy and competitive advantage" (Morville, 2000). The needs of a networked economy are driving the demand for a professional who can manage the design, development, and implementation of highly complex information environments that are easy to use yet provide satisfying experiences for users. The primary goal in building such products is generally the commercial success of the business or organization sponsoring the development activity. However, business interactions are not the only type of interaction with sophisticated electronic information environments. Such information environments are also being used increasingly to support work, learning, and recreational activities.

## MEETING A DEMAND

To meet the demands of information-intensive organizations in an information-intensive society, educational institutions are recognizing the need for the preparation of a new breed of multidisciplinary information professional. The demand for this new type of professional is being "facilitated by the emergence and explosion of digital information and electronic networks" (Kent State, 2001). Courses, and in some instances

"[A] Master's in Information Architecture will become to information architects what the MBA is to business managers and administrators. The degree will not be essential to success, nor will it be a guarantee, but it will become an accepted credential, providing a valuable stepping stone on the path to a successful career."

*Peter Morville*

### KEYWORDS

information architecture, education

information architecture, education theory

IA education, Andrew Dillon

IA education, Peter Morville

entire multidisciplinary degree programs, are being developed and organized by universities and colleges within and across a broad range of disciplines: communications, library science, information studies, computer science, and visual design. In most cases these courses and programs are offered by graduate library and information science programs under the rubric of information architecture.

## TRENDS IN IA CURRICULA DEVELOPMENT

Building upon existing core courses currently offered in their programs, library and information science programs are also developing new courses as well as collaborating with other departments in their institutions to satisfy the corporate world's requirements for educating a multidisciplinary information professional.

When evaluating current IA curricula for the purpose of developing their own curriculum, the Graduate School of Library and Information Science at the University of Texas at Austin (GSIS-UTA), examined the core requirements of six prominent universities offering masters level specializations in IA: Drexel, Kent State, San Jose State, Indiana, UC Berkeley, and Michigan. They found that "there are seven visible trends in the core requirements from program to program," and "although each program seems to employ its own nomenclature, most of the classes seek to impart the same knowledge to the student." The seven trends in core courses identified for a specialization in IA fell within the following subject areas:

- Information systems/Management/Organization
- Information searching/Retrieval
- Database management
- Research methodology/Statistics
- Human–computer interaction
- Networking
- Project management/Problem solving
  (Ewing, 2002)

The University of Texas at Austin also examined the elective courses offered among the six universities mentioned above and two universities that did not require core courses: Florida State and the University of Illinois. A number of trends were apparent in the types of courses offered as electives:

- Cognitive psychology/Human behavior
- Software engineering/User interface design/HCI
- Database management
- Programming
- Classification/Indexing/Cataloging
- Networking
- Public policy

> "The educational approach of the School [Harvard School of Design] during this period [1950s and 1960s] was to teach an interdisciplinary general program of design to first-year students in architecture, landscape architecture, and city planning. The goal of this approach was to develop within the student an orientation 'toward the unified field of design that would serve him as a broad and flexible basis for creative work in the context of his own future.' This sense of the creative usefulness of a general design education, augmented by the professional attitude and skills necessary to a particular field, has much to offer information architecture as a field."
>
> *Keith Belton*

- Management/Administration
- Search behavior/User needs
- System analysis

(Ewing, 2002)

## LEARNING OBJECTIVES OF AN IA CURRICULUM

Based upon their research into corporate requirements for IAs and the curricula of the universities mentioned above, the University of Texas School of Library and Information Science developed the following learning objectives:

- Understand and apply theories of information organization and retrieval as they relate to managing electronic resources.
- Have a basic knowledge of a Web programming language and the software design process.
- Design, implement, and analyze data from social research projects.
- Understand and apply the concepts of user-centered design and Web site usability.
- Research, plan, and manage IA projects.
- Be familiar with key aspects of the application of electronic information resources in educational and/or business environments.
- Develop and practice the soft skills of working in a team environment, critical thinking, and problem solving.
- Effectively communicate ideas and concepts (both orally and in writing) on many different levels of understanding, from end users to clients to corporate sponsors.

(Ewing, 2002)

Currently, most information architecture courses and curricula are being offered by library and information science programs (LIS). Many of them acknowledge that the IA process is informed by several disciplines and attempt to structure their programs accordingly. However, quite naturally, their IA curricula emphasize the strengths of their own LIS programs, and the end product is typically an IA specialization wrapped around a LIS core. The descriptions below of existing graduate-level IA curricula, and one proposed curriculum, were taken from the following institutions:

- Illinois Institute of Technology Institute of Design
- Indiana University School of Library and Information Science
- Kent State University School of Library and Information Science
- University of Michigan School of Information
- State University of New York (Buffalo) School of Information Studies
- University of Texas, Austin, Graduate School of Library and Information Studies

"We have state of the art facilities [at the Indiana University School of Library and Information Studies] and a first rate faculty who research as well as teach IA, even if they have always called it computer science, information science, library science, or something else. At Indiana we have worked hard at building a cross-disciplinary program informatics that bridges these disciplines so the we can best teach and study issues fundamental to IA."

*Andrew Dillon*

"The field [of information architecture] is adapting ad hoc methods from various sources, and, although there seem to be relatively rich ways to formalize adaptations of methods and models from other design professions, there has been no systematic exploration or development of how such adaptations might best be implemented."

*Keith Belton*

## INFORMATION ARCHITECTURE DEGREE PROGRAMS AND PROGRAM DESCRIPTIONS

Several IA graduate-level degrees are currently being offered. Among them are

- Master of Design (human-centered product and communication design tracks),
- Master of Science in Information (specialization in human–computer interaction),
- Master of Information Science (specialization in information architecture),
- Master of Interaction Design and Information Architecture,
- Master of Arts in Information and Communication (information architecture track),
- Master of Science in Information Architecture and Knowledge Management (IAKM),
- Master of Science in IAKM (information architecture concentration),
- Master of Science in IAKM (information use concentration), and a
- Master of Science in IAKM (knowledge management concentration).

**Institution:** Illinois Institute of Technology Institute of Design

**Degree:** Master of Design (human-centered product and communication design tracks)

**Description:** "The Master of Design (M. Des.) program is a two-year, 64-credit-hour degree program. It is intended for those who wish to achieve mastery at the highest levels of product design, communication design, or design planning."

"The human-centered product and communication design tracks focus on user-centered methods of designing messages, products, services, systems, environments, and software. Master of Design courses draw upon analytic methods from the social sciences and methods developed at the Institute of Design and other design organizations. The goals are to understand how people comprehend and use the built environment, to evaluate their expressed and unexpressed needs, and to add value to their lives."

**Institution:** Indiana University School of Library and Information Science

**Degree:** Master of Information Science Programs

**Description:** "Our MIS program helps to educate a distinctive and rare kind of professional whose expertise assists them in understanding the human side of information and information technologies and in applying this understanding to practical problems. Our new curriculum has been designed to provide both a sound conceptual foundation for developing leadership-oriented careers and to enable students to develop expertise in one or more specific areas."

"Our goal is to equip information architects with the skills to have a career, not just a job. Thus, we encourage students to think about theories of human behavior and how they apply to interaction design, and we teach them how to test out ideas and use statistics to estimate confidence in their findings. Such skills are essential for information architects and are really only likely to be acquired in an academic setting."

*Andrew Dillon*

One of the areas is information architecture and design. "It is the user-centered approach to Information Science at Indiana University that makes IU and Information Architecture such a good fit. While taking courses from this area, you will investigate information architecture as a social and technological phenomenon, focusing on the ways in which organizations are making use of electronic information networking and the impacts that networking is having on communication activities, productivity, and information seeking behavior."

**Institution:** Indiana University School of Library and Information Science

**Degree:** Master of Science in Interaction Design and Information Architecture

**Description:** "Students pursing this degree will become proficient in specific applications of significant information technologies, well-versed in methods for understanding and structuring human interactions with those technologies, and critically aware of social and cultural implications arising from technological developments." Graduates of the program will be able to

- develop structures of information directly related to specific audiences;
- describe the content and interactive features of computer-mediated communication systems;
- define the organization, navigation, and labeling systems;
- apply the principles of user-centered and iterative design to the development process;
- plan for change and growth over time;
- understand social and cultural effects of information systems and their implementations; and
- develop new media genres.

**Institution:** Kent State University School of Library and Information Science

**Degree:** Master of Science in Information Architecture and Knowledge Management (IAKM)

**Description:** The M.S. in IAKM is administered by the School of Library and Information Science, but communication studies, journalism and mass communication, management and information systems, mathematics and computer science, and visual design departments are all major participants in this program. "With the rapid evolution of the information society, facilitated by the emergence of digital information and electronic networks, there has been tremendous growth in the information-related disciplines. At the same time, there has been a convergence of the activities of these disciplines in electronic information and a need for information professionals who span many fields or who are establishing new roles in information-intensive organizations."

> "If educators are serious about providing educational pathways for IA professionals, the give-and-take of the studio "crit" that gives rise to both the ability to develop and deliver a solution in context, and to the development of the designer, may be an essential part of the educational process."
>
> *Keith Belton*

"Kent State University recognizes this growth within and across disciplines. It is the latter need for trans-disciplinary and multi-disciplinary information professionals that led to the creation of the M.S. in IAKM. . . . This degree program is designed to be nimble and flexible but rigorous: nimble and flexible through the program's continually keeping abreast of current and emerging information skills, technologies and education, yet rigorous so that graduates are equipped to assume important positions in an organization."

"Three concentrations offer flexibility for students to tailor-make a course of study to suit their interests or career objectives. This flexibility is essential to the nature of the program because of the trans-disciplinary character of information; the emerging and evolving roles for informational professionals; and the rapid and dynamic growth of information technologies, products, systems, services and networks." The concentrations are information architecture, information use, and knowledge management.

**Institution:** University of Michigan
**Degree:** Master of Science in Information (specialization in human-computer interaction)
**Description:** The School of Information offers a 48-credit-hour Master of Science in Information. The program introduces students to the foundations of the information disciplines in a new, exciting, and integrated way; offers a variety of advanced courses that prepare students for existing or newly formed specializations; and gives students venues in which to exercise their knowledge in several practical engagements.

"[The School of Information] is seeking a rich variety of multidisciplinary students. In the HCI area this includes students with a computer science background who are interested in building new systems in the networked, socially rich, multimedia world; technically adept social science students interested in understanding and designing information technology for better impact on individuals, organizations, and society; and technologically able humanities students interested in how information age resources can best serve the humanities."

**Institution:** State University of New York (Buffalo) School of Information Studies
**Degree:** Master of Arts in Information and Communication, Information Architecture Track
**Description:** "The Master of Information and Communication will be a 36-credit-hour degree preparing students for entry into knowledge-intensive organizations. The program emphasizes a concern with competencies in communication, team building, critical thinking, organizational culture, and organizational strategy. These will be in addition to, not a substitute for, technical skills. Practical experience will be emphasized along with theory."

"Why study information architecture? [Because]

1. Everyone is now a user of or potential user of IT [information technology].

2. Modern companies are built around IT.

3. [In critical applications of technology] errors are costly.

4. Studying humans interacting with artifacts can inform our theories and models of human capabilities and activities."

*Andrew Dillon*

Required courses include

Survey of Information Science/Services;
Telecommunications Infrastructure, Products, and Services;
Organizational Communication;
Policy and Legal Issues;
Information Architecture and Management; and
Information Design.

**Institution:** University of Texas, Austin, Graduate School of Library and Information Studies
**Degree:** Master of Science in Library and Information Science
**Description** (Proposed curriculum): "One important consideration for an IA curriculum is to realize IA as a process that involves the contributions of many disciplines. An LIS based curriculum in IA will provide an awareness of the practice and study of IA while allowing the specialization in organization and retrieval of information. The LIS IA curriculum will introduce the importance of the multidisciplinary team and provide the necessary skills to successfully practice IA. Students will have an appreciation for research methods and the theoretical underpinnings of IA. They will also gain a practical knowledge of using IA in real world settings."

"Graduates of the IA curriculum will be able to

- Understand and apply theories of information organization and retrieval as they relate to managing electronic information resources.
- Have a basic knowledge of a web programming language and the software design process.
- Design, implement, and analyze data from social science research projects.
- Understand and apply the concepts of user-centered design and Web site usability.
- Research, plan, and manage IA projects.
- [Understand] the key aspects of the application of electronic information resources in educational and/or business environments.
- Develop and practice the soft skills of working in a team environment, critical thinking, and problem solving.
- Effectively communicate ideas and concepts (both verbally and in writing) on many different levels of understanding, from end-users to clients to corporate sponsors."

## THE FUTURE OF IA EDUCATION

It is logical and practical that IA curricula are being built upon the foundations of existing programs. However, like the practice of IA and the IA profession that are still in formative stages, so are IA educational practices and theory. One information science educator, at Florida State University's School of Information Studies, Keith Belton, proposes that IA

"A design studio/laboratory approach to teaching IA would help to situate the discipline among design professionals, would provide models for IA pedagogy, and would also provide a path and model for the professional development of individual practitioners and for the profession as a whole."

*Keith Belton*

should be approached as a design discipline and that a "design-oriented approach to IA adds a new core discipline to Information Science as a whole."

## IA EDUCATION THEORY: A DESIGN APPROACH

"We need an entirely new kind of systems developer called an information architect who has been educated with the traditional studio method of design training and who has a strong base of skills and experience in four areas . . . software engineering, ergonomics, environmental design, and organizational design."

*Andrew Cohill*

"Design does not add value in this economy—design creates value" (Advance for Design, 2002). Many IA practitioners view the IA's primary role as that of "designer and coordinator of a process that leads to the product, deliverable, or structure, as well as the creative tasks of design per se" (Belton, 2001). This is a role very much like architects traditionally play in the built environment. In the interest of "developing coherent approaches to the theory and practice of IA and the professional needs of practitioners" (as opposed to the current ad hoc methods), some educators are proposing that a design approach to IA education would be most beneficial to students, educators, and the profession. In the following chapter, Chapter 22, "IA: Education Theory," Dr. Belton proposes that such an approach would situate IA among the design professions and would be helpful in providing models for IA pedagogy.

# IA
# Education Theory: A Design Foundation for Information Architecture

by Keith Belton

## ABSTRACT

Information architecture is currently emerging as a discipline that concerns itself with the development of systematic approaches to the organization and presentation of online information. It has emerged rapidly as a developing professional practice—more rapidly than university curricula have been able, for the most part, to develop coherent approaches to the theory and practice of IA and to the professional needs of practitioners. An "architecture" analogy is appropriate for information architecture since it provides methods and models for education and professional development.

## INTRODUCTION

Information architecture is currently emerging as a discipline that concerns itself with the development of systematic approaches to the organization and presentation of online information. It has emerged rapidly as a developing professional practice—more rapidly than university curricula have been able, for the most part, to develop coherent approaches to the theory and practice of IA and to the professional needs of practitioners. The field is adapting ad hoc methods from various sources, and there seem to be relatively rich ways to formalize adaptations of methods and models from other design professions. A design studio approach to teaching IA would help to situate the discipline among the design professions, would provide models for IA pedagogy, and would also provide a path and model both for the professional development of individual practitioners and for the profession as a whole.

**KEYWORDS**

Christompher Alexander, design
Ken Friedman, design
Norman Newton, design
Peter Rowe, design
Herbert Simon, design

In defining the field as information architecture, there are probably productive analogies to other professions that are being ignored—*information engineering,* or *information therapy,* for example. Although it may be too soon to eliminate the possibilities that other professional analogies might present to the profession, the fit of *architecture* among the various possible professional analogies seems to have a lot of resonance among its practitioners.[1] The architecture analogy may be very appropriate: areas that could be developed include the architect's role as the designer and coordinator of a process that leads to the product, deliverable, or structure, as well as the creative tasks of design per se. Design and planning education have developed explicit methods for design and implementation processes, as well as pedagogical methods for professional role development, such as manager, designer, evaluator, mediator, advocate, teacher, facilitator, and technical expert. The orientation in design training and education emphasizes studio/lab/project learning, critiques of works-in-progress, and theory, which provide a useful model for educators in information architecture. This chapter outlines the history of design pedagogy from the perspective of the Harvard School of Design (1955–1975) and posits its appropriateness for the development of pedagogical methods and models for information architecture. The chapter concludes by noting where the processes and methods of traditional design disciplines may be most appropriate to information architecture, and where they may be less so, and outlines a possible undergraduate curriculum for IA based on areas of convergence.

## BUT IS IT ARCHITECTURE?

In what sense is information architecture *architecture?* Is it related to the profession of architecture by metaphor and analogy, or is there some basis for seeing IA and "A" as components of some broader domain of theory and practice? Wordnet[2] gives four senses for *architecture*:

1. *architecture*—(an architectural product or work)
2. *architecture*—(the discipline dealing with the principles of design and construction and ornamentation of fine buildings; "*architecture and eloquence are mixed arts whose end is sometimes beauty and sometimes use*"
3. *architecture*—(the profession of designing buildings and environments with consideration for their esthetic effect)
4. structure, *architecture*—(the manner of construction of something and the disposition of its parts; "*artists must study the structure of the human body*"; "*the architecture of a computer's system software*")

Current usage of the term *architecture* in computer and information science is limited to the fourth sense above related to structure.[3] The current usage of the term IA seems broader than simply an adaptation of a generic meaning of structure and relations; it also connotes the traditional professional usages referring to the architectural design process and the architect/designer as a person. If we accept the word *architecture* in IA as an accurate descriptor rather than a metaphor, what implications does that have for the theory, practice, and professional development of IA?

## A DESIGN APPROACH TO IA

Norman Newton, who presented the approach of the Harvard School of Design in his *An Approach to Design,* notes that architecture is a process, not an instance or manifestation of its results (1951, 75). For those familiar with the design approach of the School in the 1950s and 1960s, it might be fair to modify the third sense of *architecture* given above to state "the *process* of designing buildings and environments with consideration for their esthetic effect." The educational approach of the school during this period was to teach an interdisciplinary general program of design to first-year students in architecture, landscape architecture, and city planning. The goal of this approach was to develop within the student an orientation "toward the *unified field* of design that would serve him as a broad and soundly flexible basis for creative work in the context of his own future" (Newton 1951, vii). This sense of the creative usefulness of a general design education, augmented by the professional attitude and skills necessary to a particular field, has much to offer information architecture as a field.

Although this integrated interdisciplinary approach has since been discontinued at Harvard, it has had tremendous influence in design education in the United States. These early attempts to formalize a general approach to design seem rather soft when compared with today's more procedural methods, perhaps the best known of which in this context is Christopher Alexander's work.[4] However, the approach developed by the school pre-sages current thinking about the need for universal approaches to design education. Proponents of the emerging field of design research make persuasive arguments for a general design education even at the doctoral level (Durling and Friedman, 2000). Friedman (2000, 12) also presents a conceptual model for aligning design professions dealing with the "material" with those concerned with the "immaterial" as a necessary component of design in a knowledge economy.

The method that the Harvard School of Design promulgated in the 1950s and 1960s consisted of a three-phased approach to design:

1. *Programming,* "a phase of recognizing and delimiting the basic problem in terms of human need, and of deciding in a general way what sort of action or provision is most likely to effect a solution."
2. *Analysis,* "in which the designer analyzes carefully the relationships among the various activities involved in the problem and, by means of

a persona, visual, imaginative synthesis, evolves the specific structure—the specific form and arrangement—of the concrete physical solution that will accommodate that complex of activities."

3. *Representation and implementation,* "in order that this creature of his imagination may be brought to full actuality, the designer prepares working drawings and other contract documents and furnishes supervision, all as directives to the men whose combined efforts will result in construction of the finished product, the work of design" (Newton 1951, 5–6).

These three phases themselves were broken down into various component processes. The emphasis of most design education and of most designers has been on the "creative" middle phase. Over time, all aspects of this process have been subject to more rigorous procedural development in the design professions, but one may still recognize these basic processes in most of them.[5] This process is also implicit in the more design-oriented of the commercial information architecture firms, such as Sapient's 'Discover—Define—Concept—Design—Implement' process (Svec, 2000). It may be worth quoting from Newton's instructions to beginning designers for the middle phase to see how relevant this approach may be for information architects today:

> As a procedure, therefore, I suggest that you try, as the first step in the middle creative phase of your designing, to draw a *structural diagram* (some prefer to call it a relational diagram or a functional analysis) of the *activities* to be provided for in the solution of your problem. The aim of such a diagram is to enable you to visualize and to relate to each other the kinds or phases of activity, to come to a tentative conclusion as to which of these are in their nature closely connected (as, say, cooking and eating), which ones less closely (as, say, playing ball and sleeping), and so on toward the establishment of a workable *structure*—an optimal set of relations and order—of the various *activities* concerned). (Newton 1951, 138–9)

Newton also advises against prematurely forming a structure before all the analytic and synthetic processes are complete:

> In setting up this structural diagram of activities . . . you will avoid as completely as possible any premature visualization of the specific spatial form or forms in which the activities are to go on . . . [Newton then goes on to give specific recommendations for the kinds of symbols to be used].
>
> All of these factors, and any others appropriate to the individual case, will help you to visualize the entire complex of activities as something occupying roughly determinable plastic spaces related to each other in many dimensions. But keep your attention continually on the *activities,* seeing them occur freely in space without physical restriction, and hold off as long as you can your finally visualized realization of specific form.

> From this point on there are no doubt many sound ways of going forward with the problem of creating the spatial complex that your analysis has indicated as desirable. You will surely need to ask yourself early how the spaces thus far determined can be built with construction methods and materials available to you—or capable of invention—and how these would best be used to accomplish their space-forming purpose with sensible economy of means. . . . Little by little, swiftly or slowly, depending on how fast the light of your vision enables you to go, you will be bringing into form a tentative graphic statement in plans, elevations, and sections—and you will be well under way in the creative middle phase of the process of design. (Newton 1979, 131–3)

This design approach for developing relationships of functions, activities, and structure in spatial design maps very well as an overview of the information architecture process as well. That it maps so well supports Newton's (and later Friedman's) arguments about the value of a general design education for the design professions.

The Harvard School's early formalization of the design process may be viewed as an expression of what Friedman (1997) sees as the transition from design as "craft" to design as a "knowledge profession" comprising "a knowledge-intensive process that involves selecting goals, then developing and executing strategies to meet those goals." This is also part of the process that Herbert Simon (1981, 112) presents as the transformation, in order to gain academic respectability, of "the intellectually soft, intuitive, informal, and cook-booky" approach to design into "subject matter that is intellectually tough, analytic, formalizable, and teachable."

Rowe (1987, 46–50) describes this transition in focus and methods as one from a "behaviorist" method that saw design in terms of a series of overt stages of the activities of "analysis, synthesis, evaluation, and so on," to an "information processing model" that sees the design process as a frame for problem-solving behavior with "three subclasses of activity:"

1. The "problem representation problem";
2. The "solution generation problem"; and
3. The "solution evaluation problem."

These lead to a view of design as "problem-space planning" wherein the types of decision making that are appropriate to particular design problems become the subject of design. This information processing is shown in the early work of Alexander where the design approach is an algorithmic one based on decision trees.[6] The reaction to the more deterministic and procedural of these information processing models, which seemed to diminish the role of the traditional, intuitive, creative part of the design process, led to the perception "that design, like other disciplines, involves a kind of procedural knowledge—that is, both tactical understanding and know-how—and a kind of substantive knowledge outside the procedures themselves" (Rowe, 1987, 112). Taken as a whole, the evolution of design theory and design education provides useful hints and explicit pedagogical models for the development of information architecture educational practice.

## AN EDUCATIONAL ARCHITECTURE

This tension between the procedural aspects of design and the knowledge of the creative substance of design outside those procedures has affected, I would argue, the development of pedagogy in the design professions. Most design education has its share of traditional classroom lecture-style learning where one gets to know the nuts and bolts of history, construction materials, theory, and so on. But there is also the studio environment where the budding design professional develops her own "substantive knowledge" of a way of working that is necessarily a personal synthesis and application of all the other components. This is the crux of professional development where theory, content, and procedure are integrated in a continual refinement of both a product (as an instance) and a personal synthesis of the design process. This results, ideally, not only in the designer's ability to approach a given design context in a creative and productive manner, but also in the realization that each design "episode" may call for variations in technique and method in the process itself. As Rowe (1987, 34–35) observes, "We might say that the organizing principles involved in each episode take on a life of their own, as the designer becomes absorbed in the possibilities that they promise. Here a 'dialogue' between the designer and the situation is evident."

To enable this dialogue for future design professionals in IA, it may be helpful for IA education to model the studio orientation of the other design professions. If educators are serious about providing educational pathways for IA professionals, the give-and-take of the studio "crit" that gives rise to both the ability to develop and deliver a solution in context, and to the development of the designer, may be an essential part of the educational process. This ability to integrate the performative, "problem-solving, know-how," and what Peter Rowe (1996, 243) calls the "tectonic imagination" into an ideal "design thinking" should be the goal of a professional design education. According to Rowe, "Moreover, this thinking is probably epistemologically unique, and therefore warrants continued institutional recognition and support" (1996, 243).

In this respect, the emerging profession of IA may be (oxymoronically) a new archetype for the professional information scientist, since many practicing information architects are already at the point Marcia Bates (1999, 1045) describes as an essential transformation for an information professional:

> Most people outside our field do not realize that there is a content to the study of form and organization. . . .

> People who come into this field, whether formally educated in it or
> who drift in through a job, sooner or later go through a transformation,
> wherein they shift their primary focus of attention from the information
> content to the information form, organization, and structure.

This focusing of attention on the "form, organization, and structure" of
information is what information architects do. As an emerging subdisci-
pline of information science, one educational goal of information architecture should be to emphasize and reinforce this focus on form and
structure as a core component of the field.

Herbert Simon lamented (113) the "loss of design" in professional
curricula that occurred when the professions were striving for more academic legitimacy by transforming trade schools to schools of applied science. He noted that "the older kind of professional school did not know
how to educate for professional design at an intellectual level appropriate to a university; the newer kind of school nearly abdicated responsibility for training in the core professional skill."

The development of a design-oriented approach to information architecture adds a new core discipline to information science as a whole—
one that would explicitly fill the need for Bates' idea of "a content to the
study of form and organization" of information. Information science as
a field has tended to take a passive approach to information structure,
studying information form and structure as given or as developed in
other fields. As the knowledge economy expands, a more active approach is needed. Information architecture as a design profession would
radically expand Bates' notion by not only studying the form and organization of information as it already exists, but also by further developing
principles of information architecture and design for the proactive structuring of information. The educational structure supporting such activity would include not only the general problem-solving skills provided by
a design education, but also the specific development of design skills for
information architecture. The challenge is to develop interdisciplinary
languages and skills for design practice while also developing the methods and skills specifically appropriate to information architecture. As
Rowe (1996, II 245) notes:

> Undoubtedly there will always be a certain artificial compartmentaliza-
> tion of design knowledge and understanding for effective didactic pur-
> poses. There are, however, pressing needs in educational circles for
> decent role models and for case studies of good practice. There is also
> a need for reasonable amounts of integration and inclusiveness, with-
> out inundating design studios with constraints and responsibilities that
> cannot possibly be addressed. The choice of subject matter is certainly
> important and should reflect important facets of the surrounding social
> and technical context. Nevertheless, design is a way of thinking about
> and of knowing the world, and it has its own considerations and prac-
> tices that require mastery.

In addition to mastering design practices in general and skills appropriate to one's field, another principle of professional activity is that it exists for the overall public good. Newton (1979, 91) describes: "the common goal" of the design professions is to study "*people in their environments,* and . . . we evaluate our work in terms of its positive contribution to the longer, healthier, happier survival of humans." Although the fields of human computer interaction and usability design share this orientation, the development of a professional structure and ethical basis for research, design, and implementation is still in its infancy.

## DEVELOPMENT OF AN EMERGING PROFESSION

> [P]rofessions are occupations with special power and prestige. Society grants these rewards because professions have special competence in esoteric bodies of knowledge linked to central needs and values of the social system, and because professions are devoted to the service of the public, above and beyond material incentives (Larson, 1977).

According to a recent survey (ACIA, 2001a), 51 percent of respondents to a survey of those who call themselves information architects "seek certification or some other type of professional recognition." In a separate survey (ACIA, 2001b), 228 respondents who identified themselves as information architects had no less than 116 distinct job titles. In yet another survey (ACIA 2000), respondents indicated that while 37 percent currently have no formal educational credentials in IA, the respondents expect this number to drop to 10 percent by 2005, with 47 percent expecting that the increase in formal credentials will come from graduate courses in IA or related fields. Dodging for the moment the question of whether the educational system is prepared to meet these expectations, it seems apparent that there does exist a more-or-less self-organizing professional movement in IA. Reciprocal to the need in the field of information science for active designers and architects for information structures, there is a need for professional recognition and social recognition of the importance of this activity in the emerging knowledge economy for its practitioners. At the nexus of these two reciprocal needs is the social value of giving incentives to a profession to make the kinds of positive contributions to the social fabric that have historically been expected of professional activity.

The recent evolution of information architecture seems to have more parallels to guild formation than to the formation of a profession:

> The craft guilds, which were organized everywhere by the thirteenth century, were . . . devices for establishing social credit in a phase of rapid development of small commodity production. . . . The assem-

bling of producers along craft lines was encouraged by the public authorities as a means of regulating the new urban markets. (Larson,
1977, 15)

To participants of the ASIS-sponsored listserv on information architecture, the craft-supporting nature of the self-organization of information
architects is apparent—much of the list discussion is about technique,
relations with others in production, process standards, and markets.
There is also a good deal of discussion about the need for more formal
training for and recognition of IA skills.[7] These kinds of discussion, together with the needs expressed in the surveys discussed above, reinforce the perspective that IA is an emerging profession that may benefit
from the "social credit" and recognition that formalizing the educational process may provide. Such a process would also provide a mechanism for social input regarding what the social expectations for such a
profession would be.

If information architecture as a profession develops along the lines
of other traditional professions, one would expect education to support
what Larson describes as three "dimensions" of professional attributes—
the cognitive, the normative, and the evaluative:

> The cognitive dimension is centered on the body of knowledge and
> techniques which the professionals apply in their work, and on the
> training necessary to master such knowledge and skills; the normative
> dimension covers the service orientation of professionals and their dis-
> tinctive ethics, which justify the privilege of self-regulation granted
> them by society; the evaluative dimension implicitly compares profes-
> sions to other occupations, underscoring the professions' singular char-
> acteristics of autonomy and prestige. . . .
>
> These communities are concretely identified by typical organiza-
> tions and institutional patterns: professional associations, professional
> schools, and self-administered codes of ethics. (Larson, 1977, x)

These three dimensions correspond closely with architect Peter Rowe's
description of the threefold relationship of a design school to professional practice:

> First, there is the direct education of would-be professionals. Second,
> there is a critical appraisal and reappraisal of architecture, including
> the circumstances and agents that brought it into being, as well as its
> practices. Third, there is public education about architecture, how it is
> produced and what might be expected of it. (Rowe, 1996, 242)

Rowe cautions against thinking "the educational mission of most architecture schools and the well-rounded development of practicing professionals" to be "fully coincidental or isomorphic." "As much as anything,"
Rowe continues, "this education concerns a way of thinking about the
world and about architecture in an intellectual as well as a practical
sense" (Rowe, 1996, 242).

## CONCLUSION

As educators and professional designers, we are already, as Phil Agre notes, "latecomers to the scene of the accident. The real design has been done by poets, and intellectuals, and propagandists. . . . The designer becomes a representative for all of the people whose attentions are still elsewhere, who don't know the stakes in a design process whose results will become irreversible by the time they ever hear about it." Information architecture already is a vibrant field of practice. Some of its practitioners might take umbrage at being included in the realm of "poets, and intellectuals, and propagandists," but I think more would identify with the edgy, countercultural aspects of their design practice. As a discipline it finds itself in a mediating space between the artistic aspects of design practice as cultural production and the economic field of production of most of their clients and employers. The professional practices of information architecture are being developed by a cohesive group of committed individuals. Its core practices of analyzing, designing, and building information structures are not only central to the present and future needs and concerns of the information sciences as a whole, but also central to the needs and concerns of society in an information economy.

Newton's (1979, ii) goal "of design as an integral part of modern life and as an approach to positive creative action" can be seen as a manifesto for the professionalization of information architecture, which would be enabled through the development of a design-oriented profession and accompanying professional standards, educational practices, and professional mission and ethics. The professional goals of information architects are parallel to those that Rowe (1996, 243) posits for architecture: to "have the understanding and the wherewithal to deal effectively with the institutional setting in which their professional actions take place," and above all to "get the job done properly, responsibly, and beautifully."

---

[1]These thoughts were initiated by Lou Rosenfeld's (somewhat tongue-in-cheek) comments at the ASIS IA session on the possibilities that might be afforded by looking at ourselves as "Information Therapists" in addition to Information Architects.

[2](http://www.cogsci.princeton.edu/cgi-bin/webwn/?stage=1&word=architecture)

[3]The ACM thesaurus has many uses of architecture: Modeling of computer architecture; system architectures; processor architectures; network architecture and design; software architectures; hyptertext/hypermedia architectures; hardware architectures. The ASIS thesaurus refers only to architecture as a profession and computer architecture. ACM Classification system: (http://www.acm.org/class/1998/ccs98.html; ASIS Thesaurus http://www.asis.org/Publications/Theszyrus/tnhome.htm

[4]Alexander wrote his *Notes on the Synthesis of Form* while at the school. His later work, *A Pattern Language* was written partly as a rethinking of what he came to see as an overly algorithmic approach to design.

[5]See Rowe (1987) for an excellent discussion of this evolution.

[6]Alexander, *Notes on the Synthesis of Form.* The sigia-l archives can be found at http://www.listquest.com/lq/search.html?ln=sigia.

[7]The sigia-l archives can be found at http://www.listquest.com/lq/search. html?ln=sigia.

# Information Architects
## Envisioning the Future of IA

In the next decade, as the use of new technologies extends deeper into everyday life, the workplace, schools, and homes will be fertile grounds for experimentation and the development of new concepts of information and communication systems. Hundreds of information architects are leading the way in this experimentation. From these experiments will evolve new models for creating and disseminating information that will help guide the practice of information architecture, promote the emerging IA profession, and benefit the public in general.

## TECHNOLOGY, SOCIETY, AND THE FUTURE

Forecasting the future of new technologies, or the benefits (and ills) of new technologies, is risky business. More often than not, these types of predictions about the future are overly optimistic: domestic robots in every home, a flying car in every garage, and permanent colonies under the sea and on the moon by the end of the year 2000. There are also notable instances where visions of the future were realized well before anticipated. For example, in 1901 Wilbur Wright estimated that it would be another 50 years before mechanized flight was possible. Beating his own prediction by 48 years, he and his brother Orville took to the skies from Kitty Hawk in their flying machine. Another example is an entire industry, the computer industry. The history of computing is punctuated by gross underestimations such as IBM's boast that the world market for personal computers in the 1980s would rise to 300,000. The actual number turned out to be closer to 60 million. What IBM could not anticipate over that decade were the rapid improvements in computing technology, the resulting steady decline in the cost of faster and more powerful personal computers, and the development of a broad range of software applications that would make computers easier to use and more useful both at home and work.

Unanticipated technological breakthroughs will more than likely continue to make predicting the future of information and communi-

> "In the past, people have outlived and outwitted monumental media transformations, and we'll survive this [information age] chaos too. There are no quick answers, though, because the future is wrapped in the design process, only to be unveiled by teams of people from multiple disciplines, all asking What is valuable? What is usable? What is better?"
> *Clement Mok*

**KEYWORDS**

information architecture, future

information architecture, pioneers

information technology, influences

information technology, unintended consequences

cation technologies, and the resulting social influences, difficult. For instance, as recently as November 2001, Bell Labs scientists announced the development of a transistor from a single molecule. First invented by Bell Labs in 1947, early transistors were an inch or more long. Since that time, continuous improvements in transistor design have led to the development of tiny microprocessors each with millions of transistors called *chips*. This most recent breakthrough in transistor technology miniaturization will make possible the placement of about 10 million transistors on an area the size of a pinhead. Equally important as miniaturization, as far as implications for the future of computing technology is concerned, is the simpler and less-expensive process by which these new transistors were made. Historically this has resulted in cheaper computers and that, in turn, fueled their diffusion and fusion into the everyday things in our lives.

## TECHNOLOGICAL INNOVATION CAN HAVE UNINTENDED CONSEQUENCES

Many, if not most, technological innovations have had unforeseen and unintended consequences on the way we live and can contribute to:

- changes in the location of human activities,
- changes in the character of activities, and
- changes in the way such activities are organized.

The telephone affected such changes early in the 20th century. It has even been said that Alexander Graham Bell was the father of the skyscraper. The implication is that, without telephones, it was difficult for architects to imagine how internal and external communication systems would work in tall buildings. Sending messengers running up and down scores of flights of stairs was not a practical solution. Acutally there were other technological innovations that transformed architecture in the mid-1800s: girders made of strong but light metals; reinforced concrete; plate glass; advances in elevator and escalator engineering; and the development of new techniques for distributing power, water, and light. These innovations were not driven by the desires of architects to build skyscrapers. Seeing how these new technologies changed what was architecturally possible, architects made optimal use of them—changing the skylines of cities around the world dramatically.

It is the same today with new information and communication technologies. During the Cold War, the Department of Defense set out to develop an intergovernmental computer network that was capable of surviving a nuclear attack: ARPAnet. In the course of its development, designers saw the potential for a new type of global communications system: the Internet. Seeing the potential in the Internet for improving communication and resource sharing among fellow CERN researchers around

"Thomas Edison invented his phonograph as a machine for dictating letters, teaching speech, and archiving voices of famous people. Initially, he resisted the idea of using the phonograph for reproducing music."

*The Star Tribune,* 1996

In the next decade, as the use of new technologies extends deeper into everyday life, the workplace, schools, and homes will be fertile grounds for experimentation and the development of new concepts of information and communication systems. Hundreds of information architects are leading the way in this experimentation. From these experiments will evolve new models for creating and disseminating information that will help guide the creative endeavors of information designers, promote the emerging profession of information architecture, and benefit the public in general.

the world, Tim Berners-Lee developed the first Internet browser application that he named the World Wide Web. More sophisticated commercial browsers such as Netscape's Navigator and Microsoft's Internet Explorer soon followed.

With access and navigation simplified and improved, Internet use and the Internet infrastructure grew at an unanticipated rate. However, even as late as 1994 no one imagined the explosive growth that was yet to come. In 1997 19 million Americans were using the Internet. Within one year that number would triple. In the first quarter of 2000, Americans were getting online at the rate of 55,000 new users per day, 2,289 per hour, 38 per minute. Such widespread acceptance of this networked technology increased its potential to "provide more communication power, purchasing power, and knowledge-gathering outreach than print and electronic media combined" (UCLA, 2000). Time and time again, because of unanticipated technological advances and complex social forces, new technologies have had unexpected and unintended influences on the way we live.

## SOCIALIZING NEW TECHNOLOGIES

History tells us that new technologies can influence societies culturally, politically, even physically. We have also learned from history that the integration and acceptance of new technologies and systems into everyday life—socialization—usually comes after numerous cycles of failure followed by improvement. This trial-and-error process is slow. It is safe to assume that the maximum human utilization of new information and communication technologies by such a process will always lag behind the rapid pace of technological innovation. However, the socialization of new information and communication technologies can be nurtured and expedited by developing an orienting vision or conceptual framework of how best to realize their greatest human potential.

## HUMAN FACTORS

In fact, an entire discipline arose in the middle of the 20th century that is concerned with the relationship between humans and technology. It is called *human factors*. Human factors is also known as *engineering psychology*, and it attempts to apply knowledge of human behavior and physical attributes to the design of products, equipment, machines, and large-scale systems for the purpose of optimizing human use. Some of the earliest human factors' work began with worker productivity studies conducted by the American Telegraph and Telephone Company (AT&T) in the 1920s and 30s. Other early human factors' concerns addressed by AT&T were the quality and intelligibility of transmitted speech. Improvements in the design of the telephone based on the static and dynamic measurements of the human body were among the success stories of user-centered design activities conducted by AT&T. Human factors' work in the telecommunication's industry soon expanded into many other areas of private industry. Not surprisingly, the human operation of computers became a natural extension of human factors' concerns, quickly developing into a specialization of human factors known as human–computer interaction (HCI).

## HUMAN–COMPUTER INTERACTION (HCI)

The field of HCI is concerned with the consideration of both the physical and psychological requirements of humans when designing computer systems and programs. The overarching goal of HCI is to make products that are practical, efficient, and easy to use. Traditional HCI practice, focused primarily on helping users translate their goals into actions and used design, research, and evaluation techniques and guidelines that resulted in great improvements in the usability of early personal computing technologies. Some notable examples of the successful application of such methods include the mouse, the graphical user interface, and the application of hypertext technology to browser applications that contributed to the explosive growth of the World Wide Web (Meyers, 1998).

Now, the design of Web sites, virtual environments, and distributed computing environments is presenting new usability challenges. Traditional HCI views the computer as an information processing tool (hardware) and situates the user outside of the computer. New information and communication technologies offer users much more freedom. They allow users to "move" to wherever they want in a computer-mediated context that contains a variety of content, including documents, media, and many soft tools for conducting everyday "real-world" activities. This change is leading designers to develop new design theories that situate users within computer-mediated information spaces and that are concerned with issues of how humans navigate in these new environments. Out of these concerns another specialized extension of the human factors field is developing. It is focused on communicating information, facilitating the storage and retrieval of data, processing data into information, structuring information, and navigating information structures. This new specialization is called *information architecture*. Like HCI, IA is also concerned with optimizing the user's experience with technology.

## IA PIONEERS AND VISIONARIES

Like human factors pioneers and visionaries of the past, IAs are working hard to articulate a conceptual framework for IA and to define research, design, and evaluation techniques that will guide both the practice of IA and the profession into the future. Information architects come from

"[*The Social Life of Information*] suggests that the really significant technologies driving large-scale social and economic change today may not be those created to assist individuals but may instead be the tools for organizational learning, creativity, and remembering. The information age is represented for most of us by consumer products like the cell phone and Palm Pilot, but perhaps it is corporate databases, project management and collaboration software and data mining tools and search engines that will be the real levers that move the world."

*Alex Soojung-Kim Pang*

"Here are some areas that I think information architects can and should take on. Some are orphans that may have gone unnoticed and therefore unowned. Some are simply not well understood by most people working on web sites today, including most IAs. Each of these areas presents us with difficult and interesting challenges that will increasingly demand our attention over time. And they fit squarely within the scope of information architecture: distinguishing users' information needs, determining content granularity, developing hybrid architectures, presenting search results better, understanding, using metadata, and rolling out enterprise-wide architectures."

*Louis Rosenfeld*

many fields, and among them are researchers, educators, and practitioners. The following statements are examples of their respective visions of IA and are quoted from interviews, conference proceedings, articles, and presentations published on the Web. They were selected as representative examples of an ongoing dialogue in the IA community and do not necessarily represent each author's current or complete views of IA. They are listed in alphabetical order.

## ANDREW DILLON

Andrew Dillon has been an active researcher of the human response to information technology for the last 15 years, starting as a Research Fellow at the Human Sciences and Advanced Technology (HUSAT) Research Institute in the United Kingdom before joining Indiana University in 1994 where he worked as an associate professor of information science and informatics and as core faculty in cognitive science until 2001. At Indiana he developed and served as director of the masters program in human–computer interaction and held adjunct positions in computer science and instructional systems technology. He joined the University of Texas at Austin in January 2002 as dean and professor in the graduate program of the School of Library and Information Science. "He is focused on user-centered design methods, usability evaluation, aesthetics and design, educational technology, information architecture, user acceptance theory, and socio-cognitive analyses of use and adoption" (IT@UT, 2002). Dillon was educated as a psychologist at University College Cork (1980–1986, B.A., M.A.) and Loughborough University of Technology (1986–1991, Ph.D.).

He made the following comments to the attendees of an information architecture summit sponsored by the American Society of Information Science and Technology (ASIST) in February 2001.

"I believe we need information architecture, because with the best of intentions in any design, it's so hard to remember what it takes for humans to use anything. If you fail to support human use, the architecture is irrelevant. Information technology is useless without people to operate it. A computer without a user somewhere is just bits of plastic and metal. The value it provides comes from its engagement with real live, flesh and blood human beings, and that's why I think we need information architects because without them, important considerations of users just get left out and the resulting designs, wonderful as they may be as feats of engineering, make life a little more difficult for humans."

He adds, "The major point I want to make today is that to design useful, usable, and socially acceptable technology is beyond the capabilities of any one field and beyond any one of us." He also went on to suggest that, ". . . IA takes and borrows from multiple disciplines and perhaps, in coming into existence, it provides a means for all of us to communicate across those boundaries."

# ALISON J. HEAD

Alison J. Head is the author of *Design Wise: A Guide for Evaluating the Interface Design of Information Resources.* She is principal of Alison J. Head & Associates, a consulting firm in Sonoma, California, specializing in interface design audits and usability testing. Dr. Head has a Ph.D. in library and information science from the University of California at Berkeley and studied human–computer interaction as a visiting scholar at Stanford University.

On November 10, 2001, Head spoke as a guest lecturer to Florida State University faculty and students. Her lecture, "Information Specialists at the Intersection of Information Architecture and Usability," focused on how and why the fields of usability and IA overlap, and in doing so, articulated her vision of the future of IA and usability. After a brief history of the origins of IA and the ongoing struggle to define IA, she stated, "At the heart of the matter, IAs and usability experts, especially those who work on information resources, have three concerns that bind them together. They are:

- A focus on users.
- Ease of use.
- Appropriate, accessible content" (Head, 2002).

She also pointed out, "Increasingly, in many settings, IAs and usability experts work closely together as the fields are viewed holistically, or as integrated parts in a larger system," and, "At many large corporations and organizations, strategies for Web development projects have demanded a holistic approach as a recipe for producing successful sites. This outcome is what many involved with Web development call user experience. IA and usability are essential nutrients to cultivating the user experience along with marketing, design, and engineering." She added, "In order to achieve high-quality user experience in a company's offerings, there must be a seamless merging of the services of multiple disciplines, including engineering, marketing, graphical and industrial design, and interface design." Noting that the " 'experience' 'economy' is well upon us [shifting from a services economy]," she explained that it's no longer good enough for companies to provide potential customers with goods and services, [and] that they must also "experientialize" products by making them memorable.

Looking beyond the experience economy, she talked about a coming "transformation" economy ("which occurs when products and services are delivered that literally alter or transform customer's lives"). She closed her lecture by suggesting that "usability and IA are, in many ways [already], transformation businesses" and that usability experts and IAs work "to see that a transformation [can] actually occur when a user interacts with an information system." In her final statement she claimed that, "In the highest regard, the intersection of IA and usability is about

"Information architecture is going to replace the management of assets and development processes as the focus of CIOs. That's because [they're] going to have to respond more to what's happening now, and so [they're] going to be running businesses more and more in project mode. Businesses will be dispatching their capabilities like a taxi company dispatches cars, rather than scheduling them in advance, like a bus company schedules stops. That means [their] organization can reconfigure itself continually on the basis of what kinds of events are happening, what kind of opportunities and threats it faces."

*Stephan H. Haeckel*

"Information architecture is entering a new stage of maturity. IA roles and responsibilities are firming up. The IA community is taking shape. While we insiders argue over the minutia, a de facto definition of information architecture has emerged and reached critical mass. There's no going back."

*Peter Morville*

delivering the promise of transformation, no matter what new medium the information is packaged in" (Head, 2002).

# ARNOLD LUND

Dr. Arnold Lund is the director of information architecture at Sapient, a leading business and technology consultancy. Lund has spent more than 20 years working in human factors, conducting user research and designing for a variety of emerging technologies. He began his career at AT&T Bell Laboratories and later served as the senior director of Human Factors and Emerging Technologies at Ameritech. Before joining Sapient, he was director of New Media Design and Usability at Qwest Advanced Technologies. In January 2002, he was named a fellow by the Human Factors and Ergonomics Society. Lund received his Ph.D. in experimental psychology, human learning and memory, in 1980 from Northwestern University, his M.A. in experimental psychology in 1977 from California State University, Fullerton, and his B.A. in Chemistry in 1972 from the University of Chicago.

Lund contributes the following on future trends in IA:

> One way to think of information architecture is to define it as the underlying organizational structure for a system of content and interactions. This allows IAs to address the design of Web, GUI, broadband, rich media, speech, and other applications. At Sapient, information architects are user experience designers that create plans for how an interactive experience works, defining both the organizational structure and the interactions. The needs of the business and the users are balanced with the capabilities of the technology (as part of a human-centered design process that includes beginning-to-end research and design). Comprehensive systems that include the organization, navigation, and interaction of the final solution are designed. The resulting plans become the foundation that other practices use to create and implement the content; visual, auditory, and rich media; and technology solutions. It is already clear, therefore, that information architects are being called to a broader charter than organizing access to libraries of hyperlinked electronic content for workstations accessing the Web. Information is more than words and numbers, and its organization is not an end in itself but in the service of diverse user and business goals. We are being called to architect experiences, and this trend is likely to continue. The structuring of experience provides the cognitive model that enables people to accomplish their goals easily and effectively, while meeting the design goals of the provider of the application. These goals might be to find a specific piece of information, to accomplish a task (e.g., ordering or making a decision), to communicate, or to have a compelling and entertaining experience. The skills of the information architect are being applied to visual and audio experiences delivered over workstations, mobile devices, interactive broadband devices, and others and to experiences that span these devices. Information archi-

tects will increasingly need to understand and apply a knowledge of the user context and the affordances of the delivery environments to the structure of the interaction and the information.

## LOUIS ROSENFELD

Lou Rosenfeld is an independent information architecture consultant. He is also the co-author of *Information Architecture for the World Wide Web.* Rosenfeld holds a masters in information and library studies and a B.A. in history, both from the University of Michigan.

In a March 2002 presentation at Michigan State University, he claimed that the Web has caused a revolution in information systems design and that several new fields are emerging to address that challenge. He places IA among these fields that include:

- content management,
- customer relationship management,
- experience design,
- information design,
- interaction design,
- knowledge management, and
- user experience.

He thinks that, "These new fields are really about how to think about information systems design and provide a framework and methodology that draw on the established [pre-Web] fields." He elaborates that, "These new fields aren't so different in goals but are more typically different due to the disciplinary and contextual biases of their 'inventors'" and that "ultimately they are trying to do the same thing: figure out how to design ambitious new information systems."

Rosenfeld is a recognized leader and inventor in the field of IA whose "disciplinary and contextual biases" have been shaped by the field of library and information science. In late 90s he defined the practice of IA as "the art and science of organizing and labeling information to improve browsing and searching," and IA products as "the structure of information and components for searching and browsing that information." Later, in 2001, he confided that, "my early view of information architecture shared too much in common with librarianship and information science. . . . Seven or eight years later and much experience later, I find myself in the same boat with many of the other commentators in this issue, grappling with issues of self-identity and disciplinary disconnectedness. Clearly the term "information architecture" is too focused on information and its structure, perhaps to the exclusion of user and contextual issues, even if in practice IA is much more inclusive."

## LILLIAN SVEC

Currently, Lillian Svec is the director of User Experience for Walmart.com, a wholly owned subsidiary of Wal-Mart Stores. She built the IA and user research practices there and now serves as discipline lead and evangelist for IA, user research, and content strategy. At Walmart.com she deals with the challenges of cross-channel integration and contributes to the development of the Walmart.com Web site and an in-store interactive kiosk system.

Svec's commitment to the field of information architecture began in 1993 when she was the first information designer hired at Studio Archetype to work on CD-ROMs and other interactive projects. Working closely with Clement Mok, she pioneered the IA role. In 1995 she was asked to expand this role into a department; this became the Information Architecture (IA) practice. In 1997 she also played a key role in establishing Studio Archetype's User Research practice.

Svec contributes the following on the future of IA:

> The 1990s Internet boom gave rise to the practice of information architecture. Commercial use of the World Wide Web has moved from the explosive phase that glorified stand-alone dot-coms to the building phase where established businesses are increasingly integrating the Internet with other channels to reach their customers. In this phase of development, IAs will be challenged with designing meta-level information architectures that span physical environments, print media, all forms of electronic and interactive media, and human systems. These will provide the infrastructure for seamless customer experience.
>
> In this model of integrated user experience, each channel has its own role to play in contributing to a successful relationship between the corporation and its clientele. For example, e-commerce is only one piece in the puzzle for a successful retailer. To truly service customer needs, businesses (and IAs) need to understand how customers utilize all channels—the web, the store, the sales associate, the catalog, the call center, and the advertising brochure—to accomplish their goals.
>
> This degree of integration is a monumental undertaking. It requires the merging of new platforms (Web, wireless), legacy systems, established channels, human organizational structures, and work practice. In order to make a significant contribution to this effort, IA as a profession needs to continue to evolve and invent:
>
> - Methodologies and practices for managing complexity that draw on its rich multidisciplinary heritage,
> - Process models for collaborative work that more successfully integrate their work with teams of specialists—social scientists and engineers; artists, writers, and designers; business strategists and managers,
> - ROI [Return On Investment] models that can be used to persuade corporations of the value of structured, user-centered approaches to system development,
> - Curricula to educate the next generation of practitioners that synthesize the most important knowledge and principles from each of their parent disciplines.

Most importantly, IAs will need to evangelize. IA offers a compelling vision: a future enabled by information technology, where the user is viewed not simply as a receiver of messages, but as a partner and collaborator in their creation. IAs need to paint that picture vividly so others can see it too.

## KARYN YOUNG

Karyn Young has been developing information architectures for online projects for seven years. Since 1999, Karyn has worked on enterprise information architecture for IBM's Software division e-business transformation team. In the role of team lead, User Experience, Karyn has been developing the process, deliverables, and roles needed to design, develop, and maintain the information architecture and user experience across various sites and portals used for IBM Software's external online presence.

Young contributes the following on the future of IA:

> Within corporations, information architecture (IA) professionals will need to increasingly understand multiple business information systems and not just those systems that may have been developed specifically to address an online presence. Corporations may use different information systems to market, sell, support products, track revenues, [and] communicate with customers, suppliers, and many other internal and external constituents. Each of these systems has an information architecture—whether it is called this or not. Today, most IA professionals are working with online projects and, in essence, an online project is just one information system or space among many within a corporation. The integration and effective communication between multiple, separate systems is critical to enabling an end-to-end customer experience that is easy, pleasant, and provides value to the information, service or product-seeking user.
>
> User goals and seeking behaviors are complex. Figuring out how to make a corporation's information systems support user goal achievement is even more complex. Corporations cannot consistently make customers happy without a solid online user experience and this cannot be achieved with ad hoc, disconnected, incoherent information architectures. More frequently, integrated information architectures will be key to corporate success and profit. While most information architects agree that a focus on user experience and user needs is absolutely critical, the information architects that can design for user needs while leveraging multiple information systems will have an additional advantage in corporate environments.

## CLOSING

As IA is a new field and still in a formative stage, it is probable that information architects will continue to struggle to define IA for many years to come. It is also probable that there will not ever be one conceptual framework to which everyone in the rapidly growing and diverse IA community subscribes. Some visions will undoubtedly attract more followers than others at different points in time. But, more than likely and as happens in other more mature professions, the practice and profession of IA will continue to change and be influenced by multiple leaders and visionaries throughout its history. It will also be influenced by continuous changes in information and communication technologies. Paradoxically, the defining mark of great information architectures may ultimately be that they are invisible to all who use them.

# Appendix A

# As We May Think

## by Vannevar Bush

July 1945

> As director of the Office of Scientific Research and Development, Dr. Vannevar Bush has coordinated the activities of some six thousand leading American scientists in the application of science to warfare. In this significant article he holds up an incentive for scientists when the fighting has ceased. He urges that men of science should then turn to the massive task of making more accessible our bewildering store of knowledge. For years inventions have extended man's physical powers rather than the powers of his mind. Trip hammers that multiply the fists, microscopes that sharpen the eye, and engines of destruction and detection are new results, but not the end results, of modern science. Now, says Dr. Bush, instruments are at hand which, if properly developed, will give man access to and command over the inherited knowledge of the ages. The perfection of these pacific instruments should be the first objective of our scientists as they emerge from their war work. Like Emerson's famous address of 1837 on "The American Scholar," this paper by Dr. Bush calls for a new relationship between thinking man and the sum of our knowledge.
>
> —The Editor, *The Atlantic Monthly*

This has not been a scientist's war; it has been a war in which all have had a part. The competition in the demand of a common cause, have shared greatly and learned much. It has been exhilarating to work in effective partnership. Now, for many, this appears to be approaching an end. What are the scientists to do next?

For the biologists, and particularly for the medical scientists, there can be little indecision, for their war has hardly required them to leave the old paths. Many indeed have been able to carry on their war research in their familiar peacetime laboratories. Their objectives remain much the same.

It is the physicists who have been thrown most violently off stride, who have left academic pursuits for the making of strange destructive gadgets, who have had to devise new methods for their unanticipated assignments.

They have done their part on the devices that made it possible to turn back the enemy, have worked in combined effort with the physicists of our allies. They have felt within themselves the stir of achievement. They have been part of a great team. Now, as peace approaches, one asks where they will find objectives worthy of their best.

# 1

Of what lasting benefit has been man's use of science and of the new instruments which his research brought into existence? First, they have increased his control of his material environment. They have improved his food, his clothing, his shelter; they have increased his security and released him partly from the bondage of bare existence. They have given him increased knowledge of his own biological processes so that he has had a progressive freedom from disease and an increased span of life. They are illuminating the interactions of his physiological and psychological functions, giving the promise of an improved mental health.

Science has provided the swiftest communication between individuals; it has provided a record of ideas and has enabled man to manipulate and to make extracts from that record so that knowledge evolves and endures throughout the life of a race rather than that of an individual.

There is a growing mountain of research. But there is increased evidence that we are being bogged down today as specialization extends. The investigator is staggered by the findings and conclusions of thousands of other workers—conclusions which he cannot find time to grasp, much less to remember, as they appear. Yet specialization becomes increasingly necessary for progress, and the effort to bridge between disciplines is correspondingly superficial.

Professionally our methods of transmitting and reviewing the results of research are generations old and by now are totally inadequate for their purpose. If the aggregate time spent in writing scholarly works and in reading them could be evaluated, the ratio between these amounts of time might well be startling. Those who conscientiously attempt to keep abreast of current thought, even in restricted fields, by close and continuous reading might well shy away from an examination calculated to show how much of the previous month's efforts could be produced on call. Mendel's concept of the laws of genetics was lost to the world for a generation because his publication did not reach the few who were capable of grasping and extending it; and this sort of catastrophe is undoubtedly being repeated all about us, as truly significant attainments become lost in the mass of the inconsequential.

The difficulty seems to be, not so much that we publish unduly in view of the extent and variety of present day interests, but rather that publication has been extended far beyond our present ability to make real use of the record. The summation of human experience is being expanded at a prodigious rate, and the means we use for threading through the consequent maze to the momentarily important item is the same as was used in the days of square-rigged ships.

But there are signs of a change as new and powerful instrumentalities come into use. Photocells capable of seeing things in a physical sense, advanced photography which can record what is seen or even what is not, thermionic tubes capable of controlling potent forces under the guidance of less power than a mosquito uses to vibrate his wings, cathode ray tubes rendering visible an occurrence so brief that by comparison a microsecond is a long time, relay combinations which will carry out involved sequences of movements more reliably than any human operator and thousands of times as fast—there are plenty of mechanical aids with which to effect a transformation in scientific records.

Two centuries ago Leibnitz invented a calculating machine which embodied most of the essential features of recent keyboard devices, but it could not then come into use. The economics of the situation were against it: the labor involved in constructing it, before the days of mass production, exceeded the labor to be saved by its use, since all it could accomplish could be duplicated by sufficient use of pencil and paper. Moreover, it would have been subject to frequent breakdown, so that it could not have been depended upon; for at that time and long after, complexity and unreliability were synonymous.

Babbage, even with remarkably generous support for his time, could not produce his great arithmetical machine. His idea was sound enough, but construction and maintenance costs were then too heavy. Had a pharaoh been given detailed and explicit designs of an automobile, and had he understood them completely, it would have taxed the resources of his kingdom to have fashioned the thousands of parts for a single car, and that car would have broken down on the first trip to Giza.

Machines with interchangeable parts can now be constructed with great economy of effort. In spite of much complexity, they perform reliably. Witness the humble typewriter, or the movie camera, or the automobile. Electrical contacts have ceased to stick when thoroughly understood. Note the automatic telephone exchange, which has hundreds of thousands of such contacts, and yet is reliable. A spider web of metal, sealed in a thin glass container, a wire heated to brilliant glow, in short, the thermionic tube of radio sets, is made by the hundred million, tossed about in packages, plugged into sockets—and it works! Its gossamer parts, the precise location and alignment involved in its construction, would have occupied a master craftsman of the guild for months; now it is built for thirty cents. The world has arrived at an age of cheap complex devices of great reliability; and something is bound to come of it.

## 2

A record if it is to be useful to science, must be continuously extended, it must be stored, and above all it must be consulted. Today we make the record conventionally by writing and photography, followed by printing; but we also record on film, on wax disks, and on magnetic wires. Even if utterly new recording procedures do not appear, these present ones are certainly in the process of modification and extension.

Certainly progress in photography is not going to stop. Faster material and lenses, more automatic cameras, finer-grained sensitive compounds to allow an extension of the minicamera idea, are all imminent. Let us project this trend ahead to a logical, if not inevitable, outcome. The camera hound of the future wears on his forehead a lump a little larger than a walnut. It takes pictures 3 millimeters square, later to be projected or enlarged, which after all involves only a factor of 10 beyond present practice. The lens is of universal focus, down to any distance accommodated by the unaided eye, simply because it is of short focal length. There is a built-in photocell on the walnut such as we now have on at least one camera, which automatically adjusts exposure for a wide range of illumination. There is film in the walnut for a hundred exposures, and the spring for operating its shutter and shifting its film is wound once for all when the film clip is inserted. It produces its result in full color. It may well be stereoscopic, and record with two spaced glass eyes, for striking improvements in stereoscopic technique are just around the corner.

The cord which trips its shutter may reach down a man's sleeve within easy reach of his fingers. A quick squeeze, and the picture is taken. On a pair of ordinary glasses is a square of fine lines near the top of one lens, where it is out of the way of ordinary vision. When an object appears in that square, it is lined up for its picture. As the scientist of the future moves about the laboratory or the field, every time he looks at something worthy of the record, he trips the shutter and in it goes, without even an audible click. Is this all fantastic? The only fantastic thing about it is the idea of making as many pictures as would result from its use.

Will there be dry photography? It is already here in two forms. When Brady made his Civil War pictures, the plate had to be wet at the time of exposure. Now it has to be wet during development instead. In the future perhaps it need not be wetted at all. There have long been films impregnated with diazo dyes which form a picture without development, so that it is already there as soon as the camera has been operated. An exposure to ammonia gas destroys the unexposed dye, and the picture can then be taken out into the light and examined. The process is now slow, but someone may speed it up, and it has no grain difficulties such as now keep photographic researchers busy. Often it would be advantageous to be able to snap the camera and to look at the picture immediately.

Another process now in use is also slow, and more or less clumsy. For fifty years impregnated papers have been used which turn dark at every point where an electrical contact touches them, by reason of the chemical change thus produced in an iodine compound included in the paper. They have been used to make records, for a pointer moving across them can leave a trail behind. If the electrical potential on the pointer is varied as it moves, the line becomes light or dark in accordance with the potential.

This scheme is now used in facsimile transmission. The pointer draws a set of closely spaced lines across the paper one after another. As it moves, its potential is varied in accordance with a varying current received over wires from a distant station, where these variations are produced by a photocell which is similarly scanning a picture. At every instant the darkness of the line being drawn is made equal to the darkness of the point on the picture being observed by the photocell. Thus, when the whole picture has been covered, a replica appears at the receiving end.

A scene itself can be just as well looked over line by line by the photocell in this way as can a photograph of the scene. This whole apparatus constitutes a camera, with the added feature, which can be dispensed with if desired, of making its picture at a distance. It is slow, and the picture is poor in detail. Still, it does give another process of dry photography, in which the picture is finished as soon as it is taken.

It would be a brave man who would predict that such a process will always remain clumsy, slow, and faulty in detail. Television equipment today transmits sixteen reasonably good pictures a second, and it involves only two essential differences from the process described above. For one, the record is made by a moving beam of electrons rather than a moving pointer, for the reason that an electron beam can sweep across the picture very rapidly indeed. The other difference involves merely the use of a screen which glows momentarily when the electrons hit, rather than a chemically treated paper or film which is permanently altered. This speed is necessary in television, for motion pictures rather than stills are the object.

Use chemically treated film in place of the glowing screen, allow the apparatus to transmit one picture only rather than a succession, and a rapid camera for dry photography results. The treated film needs to be far faster in action than present examples, but it probably could be. More serious is the objection that this scheme would involve putting the film inside a vacuum chamber, for electron beams behave normally only in such a rarefied environment. This difficulty could be avoided by allowing the electron beam to play on one side of a partition, and by pressing the film against the other side, if this partition were such as to allow the electrons to go through perpendicular to its surface, and to prevent them from spreading out sideways. Such partitions, in crude form, could certainly be constructed, and they will hardly hold up the general development.

Like dry photography, microphotography still has a long way to go. The basic scheme of reducing the size of the record, and examining it by projection rather than directly, has possibilities too great to be ignored. The combination of optical projection and photographic reduction is already producing some results in microfilm for scholarly purposes, and the potentialities are highly suggestive. Today, with microfilm, reductions by a linear factor of 20 can be employed and still produce full clarity when the material is re-enlarged for examination. The limits are set by the graininess of the film, the excellence of the optical system, and the efficiency of the light sources employed. All of these are rapidly improving.

Assume a linear ratio of 100 for future use. Consider film of the same thickness as paper, although thinner film will certainly be usable. Even under these conditions there would be a total factor of 10,000 between the bulk of the ordinary record on books, and its microfilm replica. The *Encyclopaedia Britannica* could be reduced to the volume of a matchbox. A library of a million volumes could be compressed into one end of a desk. If the human race has produced since the invention of movable type a total record, in the form of magazines, newspapers, books, tracts, advertising blurbs, correspondence, having a volume corresponding to a billion books, the whole affair, assembled and compressed, could be lugged off in a moving van. Mere compression, of course, is not enough; one needs not only to make and store a record but also be able to consult it, and this aspect of the matter comes later. Even the modern great library is not generally consulted; it is nibbled at by a few.

Compression is important, however, when it comes to costs. The material for the microfilm *Britannica* would cost a nickel, and it could be mailed anywhere for a cent. What would it cost to print a million copies? To print a sheet of newspaper, in a large edition, costs a small fraction of a cent. The entire material of the *Britannica* in reduced microfilm form would go on a sheet eight and one-half by eleven inches. Once it is available, with the photographic reproduction methods of the future, duplicates in large quantities could probably be turned out for a cent apiece beyond the cost of materials. The preparation of the original copy? That introduces the next aspect of the subject.

## 3

To make the record, we now push a pencil or tap a typewriter. Then comes the process of digestion and correction, followed by an intricate process of typesetting, printing, and distribution. To consider the first stage of the procedure, will the author of the future cease writing by hand or typewriter and talk directly to the record? He does so indirectly, by talking to a stenographer or a wax cylinder; but the elements are all present if he wishes to have his talk directly produce a typed record. All he needs to do is to take advantage of existing mechanisms and to alter his language.

At a recent World Fair a machine called a Voder was shown. A girl stroked its keys and it emitted recognizable speech. No human vocal chords entered into the procedure at any point; the keys simply combined some electrically produced vibrations and passed these on to a loudspeaker. In the Bell Laboratories there is the converse of this machine, called a Vocoder. The loudspeaker is replaced by a microphone, which picks up sound. Speak to it, and the corresponding keys move. This may be one element of the postulated system.

The other element is found in the stenotype, that somewhat disconcerting device encountered usually at public meetings. A girl strokes its keys languidly and looks about the room and sometimes at the speaker with a disquieting gaze. From it emerges a typed strip which records in a phonetically simplified language a record of what the speaker is supposed to have said. Later this strip is retyped into ordinary language, for in its nascent form it is intelligible only to the initiated. Combine these two elements, let the Vocoder run the stenotype, and the result is a machine which types when talked to. Our present languages are not especially adapted to this sort of mechanization, it is true. It is strange that the inventors of universal languages have not seized upon the idea of producing one which better fitted the technique for transmitting and recording speech. Mechanization may yet force the issue, especially in the scientific field; whereupon scientific jargon would become still less intelligible to the layman.

One can now picture a future investigator in his laboratory. His hands are free, and he is not anchored. As he moves about and observes, he photographs and comments. Time is automatically recorded to tie the two records together. If he goes into the field, he may be connected by radio to his recorder. As he ponders over his notes in the evening, he again talks his comments into the record. His typed record, as well as his photographs, may both be in miniature, so that he projects them for examination.

Much needs to occur, however, between the collection of data and observations, the extraction of parallel material from the existing record, and the final insertion of new material into the general body of the common record. For mature thought there is no mechanical substitute. But creative thought and essentially repetitive thought are very different things. For the latter there are, and may be, powerful mechanical aids.

Adding a column of figures is a repetitive thought process, and it was long ago properly relegated to the machine. True, the machine is sometimes controlled by a keyboard, and thought of a sort enters in reading the figures and poking the corresponding keys, but even this is avoidable. Machines have been made which will read typed figures by photocells and then depress the corresponding keys; these are combinations of photocells for scanning the type, electric circuits for sorting the consequent variations, and relay circuits for interpreting the result into the action of solenoids to pull the keys down.

All this complication is needed because of the clumsy way in which we have learned to write figures. If we recorded them positionally, simply by the configuration of a set of dots on a card, the automatic reading mechanism would become comparatively simple. In fact if the dots are holes, we have the punched-card machine long ago produced by Hollorith for the purposes of the census, and now used throughout business. Some types of complex businesses could hardly operate without these machines.

Adding is only one operation. To perform arithmetical computation involves also subtraction, multiplication, and division, and in addition some method for temporary storage of results, removal from storage for further manipulation, and recording of final results by printing. Machines for these purposes are now of two types: keyboard machines for accounting and the like, manually controlled for the insertion of data, and usually automatically controlled as far as the sequence of operations is concerned; and punched-card machines in which separate operations are usually delegated to a series of machines, and the cards then transferred bodily from one to another. Both forms are very useful; but as far as complex computations are concerned, both are still in embryo.

Rapid electrical counting appeared soon after the physicists found it desirable to count cosmic rays. For their own purposes the physicists promptly constructed thermionic-tube equipment capable of counting electrical impulses at the rate of 100,000 a second. The advanced arithmetical machines of the future will be electrical in nature, and they will perform at 100 times present speeds, or more.

Moreover, they will be far more versatile than present commercial machines, so that they may readily be adapted for a wide variety of operations. They will be controlled by a control card or film, they will select their own data and manipulate it in accordance with the instructions thus inserted, they will perform complex arithmetical computations at exceedingly high speeds, and they will record results in such form as to be readily available for distribution or for later further manipulation. Such machines will have enormous appetites. One of them will take instructions and data from a whole roomful of girls armed with simple keyboard punches, and will deliver sheets of computed results every few minutes. There will always be plenty of things to compute in the detailed affairs of millions of people doing complicated things.

# 4

The repetitive processes of thought are not confined, however, to matters of arithmetic and statistics. In fact, every time one combines and records facts in accordance with established logical processes, the creative aspect of thinking is concerned only with the selection of the data and the process to be employed and the manipulation thereafter is repetitive in nature and hence a fit matter to be relegated to the machine. Not so much has been done along these lines, beyond the bounds of arithmetic, as might be done, primarily because of the economics of the situation. The needs of business and the extensive market obviously waiting, assured the advent of mass-produced arithmetical machines just as soon as production methods were sufficiently advanced.

With machines for advanced analysis no such situation existed; for there was and is no extensive market; the users of advanced methods of manipulating data are a very small part of the population. There are, however, machines for solving differential equations—and functional and integral equations, for that matter. There are many special machines, such as the harmonic synthesizer which predicts the tides. There will be many more, appearing certainly first in the hands of the scientist and in small numbers.

If scientific reasoning were limited to the logical processes of arithmetic, we should not get far in our understanding of the physical world. One might as well attempt to grasp the game of poker entirely by the use of the mathematics of probability. The abacus, with its beads strung on parallel wires, led the Arabs to positional numeration and the concept of zero many centuries before the rest of the world; and it was a useful tool—so useful that it still exists.

It is a far cry from the abacus to the modern keyboard accounting machine. It will be an equal step to the arithmetical machine of the future. But even this new machine will not take the scientist where he needs to go. Relief must be secured from laborious detailed manipulation of higher mathematics as well, if the users of it are to free their brains for something more than repetitive detailed transformations in accordance with established rules. A mathematician is not a man who can readily manipulate figures; often he cannot. He is not even a man who can readily perform the transformations of equations by the use of calculus. He is primarily an individual who is skilled in the use of symbolic logic on a high plane, and especially he is a man of intuitive judgment in the choice of the manipulative processes he employs.

All else he should be able to turn over to his mechanism, just as confidently as he turns over the propelling of his car to the intricate mechanism under the hood. Only then will mathematics be practically effective in bringing the growing knowledge of atomistics to the useful solution of the advanced problems of chemistry, metallurgy, and biology. For this reason there still come more machines to handle advanced mathematics for the scientist. Some of them will be sufficiently bizarre to suit the most fastidious connoisseur of the present artifacts of civilization.

# 5

The scientist, however, is not the only person who manipulates data and examines the world about him by the use of logical processes, although he sometimes preserves this appearance by adopting into the fold anyone who becomes logical, much in the manner in which a British labor leader is elevated to knighthood. Whenever logical processes of thought are employed—that is, whenever thought for a time runs along an accepted groove—there is an opportunity for the machine. Formal logic used to be a keen instrument in the hands of the teacher in his trying of students' souls. It is readily possible to construct a machine which will manipulate premises in accordance with formal logic, simply by the clever use of relay circuits. Put a set of premises into such a device and turn the crank, and it will readily pass out conclusion after conclusion, all in accordance with logical law, and with no more slips than would be expected of a keyboard adding machine.

Logic can become enormously difficult, and it would undoubtedly be well to produce more assurance in its use. The machines for higher analysis have usually been equation solvers. Ideas are beginning to appear for equation transformers, which will rearrange the relationship expressed by an equation in accordance with strict and rather advanced logic. Progress is inhibited by the exceedingly crude way in which mathematicians express their relationships. They employ a symbolism which grew like Topsy and has little consistency; a strange fact in that most logical field.

A new symbolism, probably positional, must apparently precede the reduction of mathematical transformations to machine processes. Then, on beyond the strict logic of the mathematician, lies the application of logic in everyday affairs. We may some day click off arguments on a machine with the same assurance that we now enter sales on a cash register. But the machine of logic will not look like a cash register, even of the streamlined model.

So much for the manipulation of ideas and their insertion into the record. Thus far we seem to be worse off than before—for we can enormously extend the record; yet even in its present bulk, we can hardly consult it. This is a much larger matter than merely the extraction of data for the purposes of scientific research; it involves the entire process by which man profits by his inheritance of acquired knowledge. The prime action of use is selection, and here we are halting indeed. There may be millions of fine thoughts, and the account of the experience on which they are based, all encased within stone walls of acceptable architectural form; but if the scholar can get at only one a week by diligent search, his syntheses are not likely to keep up with the current scene.

Selection, in this broad sense, is a stone adze in the hands of a cabinetmaker. Yet, in a narrow sense and in other areas, something has already been done mechanically on selection. The personnel officer of a factory drops a stack of a few thousand employee cards into a selecting machine, sets a code in accordance with an established convention, and produces in a short time a list of all employees who live in Trenton and know Spanish. Even such devices are much too slow when it comes, for example, to matching a set of fingerprints with one of five million on file. Selection devices of this sort will soon be speeded up from their present rate of reviewing data at a few hundred a minute. By the use of photocells and microfilm they will survey items at the rate of a thousand a second, and will print out duplicates of those selected.

This process, however, is simple selection: it proceeds by examining in turn every one of a large set of items, and by picking out those which have certain specified characteristics. There is another form of selection best illustrated by the automatic telephone exchange. You dial a number and the machine selects and connects just one of a million possible stations. It does not run over them all. It pays attention only to a class given by a first digit, then only to a subclass of this given by the second digit, and so on; and thus proceeds rapidly and almost unerringly to the selected station. It requires a few seconds to make the selection, although the process could be speeded up if increased speed were economically warranted. If necessary, it could be made extremely fast by substituting thermionic-tube switching for mechanical switching, so that the full selection could be made in one one-hundredth of a second. No one would wish to spend the money necessary to make this change in the telephone system, but the general idea is applicable elsewhere.

Take the prosaic problem of the great department store. Every time a charge sale is made, there are a number of things to be done. The inventory needs to be revised, the salesman needs to be given credit for the sale, the general accounts need an entry, and, most important, the customer needs to be charged. A central records device has been developed in which much of this work is done conveniently. The salesman places on a stand the customer's identification card, his own card, and the card taken from the article sold—all punched cards. When he pulls a lever, contacts are made through the holes, machinery at a central point makes the necessary computations and entries, and the proper receipt is printed for the salesman to pass to the customer.

But there may be ten thousand charge customers doing business with the store, and before the full operation can be completed someone has to select the right card and insert it at the central office. Now rapid selection can slide just the proper card into position in an instant or two, and return it afterward. Another difficulty occurs, however. Someone must read a total on the card, so that the machine can add its computed item to it. Conceivably the cards might be of the dry photography type I have described. Existing totals could then be read by photocell, and the new total entered by an electron beam.

The cards may be in miniature, so that they occupy little space. They must move quickly. They need not be transferred far, but merely into position so that the photocell and recorder can operate on them. Positional dots can enter the data. At the end of the month a machine can readily be made to read these and to print an ordinary bill. With tube selection, in which no mechanical parts are involved in the switches, little time need be occupied in bringing the correct card into use—a second should suffice for the entire operation. The whole record on the card may be made by magnetic dots on a steel sheet if desired, instead of dots to be observed optically, following the scheme by which Poulsen long ago put speech on a magnetic wire. This method has the advantage of simplicity and ease of erasure. By using photography, however one can arrange to project the record in enlarged form and at a distance by using the process common in television equipment.

One can consider rapid selection of this form, and distant projection for other purposes. To be able to key one sheet of a million before an operator in a second or two, with the possibility of then adding notes thereto, is suggestive in many ways. It might even be of use in libraries, but that is another story. At any rate, there are now some interesting combinations possible. One might, for example, speak to a microphone, in the manner described in connection with the speech controlled typewriter, and thus make his selections. It would certainly beat the usual file clerk.

# 6

The real heart of the matter of selection, however, goes deeper than a lag in the adoption of mechanisms by libraries, or a lack of development of devices for their use. Our ineptitude in getting at the record is largely caused by the artificiality of systems of indexing. When data of any sort are placed in storage, they are filed alphabetically or numerically, and information is found (when it is) by tracing it down from subclass to subclass. It can be in only one place, unless duplicates are used; one has to have rules as to which path will locate it, and the rules are cumbersome. Having found one item, moreover, one has to emerge from the system and re-enter on a new path.

The human mind does not work that way. It operates by association. With one item in its grasp, it snaps instantly to the next that is suggested by the association of thoughts, in accordance with some intricate web of trails carried by the cells of the brain. It has other characteristics, of course; trails that are not frequently followed are prone to fade, items are not fully permanent, memory is transitory. Yet the speed of action, the intricacy of trails, the detail of mental pictures, is awe-inspiring beyond all else in nature.

Man cannot hope fully to duplicate this mental process artificially, but he certainly ought to be able to learn from it. In minor ways he may even improve, for his records have relative permanency. The first idea, however, to be drawn from the analogy concerns selection. Selection by association, rather than indexing, may yet be mechanized. One cannot hope thus to equal the speed and flexibility with which the mind follows an associative trail, but it should be possible to beat the mind decisively in regard to the permanence and clarity of the items resurrected from storage.

Consider a future device for individual use, which is a sort of mechanized private file and library. It needs a name, and, to coin one at random, "memex" will do. A memex is a device in which an individual stores all his books, records, and communications, and which is mechanized so that it may be consulted with exceeding speed and flexibility. It is an enlarged intimate supplement to his memory.

It consists of a desk, and while it can presumably be operated from a distance, it is primarily the piece of furniture at which he works. On the top are slanting translucent screens, on which material can be projected for convenient reading. There is a keyboard, and sets of buttons and levers. Otherwise it looks like an ordinary desk.

In one end is the stored material. The matter of bulk is well taken care of by improved microfilm. Only a small part of the interior of the memex is devoted to storage, the rest to mechanism. Yet if the user inserted 5000 pages of material a day it would take him hundreds of years to fill the repository, so he can be profligate and enter material freely.

Most of the memex contents are purchased on microfilm ready for insertion. Books of all sorts, pictures, current periodicals, newspapers, are thus obtained and dropped into place. Business correspondence takes the same path. And there is provision for direct entry. On the top of the memex is a transparent platen. On this are placed longhand notes, photographs, memoranda, all sorts of things. When one is in place, the depression of a lever causes it to be photographed onto the next blank space in a section of the memex film, dry photography being employed.

There is, of course, provision for consultation of the record by the usual scheme of indexing. If the user wishes to consult a certain book, he taps its code on the keyboard, and the title page of the book promptly appears before him, projected onto one of his viewing positions. Frequently-used codes are mnemonic, so that he seldom consults his code book; but when he does, a single tap of a key projects it for his use. Moreover, he has supplemental levers. On deflecting one of these levers to the right he runs through the book before him, each page in turn being projected at a speed which just allows a recognizing glance at each. If he deflects it further to the right, he steps through the book 10 pages at a time; still further at 100 pages at a time. Deflection to the left gives him the same control backwards.

A special button transfers him immediately to the first page of the index. Any given book of his library can thus be called up and consulted with far greater facility than if it were taken from a shelf. As he has several projection positions, he can leave one item in position while he calls up another. He can add marginal notes and comments, taking advantage of one possible type of dry photography, and it could even be arranged so that he can do this by a stylus scheme, such as is now employed in the telautograph seen in railroad waiting rooms, just as though he had the physical page before him.

# 7

All this is conventional, except for the projection forward of present-day mechanisms and gadgetry. It affords an immediate step, however, to associative indexing, the basic idea of which is a provision whereby any item may be caused at will to select immediately and automatically another. This is the essential feature of the memex. The process of tying two items together is the important thing.

When the user is building a trail, he names it, inserts the name in his code book, and taps it out on his keyboard. Before him are the two items to be joined, projected onto adjacent viewing positions. At the bottom of each there are a number of blank code spaces, and a pointer is set to indicate one of these on each item. The user taps a single key, and the items are permanently joined. In each code space appears the code word. Out of view, but also in the code space, is inserted a set of dots for photocell viewing; and on each item these dots by their positions designate the index number of the other item.

Thereafter, at any time, when one of these items is in view, the other can be instantly recalled merely by tapping a button below the corresponding code space. Moreover, when numerous items have been thus joined together to form a trail, they can be reviewed in turn, rapidly or slowly, by deflecting a lever like that used for turning the pages of a book. It is exactly as though the physical items had been gathered together from widely separated sources and bound together to form a new book. It is more than this, for any item can be joined into numerous trails.

The owner of the memex, let us say, is interested in the origin and properties of the bow and arrow. Specifically he is studying why the short Turkish bow was apparently superior to the English long bow in the skirmishes of the Crusades. He has dozens of possibly pertinent books and articles in his memex. First he runs through an encyclopedia, finds an interesting but sketchy article, leaves it projected. Next, in a history, he finds another pertinent item, and ties the two together. Thus he goes, building a trail of many items. Occasionally he inserts a comment of his own, either linking it into the main trail or joining it by a side trail to a particular item. When it becomes evident that the elastic properties of available materials had a great deal to do with the bow, he branches off on a side trail which takes him through textbooks on elasticity and tables of physical constants. He inserts a page of longhand analysis of his own. Thus he builds a trail of his interest through the maze of materials available to him.

And his trails do not fade. Several years later, his talk with a friend turns to the queer ways in which a people resist innovations, even of vital interest. He has an example, in the fact that the outraged Europeans still failed to adopt the Turkish bow. In fact he has a trail on it. A touch brings up the code book. Tapping a few keys projects the head of the trail. A lever runs through it at will, stopping at interesting items, going off on side excursions. It is an interesting trail, pertinent to the discussion. So he sets a reproducer in action, photographs the whole trail out, and passes it to his friend for insertion in his own memex, there to be linked into the more general trail.

# 8

Wholly new forms of encyclopedias will appear, ready made with a mesh of associative trails running through them, ready to be dropped into the memex and there amplified. The lawyer has at his touch the associated opinions and decisions of his whole experience, and of the experience of friends and authorities. The patent attorney has on call the millions of issued patents, with familiar trails to every point of his client's interest. The physician, puzzled by a patient's reactions, strikes the trail established in studying an earlier similar case, and runs rapidly through analogous case histories, with side references to the classics for the pertinent anatomy and histology. The chemist, struggling with the synthesis of an organic compound, has all the chemical literature before him in his laboratory, with trails following the analogies of compounds, and side trails to their physical and chemical behavior.

The historian, with a vast chronological account of a people, parallels it with a skip trail which stops only on the salient items, and can follow at any time contemporary trails which lead him all over civilization at a particular epoch. There is a new profession of trail blazers, those who find delight in the task of establishing useful trails through the enormous mass of the common record. The inheritance from the master becomes, not only his additions to the world's record, but for his disciples the entire scaffolding by which they were erected.

Thus science may implement the ways in which man produces, stores, and consults the record of the race. It might be striking to outline the instrumentalities of the future more spectacularly, rather than to stick closely to methods and elements now known and undergoing rapid development, as has been done here. Technical difficulties of all sorts have been ignored, certainly, but also ignored are means as yet unknown which may come any day to accelerate technical progress as violently as did the advent of the thermionic tube. In order that the picture may not be too commonplace, by reason of sticking to present-day patterns, it may be well to mention one such possibility, not to prophesy but merely to suggest, for prophecy based on extension of the known has substance, while prophecy founded on the unknown is only a doubly involved guess.

All our steps in creating or absorbing material of the record proceed through one of the senses—the tactile when we touch keys, the oral when we speak or listen, the visual when we read. Is it not possible that some day the path may be established more directly? We know that when the eye sees, all the consequent information is transmitted to the brain by means of electrical vibrations in the channel of the optic nerve. This is an exact analogy with the electrical vibrations which occur in the cable of a television set: they convey the picture from the photocells which see it to the radio transmitter from which it is broadcast. We know further that if we can approach that cable with the proper instruments, we do not need to touch it; we can pick up those vibrations by electrical induction and thus discover and reproduce the scene which is being transmitted, just as a telephone wire may be tapped for its message.

The impulses which flow in the arm nerves of a typist convey to her fingers the translated information which reaches her eye or ear, in order that the fingers may be caused to strike the proper keys. Might not these currents be intercepted, either in the original form in which information is conveyed to the brain, or in the marvelously metamorphosed form in which they then proceed to the hand?

By bone conduction we already introduce sounds: into the nerve channels of the deaf in order that they may hear. Is it not possible that we may learn to introduce them without the present cumbersomeness of first transforming electrical vibrations to mechanical ones, which the human mechanism promptly transforms back to the electrical form? With a couple of electrodes on the skull the encephalograph now produces pen-and-ink traces which bear some relation to the electrical phenomena going on in the brain itself. True, the record is unintelligible, except as it points out certain gross misfunctioning of the cerebral mechanism; but who would now place bounds on where such a thing may lead?

In the outside world, all forms of intelligence whether of sound or sight, have been reduced to the form of varying currents in an electric circuit in order that they may be transmitted. Inside the human frame exactly the same sort of process occurs. Must we always transform to mechanical movements in order to proceed from one electrical phenomenon to another? It is a suggestive thought, but it hardly warrants prediction without losing touch with reality and immediateness.

Presumably man's spirit should be elevated if he can better review his shady past and analyze more completely and objectively his present problems. He has built a civilization so complex that he needs to mechanize his records more fully if he is to push his experiment to its logical conclusion and not merely become bogged down part way there by overtaxing his limited memory. His excursions may be more enjoyable if he can reacquire the privilege of forgetting the manifold things he does not need to have immediately at hand, with some assurance that he can find them again if they prove important.

The applications of science have built man a well-supplied house, and are teaching him to live healthily therein. They have enabled him to throw masses of people against one another with cruel weapons. They may yet allow him truly to encompass the great record and to grow in the wisdom of race experience. He may perish in conflict before he learns to wield that record for his true good. Yet, in the application of science to the needs and desires of man, it would seem to be a singularly unfortunate stage at which to terminate the process, or to lose hope as to the outcome.

*The Atlantic Monthly;* July, 1945; "As We May Think," Volume 176, No. 1, pp. 101–108.

# Appendix B

# Software Engineering
## Code of Ethics and Professional Practice

**IEEE-CS/ACM Joint Task Force on Software Engineering Ethics and Professional Practices**

## PREAMBLE

Computers have a central and growing role in commerce, industry, government, medicine, education, entertainment and society at large. Software engineers are those who contribute by direct participation or by teaching, to the analysis, specification, design, development, certification, maintenance and testing of software systems. Because of their roles in developing software systems, software engineers have significant opportunities to do good or cause harm, to enable others to do good or cause harm, or to influence others to do good or cause harm. To ensure, as much as possible, that their efforts will be used for good, software engineers must commit themselves to making software engineering a beneficial and respected profession. In accordance with that commitment, software engineers shall adhere to the following Code of Ethics and Professional Practice.

The Code contains eight Principles related to the behavior of and decisions made by professional software engineers, including practitioners, educators, managers, supervisors and policy makers, as well as trainees and students of the profession. The Principles identify the ethically responsible relationships in which individuals, groups, and organizations participate and the primary obligations within these relationships. The Clauses of each Principle are illustrations of some of the obligations included in these relationships. These obligations are founded in the software engineer's humanity, in special care owed to people affected by the work of software engineers, and in the unique elements of the practice of software engineering. The Code prescribes these as obligations of anyone claiming to be or aspiring to be a software engineer.

It is not intended that the individual parts of the Code be used in isolation to justify errors of omission or commission. The list of Principles and Clauses is not exhaustive. The Clauses should not be read as separating the acceptable from the unacceptable in professional conduct in all practical situations. The Code is not a simple ethical algorithm that generates ethical decisions. In some situations, standards may be in tension with each other or with standards from other sources. These situations require the software engineer to use ethical judgment to act in a manner which is most consistent with the spirit of the Code of Ethics and Professional Practice, given the circumstances.

Ethical tensions can best be addressed by thoughtful consideration of fundamental principles, rather than blind reliance on detailed regulations. These Principles should influence software engineers to consider broadly who is affected by their work; to examine if they and their colleagues are treating other human beings with due respect; to consider how the public, if reasonably well informed, would view their decisions; to analyze how the least empowered will be affected by their decisions; and to consider whether their acts would be judged worthy of the ideal professional working as a software engineer. In all these judgments concern for the health, safety and welfare of the public is primary; that is, the "Public Interest" is central to this Code.

The dynamic and demanding context of software engineering requires a code that is adaptable and relevant to new situations as they occur. However, even in this generality, the Code provides support for software engineers and managers of software engineers who need to take positive action in a specific case by documenting the ethical stance of the profession. The Code provides an ethical foundation to which individuals within teams and the team as a whole can appeal. The Code helps to define those actions that are ethically improper to request of a software engineer or teams of software engineers.

The Code is not simply for adjudicating the nature of questionable acts; it also has an important educational function. As this Code expresses the consensus of the profession on ethical issues, it is a means to educate both the public and aspiring professionals about the ethical obligations of all software engineers.

## PRINCIPLES

*Principle 1. Public*—Software engineers shall act consistently with the public interest. In particular, software engineers shall, as appropriate:

1.01.  Accept full responsibility for their own work.

1.02.  Moderate the interests of the software engineer, the employer, the client and the users with the public good.

1.03.  Approve software only if they have a well-founded belief that it is safe, meets specifications, passes appropriate tests, and does not diminish quality of life, diminish privacy or harm the environment. The ultimate effect of the work should be to the public good.

1.04.  Disclose to appropriate persons or authorities any actual or potential danger to the user, the public, or the environment, that they reasonably believe to be associated with software or related documents.

1.05. Cooperate in efforts to address matters of grave public concern caused by software, its installation, maintenance, support or documentation.

1.06. Be fair and avoid deception in all statements, particularly public ones, concerning software or related documents, methods and tools.

1.07. Consider issues of physical disabilities, allocation of resources, economic disadvantage and other factors that can diminish access to the benefits of software.

1.08. Be encouraged to volunteer professional skills to good causes and to contribute to public education concerning the discipline.

*Principle 2. Client and Employer*—Software engineers shall act in a manner that is in the best interests of their client and employer, consistent with the public interest. In particular, software engineers shall, as appropriate:

2.01. Provide service in their areas of competence, being honest and forthright about any limitations of their experience and education.

2.02. Not knowingly use software that is obtained or retained either illegally or unethically.

2.03. Use the property of a client or employer only in ways properly authorized, and with the client's or employer's knowledge and consent.

2.04. Ensure that any document upon which they rely has been approved, when required, by someone authorized to approve it.

2.05. Keep private any confidential information gained in their professional work, where such confidentiality is consistent with the public interest and consistent with the law.

2.06. Identify, document, collect evidence and report to the client or the employer promptly if, in their opinion, a project is likely to fail, to prove too expensive, to violate intellectual property law, or otherwise to be problematic.

2.07. Identify, document, and report significant issues of social concern, of which they are aware, in software or related documents, to the employer or the client.

2.08. Accept no outside work detrimental to the work they perform for their primary employer.

2.09. Promote no interest adverse to their employer or client, unless a higher ethical concern is being compromised; in that case, inform the employer or another appropriate authority of the ethical concern.

*Principle 3. Product*—Software engineers shall ensure that their products and related modifications meet the highest professional standards possible. In particular, software engineers shall, as appropriate:

3.01. Strive for high quality, acceptable cost, and a reasonable schedule, ensuring significant tradeoffs are clear to and accepted by the employer and the client, and are available for consideration by the user and the public.

3.02. Ensure proper and achievable goals and objectives for any project on which they work or propose.

3.03. Identify, define and address ethical, economic, cultural, legal and environmental issues related to work projects.

3.04. Ensure that they are qualified for any project on which they work or propose to work, by an appropriate combination of education, training, and experience.

3.05. Ensure that an appropriate method is used for any project on which they work or propose to work.

3.06. Work to follow professional standards, when available, that are most appropriate for the task at hand, departing from these only when ethically or technically justified.

3.07. Strive to fully understand the specifications for software on which they work.

3.08. Ensure that specifications for software on which they work have been well documented, satisfy the users' requirements and have the appropriate approvals.

3.09. Ensure realistic quantitative estimates of cost, scheduling, personnel, quality and outcomes on any project on which they work or propose to work and provide an uncertainty assessment of these estimates.

3.10. Ensure adequate testing, debugging, and review of software and related documents on which they work.

3.11. Ensure adequate documentation, including significant problems discovered and solutions adopted, for any project on which they work.

3.12. Work to develop software and related documents that respect the privacy of those who will be affected by that software.

3.13. Be careful to use only accurate data derived by ethical and lawful means, and use it only in ways properly authorized.

3.14. Maintain the integrity of data, being sensitive to outdated or flawed occurrences.

3.15. Treat all forms of software maintenance with the same professionalism as new development.

*Principle 4. Judgment*—Software engineers shall maintain integrity and independence in their professional judgment. In particular, software engineers shall, as appropriate:

4.01. Temper all technical judgments by the need to support and maintain human values.

4.02. Only endorse documents either prepared under their supervision or within their areas of competence and with which they are in agreement.

4.03. Maintain professional objectivity with respect to any software or related documents they are asked to evaluate.

4.04. Not engage in deceptive financial practices such as bribery, double billing, or other improper financial practices.

4.05. Disclose to all concerned parties those conflicts of interest that cannot reasonably be avoided or escaped.

4.06. Refuse to participate, as members or advisors, in a private, governmental or professional body concerned with software related issues, in which they, their employers or their clients have undisclosed potential conflicts of interest.

*Principle 5. Management*—Software engineering managers and leaders shall subscribe to and promote an ethical approach to the management of software development and maintenance. In particular, those managing or leading software engineers shall, as appropriate:

5.01. Ensure good management for any project on which they work, including effective procedures for promotion of quality and reduction of risk.

5.02. Ensure that software engineers are informed of standards before being held to them.

5.03. Ensure that software engineers know the employer's policies and procedures for protecting passwords, files and information that is confidential to the employer or confidential to others.

5.04. Assign work only after taking into account appropriate contributions of education and experience tempered with a desire to further that education and experience.

5.05. Ensure realistic quantitative estimates of cost, scheduling, personnel, quality and outcomes on any project on which they work or propose to work, and provide an uncertainty assessment of these estimates.

5.06. Attract potential software engineers only by full and accurate description of the conditions of employment.

5.07. Offer fair and just remuneration.

5.08. Not unjustly prevent someone from taking a position for which that person is suitably qualified.

5.09. Ensure that there is a fair agreement concerning ownership of any software, processes, research, writing, or other intellectual property to which a software engineer has contributed.

5.10. Provide for due process in hearing charges of violation of an employer's policy or of this Code.

5.11. Not ask a software engineer to do anything inconsistent with this Code.

5.12. Not punish anyone for expressing ethical concerns about a project.

*Principle 6. Profession*—Software engineers shall advance the integrity and reputation of the profession consistent with the public interest. In particular, software engineers shall, as appropriate:

6.01. Help develop an organizational environment favorable to acting ethically.

6.02. Promote public knowledge of software engineering.

6.03. Extend software engineering knowledge by appropriate participation in professional organizations, meetings and publications.

6.04. Support, as members of a profession, other software engineers striving to follow this Code.

6.05. Not promote their own interest at the expense of the profession, client or employer.

6.06. Obey all laws governing their work, unless, in exceptional circumstances, such compliance is inconsistent with the public interest.

6.07. Be accurate in stating the characteristics of software on which they work, avoiding not only false claims but also claims that might reasonably be supposed to be speculative, vacuous, deceptive, misleading, or doubtful.

6.08. Take responsibility for detecting, correcting, and reporting errors in software and associated documents on which they work.

6.09. Ensure that clients, employers, and supervisors know of the software engineer's commitment to this Code of ethics, and the subsequent ramifications of such commitment.

6.10. Avoid associations with businesses and organizations which are in conflict with this code.

6.11. Recognize that violations of this Code are inconsistent with being a professional software engineer.

6.12. Express concerns to the people involved when significant violations of this Code are detected unless this is impossible, counterproductive, or dangerous.

6.13. Report significant violations of this Code to appropriate authorities when it is clear that consultation with people involved in these significant violations is impossible, counter-productive or dangerous.

*Principle 7. Colleagues*—Software engineers shall be fair to and supportive of their colleagues. In particular, software engineers shall, as appropriate:

7.01. Encourage colleagues to adhere to this Code.

7.02. Assist colleagues in professional development.

7.03. Credit fully the work of others and refrain from taking undue credit.

7.04. Review the work of others in an objective, candid, and properly documented way.

7.05. Give a fair hearing to the opinions, concerns, or complaints of a colleague.

7.06. Assist colleagues in being fully aware of current standard work practices including policies and procedures for protecting passwords, files and other confidential information, and security measures in general.

7.07. Not unfairly intervene in the career of any colleague; however, concern for the employer, the client or public interest may compel software engineers, in good faith, to question the competence of a colleague.

7.08. In situations outside of their own areas of competence, call upon the opinions of other professionals who have competence in that area.

*Principle 8. Self*—Software engineers shall participate in lifelong learning regarding the practice of their profession and shall promote an ethical approach to the practice of the profession. In particular, software engineers shall continually endeavor to:

8.01. Further their knowledge of developments in the analysis, specification, design, development, maintenance and testing of software and related documents, together with the management of the development process.

8.02. Improve their ability to create safe, reliable, and useful quality software at reasonable cost and within a reasonable time.

8.03. Improve their ability to produce accurate, informative, and well-written documentation.

8.04. Improve their understanding of the software and related documents on which they work and of the environment in which they will be used.

8.05. Improve their knowledge of relevant standards and the law governing the software and related documents on which they work.

8.06. Improve their knowledge of this Code, its interpretation, and its application to their work.

8.07. Not give unfair treatment to anyone because of any irrelevant prejudices.

8.08. Not influence others to undertake any action that involves a breach of this Code.

8.09. Recognize that personal violations of this Code are inconsistent with being a professional software engineer.

This Code was developed by the IEEE-CS/ACM joint task force on Software Engineering Ethics and Professional Practices (SEEPP): Executive Committee:

Donald Gotterbarn (Chair), Keith Miller and Simon Rogerson;

Members:

Steve Barber, Peter Barnes, Ilene Burnstein, Michael Davis, Amr El_Kadi, N. Ben Fairweather, Milton Fulghum, N. Jayaram, Tom Jewett, Mark Kanko, Ernie Kallman, Duncan Langford, Joyce Currie Little, Ed Mechler, Manuel J. Norman, Douglas Phillips, Peter Ron Prinzivalli, Patrick Sullivan, John Weckert, Vivian Weil, S. Weisband and Laurie Honour Werth.

# References

Abbate, J. (1999). *Inventing the Internet.* Cambridge: MIT Press.

Achenbach, J. (December 4, 1996). Reality Check; You Can't Believe Everything You Read. But You Better Believe This. *Washington Post,* pp. C01.

ACIA. (2000). Formal educational credentials for information architects. *http://argusacia.com/iask/survey001107.html*

ACIA. (2001a). Education and training needs for information architects. *http://argusacia.com/iask/survey010301.html*

ACIA. (2001b). Salaries and benefits for information architects. *http://argusacia.com/iask/survey010124titles.html*

Agre, P. (2000). Notes on the new design space. Unpublished ms., circulated on RRE mailing list. *http://dlis.gseis.ucla.edu/people/pagre/rre.html*

Alexander, C. (1971). Notes on the synthesis of form. Cambridge: Harvard University Press.

Alexander, C., Ishikawa, S., and Silverstein, M. (1977). A pattern language: towns, buildings, construction. New York: Oxford University Press.

Allinson, K. (1997). *Getting There by Design.* Oxford: Architectural Press.

Allision, D. K. (1996). *Using the Computer: Episodes Across 50 Years.* Paper presented at the Annual Meeting of the Association of Computing Machinery.

American Society for Information Science and Technology, Information Architecture Special Interest Group (2000). *Call for Contributions.* Available: *http://www.asis.org/AboutASIS/asis-sigs.html#SIGIA*

American Society for Information Science and Technology, Information Architecture Summit (2001). Panel Discussion: *Reflections and Projections,* [Web site]. Available: *www.asis.org/Conferences/Summit2001/reflections.html*

Barnouw, E. (1975). *Tube of Plenty.* New York/Oxford: Oxford University Press.

Bates, M. J. (1999). The invisible substrate of information science. JASIS (50)12:1043–1050.

Belton, B. K. (2001). *A Design Foundation for Information Architecture.* Unpublished manuscript, Tallahassee, Florida.

Berners-Lee, T. (1999). *The WWW: A Very Short History* [Web site] W3. Available: *http://www.w3.org/People/Berners-Lee/ShortHistory.html.*

Beyer, H., and Holtzblatt, K. (1998). Contextual design: Defining customer-centered systems. San Francisco: Morgan Kaufmann.

Borgman, C. (2000). *From Gutenberg to the Global Information Infrastructure,* [Web site]. Available: *http://commons.somewhere.com/rre/2000/RRE.From.Gutenberg.to.th.html*

Brincat, C. (2000). *Morality and the Professional Life.* Upper Saddle River: Prentice Hall.

Brooks, J. (1976). *Telephone: The First Hundred Years.* New York: Harper Row.

Brown, J. S. and Dequid, P. (2000). *The Social Life of Information.* Boston: Harvard Business School Press.

Bush, V. (July 1945). As We May Think. *The Atlantic Monthly.*

Bush, V. (1945). *As We May Think,* [Web site]. Atlantic Monthly. Available: *http://www.theatlantic.com/unbound/flashbks/computer/bushf.htm*

Chaunu, P. (1995). Foreword of *The History and Power of Writing.* Chicago: University of Chicago Press.

Coplien, J. O. (1999). *Architecture as Metaphor:* Bell Laboratories.

Crane, K. (2001). *Email Archive Management: The Emerging Issue of the Information Age,* [Web site]. Available: *http://www.document-strategy.com* [March 2002].

Das, A. (2000). *Information Architecture—A New Opportunity* [Web site]. Available: *www.webreference.com/authoring/design/information/ia* [March 2002].

Denning, D. E. (1999). *Information Warfare and Security.* New York: ACM Press.

Dertouzous, M. (1998). *What Will Be.* San Francisco: HarperEdge.

Dewar, J. A. (1998). *The Information Age and the Printing Press* [Web site] Rand. Available: *http://www.rand.org/publications/P/P8014* [2001].

Dubberly, H. (1994). *Managing Complex Design Projects.* Paper presented at the American Center for Design Conference: Living Surfaces.

Durling, D., and Friedman, K. (eds.). (2000). Doctoral education in design: Foundations for the future. Staffordshire: Staffordshire University Press.

Eisenstein, E. L. (2000). *The Printing Revolution in Early Modern Europe.* Cambridge: Cambridge University Press.

Engelbart, D. (1962). *Augmenting Human Intellect: A Conceptual Framework,* [Web site]. Bootstrap Alliance. Available: *http://www.engelbart.info/62_paper_top.html*

Erickson, T. (1995). *Notes on Design Practice: Stories and Prototypes as Catalysts for Communication* [Web site]. Available: *http://www.pliant.org/personal/Tom_Erickson/Stories.html* [March 2002].

Ewing, C. (2002). Information Architecture Proposed Curriculum, Graduate School of Library and Information Science at The University of Texas at Austin [Web site]. Available: *www.gslis.utexas.edu/~iag/resources/ia-curriculum-final* [March 2002].

Fang, I. (1997). *A History of Mass Communication.* Boston: Focal Press.

Fischer, S. R. (1999). *A History of Language.* London: Reakton Books.

Friedman, K. Design knowledge. In Durling and Friedman, 5–16. (2000).

Friedman, K. (1997). *Design and Design Education.* Paper presented at the Re-inventing Design Education in the University Conference.

Friedman, K. (1997). "Design science and design education." *http://design.curtin.edu/DesEd2000/preconference02.html.* Also in: The challenge of complexity. Peter McGrory (ed.). Helsinki: University of Art and Design Helsinki UIAH., 54–72.

Froehlich, T. J. (2001). *Information Architecture,* Kent State: School of Library and Information Science [Web site]. Available: *http://iakm.kent.edu* [2001].

Garrett, J. (2002). *The Discipline and the Role* [Web site]. Available: *http//ww.jjg.net/ia/recon* [March 2002].

Gates, B. (1996). *The Road Ahead.* New York: Penguin Books.

Hackos, J. T. (1998). *User and Task Analysis for Interface Design.* New York: John Wiley & Sons.

Hafner, K. (1996). *Where Wizards Stay Up Late.* New York: Touchstone.

Head, A. (2002). *Information Specialists at the Intersection of Information Architecture and Usability* [Web site]. Available: *http:www.ajhead.com/lecture.html* [March 2002].

Heylighen, F. (1999). *Change and Information Overload: negative effects* [Internet]. Principa Cybernetica Web.

Hill, R. (2001). SIGIA-L: Summit 2001 [Web site]. Available: *http:www.asis.org* [March 2002].

Hill, S. (1998). *An Interview with Louis Rosenfeld and Peter Morville,* [Web site]. O'Reilly. Available: *http://web.oreilly.com/news/infoarch_0100.html*

Hill, S. (2001). *An Interview with Louis Rosenfeld and Peter Morville* [Web site]. Available: *http:web.oreilly.com* [March 2002].

Horn, R. E. (2000). Information Design: Emergence of a New Profession: *Information Design* (pp. 15–33). Cambridge: Massachusetts Institute of Technology.

Horton, F. (1983). Information Literacy vs. Computer Literacy. *Bulletin of the American Society for Information Science, 9*(4).

Institute of Electrical and Electronic Engineers, Inc. and the Association for Computing Machinery (1999). *Software Engineering, Code of Ethics and Professional Practice,* [Web Site]. Available: *www.computer.org/tab/seprof/code.htm*

Johnson, J. and Roberts, T. L. (1989). *The Xerox Star: A Retrospective.* IEEE Computer, vol. 22, no. 9, pp. 11–29.

Johnson, J. and Roberts, T. (1989). The Xerox "Star": A Retrospective, *Human Computer Interaction: Toward the Year 2000.* San Francisco: Morgan Kaufmann.

Kent State University (2001). *Master of Science Information Architecture and Knowledge Management,* [Web site]. Available: *iakm.kent.edu*

Kerka, S. (1997). *Myths and Realities: Information Management* [Web site]. ERIC: Clearing house on Adult, Career, and Vocational Education [2001].

Kimen, S. (1999). *10 Questions About Information Architecture* [Web site]. Available: *http:builder.net.cnet.com/webbuilding* [March 2002].

Kling, R. (1996). *Computerization and Controversy: Value Conflicts and Social Choices,* (Second ed.). San Diego: Academic Press.

Kling, R. (1999). What Is Social Informatics and Why Does It Matter? *D-Lib Magazine, 5.*

Kling, R. (2000). Learning About Information Technologies and Social Change: The Contribution of Social Informatics. *The Information Society, 16*(3).

Lamb, R., Newby, G., and Peek, R. (1996). Analyzing Visions of Electronic Publishing and Digital Libraries. In (ed.), *Publishing: The Electronic Frontier.* Cambridge: MIT Press.

Lampson, B. W. (1988). Personal Distributed Computing: The Alto and Ethernet Software. In A. Goldberg (Ed.), *A History of Personal Workstations* (pp. 291–344). Addison Wesley.

Larsen, L. L. (1999). *Information Literacy: The Web Is Not an Encyclopedia.* College Park: University of Maryland. Available: *www.inform.umd.edu/ LibInfo/literacy* [2001].

Larson, M. (1977). The rise of professionalism: A sociological analysis. Berkeley: University of California Press.

Lazarus, R. S. (1984). *Stress, Appraisal, and Coping.* New York: Springer.

Lyman, P. (2000). *How Much Information* [Internet]. University of California at Berkeley: School of Information Management and Systems. Available: *http://www.sims.berkeley.edu/how-much-info* [2001, August 27].

Martin, H. J. (1994). *The History and Power of Writing,* L. G. Cochrane, trans. 2nd ed. Chicago: The University of Chicago Press.

McCartney, S. (2001). *Eniac: The Triumphs and Tragedies of the World's First Computer.* New York: The Berkley Publishing Book.

Mediascope. (2000). *Media Use in America* [Web site]. Available: *http://www.mediascope.org/pubs/ ibriefs/mua.htm* [2001].

Microsoft. (2001). *"Book," Microsoft Encarta Online Encyclopedia 2001.* Available: *http://encarta.msn.com* [2001].

Miller, W. R. (1996, December 15, 1996). *The Management of Design* [Web site]. Available: *http://www.tcdc.com/dphils/dphil4.htm* [2001, October 15].

Moholy-Nagy, L. (1938). *The New Vision: Fundamentals of Design, Printing, Sculpture, Architecture,* D. M. Hoffman, trans. New York: Norton.

Mok, C. (1996). *Desiging Business.* Indianapolis: Adobe Press.

Morville, P. (2000). *Educating the Information Architect,* Argus Center for Information Architecture [Web site]. Available: *http://argus-acia.com/ strange_connections/strange005.htm* [2001, September 12].

Myers, B. A. (1998). A Brief History of Human Computer Interaction Technology. J. Hollan, I. Cruz (Ed.) *ACM Interactions,* 4(1), 44–54.

Nelson, M. R. (1994). *We have the information you want, but getting it will cost you!* Association for Computing Machinery. (September) [Web site]. Available: *http://www.acm.org/crossroads/xrds1-1/ xrds1-1.html* [2001].

Newton, N. (1951). An approach to design. Cambridge: Addison-Wesley.

Newton, N. (1979). An approach to design (unpublished revised ms.). Cambridge: Harvard University.

Nielsen, J. (1998). *What Is "Usability"?* [Web site]. Available: *http://www.zdnet.com/devhead* [2001].

Norman, D. A. (1990). *The Design of Everyday Things.* New York: Doubleday.

Norman, N. (2001). *E-commerce User Experience: Methodology of the Study* [Web Site]. Available: *http://www.nngroup.com/reports/ecommerce/ methodology* [2001, September 4].

Ong, W. J. (1997). *Orality and Literacy.* London: Routledge.

Pinker, S. B. P. (1990). *Natural Language and Natural Selection* [Internet]. Available: *http://cogprints.ecs.soton.ac.uk/bbs/Archive/ bbs.pinker.html* [2001].

Postman, N. (1985). *Amusing Ourselves to Death: Public Discourse in the Age of Show Business.* New York: Viking.

Rettig, M. (2000). *Ethnography and Information Architecture.* Paper presented at the ASIST Summit on Information Architecture, Boston.

Rheingold, H. (2000). *Tools for Thought* (p. 173). Cambridge: The MIT Press.

Rhoads, B. E. (1993). Looking Back at Radio's Future. *Columbia University Media Studies Journal, 1993* (Summer), 18–19.

Robinson, A. (1999). *The Story of Writing.* New York: Thames and Hudson.

Rosenfeld, L. (2001). What's In A Name. B. Mazur (Ed.) *Design Matters,* 5(2), 8–9. [Web site download] Available: *www.stcsig.org/id/whatis.html*

Rosenfeld, L. (2002). *Why Johnny Can't Find—and How Information Architecture can help.* [Web site]. Available: *www.louisrosenfeld.com/presentations/ 020322-msu.ppt*

Rosenfield, L. and Morville, P. (1999). *Information Architecture: Designing Large-Scale Web Sites.* Sebastopol: O'Reilly.

Rowe, P. (1987). Design thinking. Cambridge: MIT Press.

Rowe, P. (1996). "Shaping design education." In W. Saunders (ed.), Reflections on architectural practices in the nineties (242–249). New York: Princeton Architectural Press.

Rowland, G. (1993). Designing and Instructional Design. *Educational Technology Research and Development Journal,* 41(1), 79–91.

Ruhlen, M. (1994). *The Origin of Language.* New York: Wiley.

Sapient, I. (2000). *Building an Integrated Information Architecture Practice at Sapient.* Paper presented at the Advance for Design Conference, Telluride, Colorado.

Schneiderman, B. (1987). *Designing the User Interface: Strategies for Effective Human-Computer Interaction.* Reading: Addison Wesley Publishing Co.

Schön, D. (1983). The reflective practitioner: How professionals think in action. New York: Basic Books.

Shedroff, N. (2000). Information Interaction Design: A Unified Field Theory of Design. In R. Jacobson (Ed.), *Information Design* (pp. 267–292). Boston: M.I.T. Press.

Shenk, D. (1997). *Data Smog.* San Francisco: HarperCollins.

Simon, H. (1996). *The Sciences of the Artificial,* 3rd ed. Cambridge: Massachusetts Institute of Technology.

Sless, D. (1996). *Transitions In Information Design.* Paper presented at the International Institute for Information Design Conference: Vision Plus 2.

Smith, A. (2001). *Why Is Usability So Hard?* Human-Computer Interaction Resource Network [Web site]. Available: *http://www.hcirn.com/reflect/ whyhard.html* [2001, October 17].

Standage, T. (1998). *The Victorian Internet.* New York: Berkley Books.

Stefik, M. (1996). *Internet Dreams.* Cambridge: Massachusetts Institute of Technology.

Stewart, W. (1997–2001). *LivingInternet.com* [Web site]. Available: *http://www.livingnet.com* [2001, July 12].

Sullivan, W. M. (1995). *Work and Integrity: The Crisis and Promise of Professionalism in America.* New York: HarperCollins Publishers.

Sutcliffe, R. J. (1992–2000). *The Fourth Civilization: Technlogy, Society, and Ethics,* 3rd ed. [Web site]. Available: *http://www.arjay.ca/EthTech/Text* [2001].

Svec, L. (2000). Building an integrated information architecture practice at Sapient. *http://advance.aiga.org/timeline/artifacts/ tArtifact_svec.pdf.*

Times, T. N. Y. (1996). *ENIAC Versus the Pentium,* [Web site]. Available: *http://mbhs.bergtraum.k12.ny.us/ cybereng.nyt/databox.htm*

Treloar, A. (1994). *Information Spaces and Affordances on the Internet* [Web site]. Available: *http:andrew.treloar.net/Research/* [March 2002].

UCLA (2000). *Surveying the Digital Future.* Los Angeles: University of California, Los Angeles.

Van Der Wal, T. (2001). *Thoughts On the Definition and Community of Information Architecture,* [Web site]. Available: *http://www.peterme.com/archives/ 00000091.html#11.*

Volti, R. (1995). *Society and Technological Change.* New York: St. Martin's Press.

Vorisek, A. M. (February 4, 1997). *Radio's Social Impact on Society During the Early Years of Popularity,* [Web site]. Mother Earth: The Activist Nexus. Available: *http://www.connix.com/~harry* [2001].

Waldrop, M. M. (2000). *Computing's Johnny Appleseed* (January/February 2000) [Web site]. *M.I.T. Technology Review.*

Williams, W. A. (1966). *The Contours of American History.* New York: W. W. Norton.

Winston, B. (1998). *Media Technology and Society: A History.* New York: Routledge.

Wisconsin-Milwaukee, U. O. (1996). *The Infancy of Printing,* University of Wisconsin-Milwaukee [Web site]. Available: *http://www.uwm.edu/Dept/ Library/special/exhibits/incunab/inctoc.htm*

Wodtke, C. (2001). *Defining the Damn Thing,* [Web site]. Elegant Hack. Available: *http:www.eleganthack.com//archives/cat_informatio n_architecture.html*

Wurman, R. S. (1997). *Information Architects.* New York: Graphis, Inc.

Wurman, R. S. (2000). *Information Anxiety 2.* Indianapolis: Que.

# Index